9-44

21143327

D0494296

GIANTS OF SCOTTISH RUGBY

GIANTS OF SCOTTISH RUGBY

JEFF CONNOR

MAINSTREAM
PUBLISHING

EDINBURGH AND LONDON

ACKNOWLEDGEMENTS

I am immensely grateful to the players who make up this book, all of whom gave time in busy lives to talk about their past and present careers. I had always wondered if international rugby turned ordinary people into special people or whether it was just special people who played international rugby. I hope the 40 players' stories in the following pages, told as far as possible in their own words, help answer that question.

My thanks go, too, to Bill Campbell and Caroline Budge of Mainstream for their encouragement and patience and to Gordon Fraser and the Scottish Rugby Union for their generous loan of archived photographs. Tracey Lawson, as always, was a source of sound advice and suggestions and I owe her a lot.

Above all, this book would not have been possible without the help, advice and inspiration of Finlay Calder, capped 34 times for Scotland and British Lions captain, 1989.

Copyright © Jeff Connor, 2000
All rights reserved
The moral right of the author has been asserted

First published in Great Britain in 2000 by
MAINSTREAM PUBLISHING COMPANY (EDINBURGH) LTD
7 Albany Street
Edinburgh EH1 3UG

This edition 2001

ISBN 1 84018 478 7

A catalogue record for this book is available from the British Library

Typeset in Bembo and Gill Sans Light
Printed and bound in Great Britain by Creative Print and Design Wales

CONTENTS

FOREWORD by Finlay Calder OBE

It's difficult to put into words what it means to play for Scotland, to pull on that blue jersey and walk out onto a rugby field as a representative of your country. That special feeling was best summed up for me by one pre-match team talk from Jim Telfer, the memory of which even now makes the hairs stand on the back of my neck. It was before a Calcutta Cup clash with the old foe, England. Jim, who saved his best speeches for special occasions like that, told us: 'To represent your country is the highlight of anyone's life, but just remember that when you are given that Scotland jersey you are only given a loan of it. It represents everyone who has played for Scotland in the past and who will play for Scotland in the future. When your career is over you hand that jersey back for future generations.'

Reading Jeff Connor's book and the stories of the lives of the 40 players in it, I think everyone will appreciate that all of the players involved have tried to live up to Jim's philosophy. I don't think it's an exaggeration to say that playing for Scotland makes you a humbler and better person. But then playing rugby at any standard allows you to find out more about yourself. You are a custodian of whatever jersey you are wearing and when the time does come to hand it back you should leave it better than you found it. There is humour and heartbreak in rugby, but above all I think Jeff's book shows that there is a lot of humility and integrity too.

Finlay Calder
Lauder
September 2000

This book is for Struan Kerr-Liddell
'Because in the end, rugby is about brave men . . .'

The Big Controller works in an office at Murrayfield hardly big enough to hold a pack of forwards stood toe to toe and Jim Telfer, even at 60, is a large, upright man whose stature and presence fill any room. In comparison to Scottish Rugby Union chief executive Bill Watson's ballroom-like premises a few doors down the corridor, Telfer's work place justifies Scott Hastings's description of 'a rabbit hutch'. But there again, as one former international put it, 'If Jim had wanted a ballroom he would have got one.' Ostentation is not one of the vices of the son of a Borders hill shepherd who became the most powerful man in the history of Scottish rugby. If Jim Telfer's name dominates this book, it is simply because he dominates Scottish rugby; virtually every life mentioned here has been touched in some way by his.

The office is decorated with wall-to-wall video tapes of every major rugby international captured on film, including the most famous Scottish black-and-white footage of all – that of Telfer dipping his shoulder into the France full-back (and now team manager) Pierre Villepreux and crashing over the line for the try that gave Scotland a 6–3 victory at Colombes on 11 January 1969. Telfer had to wait over a quarter of a century for his next win in Paris, but he has that on tape, too. He has always heeded the lessons of rugby history, but really he does not need the videotapes. Virtually every detail of every match in which he has been involved is already stored away inside his head.

The SRU Director of Rugby is famously wary of the press, but there is tea and shortbread on a little oval table and no sign of the cantankerous ogre of legend. The nerves are all in the chair opposite – the proximity of the famous can scramble one's senses at times. When Telfer, in the small talk that precedes any interview, mentions his occasional backache, some passing insanity makes me say, 'Perhaps it's because you're sat in too many committee meetings these days.'

Silence, then: 'What was that?'

'Perhaps you're spending too much time sitting in committees instead of, you know, supervising training sessions.'

Suddenly I see a mental image of myself being frogmarched back out through the South Gate, but then a smile creases those boxer's features and the man bursts into relieving laughter: 'Aye, well, maybe you're right.'

Things seemed to go swimmingly after that. I am, after all, from an era where I have seen Telfer and many of his contemporaries play and I know the magic words that might earn me an extra half-hour: 'All Blacks' and 'rucking'. True, there is a possibly pre-arranged phone call from his secretary 20 minutes into the interview, presumably offering an escape route, but he returns to pour a second cup of tea. He has the chance to talk nothing but rugby for an hour, and of course Jim Telfer would talk rugby all day given the opportunity, even to a total stranger. His enthusiasm for the game is startling. At times he finds it hard to stay seated when recalling some famous Scottish deed of the past and the voice rises gradually, from the calm reflection when talking about his beginnings, to the famous boom when expounding his rugby philosophies. One of these philosophies is personified in his favourite saying, 'The cream will always rise to the top'. It earned him the nickname 'Creamy' from his players, although no one calls him that to his face.

Born on 17 March 1940, Jim Telfer is the son of a shepherd, William Telfer, who worked on a farm near Yetholm, three miles from the English border. William and Jim's mother Peggy are still alive at the time of writing, aged 85 and 81 respectively — a clue, perhaps, to the genetics that have given their son that famous stamina, energy and longevity. He says, 'Because you didn't go to hospital in those days, I was taken to an uncle in East Lothian to be born and then back to the farm. No one in the family played rugby and, really, farm workers had no history of playing sport at all. Because we lived equidistant between Melrose and Galashiels, I was a pupil at Melrose Grammar and later went to Gala Academy. I played rugby from the age of 11, but played as much cricket and took part in athletics, too. I would say I wasn't naturally gifted at sport, but I certainly had the right attitude to be good at it.

'I took to rugby quite well, but I was a forward, so you didn't have to be very skilful. I was a leader even at that age: I was captain of the rugby team, cricket team and athletics team. I seemed to be able to give people orders and made up for everything else by working very hard at what I tried to do.

'I left school at 17 and went to Heriot-Watt University to train as a teacher, but came home at weekends to play for Melrose before taking up a teaching appointment at Gala Academy. I only ever played for one club and never thought of playing for anyone else. Even when I lived and worked in Edinburgh or Glasgow, it was always Melrose. Everything I have done in rugby I owe to Melrose.

'In the late '50s and early '60s there were some very good players at The Greenyards and I went through my career playing with Eck Hastie, David Chisholm and Frank Laidlaw. I was brought up in a place where rugby was a religion but, personally, I never thought of playing for Scotland: you just concentrated on the level you could attain. So it was the first team, then South of Scotland and I had no baggage to carry in the sense that my father or uncle had played for Scotland. I was just as surprised as anyone where I ended up. My father and mother were always very supportive. He would come and watch and tell me later I wasn't very good. He was an expert, of course, but he never played.

'I won my first cap at 23 in 1964, against France. I was leader of the pack. This was quite a big thing, quite an honour, it meant I was virtually in charge of the team. It was a wet day at Murrayfield. We were underdogs, but won 10–0. When you get to my age you can't remember what happened yesterday, but I do remember sitting next to a player called Michel Crauste at dinner. A plate of meat arrived for me, and a plate for him, and he had a knife and just helped himself to mine. He was an uncouth so-and-so. They played me at wing-forward that day and I had never played there in my life. At 17 I was a hooker, then moved to prop, then second row for six or seven seasons. Finally I must have got brainier – I went into the back row.

'My second cap was against New Zealand, with players like Meads, Wilson Whineray, Don Clarke and Brian Lochore in the side. We drew 0–0 and they were to become a very big influence on me. One of my fortes was putting my body where other people would not. Close to the line, I dived on the ball and wrapped myself round it and was duly kicked to bits, but I saved the try. They played a ferocious rucking game and there were no touch judges to stop it. Scotland teams were far better ruckers than they are now. In 1967–68 we had a very good rucking pack – you'll need a long tape for this – we had good technique, always very tightly bound.

'But it was different then. There weren't so many phases. I've got a black-and-white video here, of the 1963 South of Scotland–All Blacks match. It's like junior rugby compared to now. The All Blacks won 8–0 and there were 10,000–15,000 there at Mansfield Park. I can still name the All Blacks team.

'They got better on the '67 tour with players like Waka Nathan, Kel Tremain, Fergie McCormick. That's when I really started to be influenced by the All Blacks. Particularly the forwards. Their body position, tightness, dynamism. In a way the game is a lot looser now. Eight men in a ruck is like poetry in motion. One game against England: there was an up and under, Dusty Hare caught it, Jim Calder took the ball off him and David Leslie drove and drove and drove; as he fell, the ball came back and Roy Laidlaw gave it to John Rutherford; he picked it off his toes and put Euan Kennedy in under the posts. Oh, I can remember that one all right – want some more tea? – that was a classic, almost unopposed in a way. A ruck like that doesn't always happen. Oh, aye, I remember that.

'Against England in 1964 I scored one try and gave the scoring pass for another two. That was the first time I remember the crowd running onto the pitch. When something like that happens, you start to think you're the best thing since sliced bread, but they dropped me the year after. P. C. Brown took my place. There were no subs in those days, you just had to sit in the stand and watch, so that's where I was for the Andy Hancock try. When he got the ball he never looked as though he was going anywhere, but he beat Eck Hastie, beat Ian Laughland and then Stewart Wilson. It shouldn't have happened.

'My last season for Scotland, as it turned out, was 1969. We got beaten by France at home and beaten in Wales. I remember they were reconstructing Cardiff Arms Park and we changed in prefabs. Graham Young, the SRU Vice-President, was playing that day. He only got one cap – he was up against Gareth Edwards. When we went to Ireland my opposite number was Ken Goodall and he had a very good game, scoring at least one try. I was dropped and never got back in again, although all through 1970 I tried to fight my way back. I think I sometimes played better after I got dropped, so maybe I should have got some more caps, I was 30, I'd played a lot of rugby and injuries were taking their toll. I managed another four seasons for Melrose, 17 seasons of club rugby in all.

'Coaching? Well, when I was playing I was captain of Melrose and in charge of training, and as a teacher I was used to organising things. I retired in 1974 and became Scotland B coach the same year. I had a clear coaching philosophy: a fast, dynamic game, with the emphasis on the ruck because everything emanates from that – the quick ball and movement and so on. It was based mainly on how the All Blacks played, round the forwards. The backs were the extras. Scotland over the years have had more identity with the way the New Zealanders play the game than any other northern hemisphere country. We get credit for things we don't even do well. We get credit for rucking well. But we don't ruck well. They talk about Scotland's ferocious rucking and actually it's not very good. I'm still looking for the perfect ruck. It's a discipline as much as anything.

'The turning-point for Scottish rugby came in 1982 in Cardiff, no doubt about that. Keith Robertson was ill and in isolation and Jim Pollock arrived from Northumberland. I had never even seen him play, I'd never even met him, and he scored a try. We stayed at Chepstow, about 20 miles out: I wanted them to imagine they were the SAS, going in to do the business and coming back out again. Well, we're maybe not as efficient as the SAS; but we don't leave many dead, either.

'In team talks I try to get a theme, a rhythm of what I am going to say. I sometimes look at the papers a day or two before to get a thread of what I'll say — maybe what the opposition coach has been saying about us. I do motivate people quite well by taking players down as low as they can get, then building them up again until they think they are ten feet tall. People think I give fearsome talks now, but as a player they were far more fearsome and they weren't recorded. The players from my era — like Ian McLauchlan, Ian Robertson, Peter Brown, Frank Laidlaw — they would say some of it was near the knuckle. Once in Argentina we won 6–3, or something. I can remember that team talk when I really went at people. I've mellowed a lot now.

'At international level Scotland do work themselves up, but an hour before a game I tend to treat them all the same. For some it's like water off a duck's back, but when I go for players it's usually the best players. If we've played badly I will pick the best players. You can destroy poor players. I'll go for people I know I can get riled. I also name people individually. You go fifteen to one and if they are all mixed up you can miss one which isn't very clever. But I have changed a lot. Instead of haranguing, I get them to say the things I would want them to say, because in the professional era it's their game. Sometimes things get quite heated. I used to get knocked around because I would be shoulder-charging them, trying to get them worked up, and they were very big players, some of them.

'Another thing: I would never become too friendly. I kept players at arm's length, and never went drinking with them or anything like that.

I never tried to be one of the boys. Once they tried to take my trousers down in the bus. After two or three seconds they realised it wasn't the right thing to do. There is a difference between a player and a coach. Some coaches, young coaches, have lived to regret it because they have played alongside their players, they've come up with them, and can't get their respect after that.

'When I was a player the Grand Slam became a yoke round your neck. First, it was 30 years since we won a Grand Slam, then 31, 32, and by the time 1984 came round it was over 50 years and it had become a great burden. But I coached better teams than the '84 team and they never won a Grand Slam. In 1984 Jim Renwick and Andy Irvine were on the bench. Great players. Andy Irvine was the best player I have ever seen playing for Scotland, but he never won a Grand Slam.

'But that's rugby. It has been my life and I wouldn't change any of it. I'm still lucky to be involved, I'm thankful for that. I've played and coached some great players, men who you would happily go into any battle alongside. Because in the end, rugby is about brave men . . . and some not so brave.'

For one so young, the receptionist at the Sheraton Hotel on Edinburgh's Lothian Road demonstrates a healthy sense of priority: 'You mean Gordon Brown the rugby player?' she asks.

There are two Gordon Browns in residence that night. One is the famous Broon frae Troon, the thirty-times capped and three-times Lions tourist G. L. Brown from the West of Scotland club; the other is the Chancellor of the Exchequer. The coincidence has obviously caused a minor hiccup in the Sheraton bookings system and Brown the rugby player is in the ministerial Elgin Suite, busily throwing the contents of a suitcase into wardrobes and onto shelves while his wife Linda (who for many years has suffered from the chronic fatigue syndrome ME) relaxes in the background. As Brown reasons, quite rightly, 'They've put me in the wrong room, but the buggers won't be able to shift me once I've unpacked.'

These things tend to happen to one of the most luminous characters of any sport, let alone rugby. He's in town to fulfill an after-dinner speaking engagement for a brewery. This is his full-time occupation now and a role he could have been born for. As raconteurs go, Brown is in the superleague.

In baggy shorts and T-shirt he looks in good shape. He's bald from the chemotherapy, of course, he's lost a fair bit of weight and the voice occasionally drops to a whisper; but the humour and energy are undiminished. We have an hour before his speaking engagement, a golden hour of good cheer, outrageous stories, laughter and – on my part, at least – something close to the occasional tear.

Gordon and his older brothers, John and Peter, were brought up on a council estate in Troon, Ayrshire. Peter, another great sporting eccentric, went on to captain Scotland while John, according to Gordon, was the best rugby player of all three – a 'natural thug' – although he didn't take up the game until the age of 28. Father Jock played in goal for Clyde, Hibs, Dundee and Kilmarnock: he won the Scottish Cup with Clyde in the season 1938–39 and gained one Scotland cap. Jock was also a scratch golfer and West of Scotland badminton champion. At the time of writing Brown Sen. has turned 84 and is still a 'bandit playing golf off 19', according to Peter.

'Mum was a great hockey player, too, so there's a fair bit of pedigree there,' says Gordon.

These sporting genes produced three brawny lads with natural ball-playing skills. And, as with the Calders and the Hastings and in common with most siblings, the seeds of a competitiveness that served so well later in life were sown early on at home. In the case of the Browns, this was usually with a round ball. The early ferocious kick-arounds up and down the narrow hallway of the family home, or on the huge area of waste ground on the estate, gave way to contests of a more formal nature and Gordon played in goal for Troon Juniors until the age of 16. For his conversion, West of Scotland, Scotland and the British Lions should thank an archetypal Brown incident in a game against Irvine Meadow some 36 years ago.

Says Gordon: 'It was a West of Scotland Cup tie and the game had a huge following, around 2,000 there. We were 6–1 down – none of the goals my fault, of course – when their winger came homing in on goal. He went round me and I brought him down with a rugby tackle. Bedlam. The crowd was going mental, throwing coins and howling for my blood. There were two policemen there and for the first time in their lives they had to escort a player off the field. In the dressing-room I could hear the voices outside planning dire things for me and I ran all the way home. The Monday night, I went to the rugby club and asked to play. I honestly thought I'd be safer.'

Brown began his senior career with Marr College FP before graduating to West of Scotland, where brother Peter, Sandy Carmichael and Alastair McHarg were among the established stars. Within a year he had his first Scotland cap, although there was still a steep learning curve ahead. Brother Peter, for one, still believed he had a lot to learn.

Gordon continues: 'There was a gutter ran all the way round our house and Peter, who had this great sergeant jump, would lick his fingers, leap up and leave the wet mark there. Then he'd turn round and say: "One of these days you will be able to do that."

'I never could, until one glorious night I managed it – I left the mark on the gutter. I ran back into the house, where Peter was slumped watching TV, to tell him; but of course by the time we got outside the mark had dried. To this day he still doesn't believe I did it.' ★

Peter Brown is fond of describing his young brother as 'my best mate'. To Gordon, Peter was his hero. 'I used to watch him from the schoolboys' enclosure at Murrayfield,' he remembers, 'and dream of playing alongside my big brother, but he wasn't in the team when I won my first cap, against the Springboks in 1969. Peter wasn't in the squad because he hadn't been available for the Argentina tour the year before. He was not happy.

'I remember putting the blue jersey on and looking in the mirror. By the time we got to the tunnel I'd had it on for 45 minutes. The Boks went down the tunnel first; the steward held us back. The sounds of a piper wafted down the tunnel and we set off. The further I ran down the tunnel, the bigger and bigger I seemed to get. I was 22 years old and playing for my country. In those days we sang "God Save the Queen" and I cried and cried. I was still crying when the Boks kicked off. I caught the ball and the Boks caught me and, boy, was that a welcome to international rugby.

'The game seemed all over in a flash and there we were – we had beaten the mighty Springboks. Back in the dressing-room I was still greetin' and Big McHarg came over and said, "Who hit you?" I said, "No one, I'm just happy." He came from Irvine and Irvine guys didn't show emotions like that. But I was now upsides my brother.

'That night I had a rendezvous with a young student from Dunfermline College of PE, later to be my wife Linda, and I told her I felt so good I could play another game. Next day I couldn't get out of my bed, it took three weeks to get over it.'

The longed-for ambition to play in the same Scotland side as Peter was fulfilled in the Five Nations season of 1970, although not under the circumstances either had expected: 'I usually got a phone call from a press guy before a match who would tell me the team and, sure enough, before the match against Wales in Cardiff the phone rang,' Gordon recalls. 'It wasn't the journalist, it was Peter. "Great news," he said. "I'm back in the team."

'"Who's out?"

'"You are."

'It was the only time in my life I doubted his parentage. But then he tore a calf muscle just before half-time and the physio, who happened to

★ Peter will not be convinced. See Chapter 10.

be our dad, waved the towel as a sign to the selectors for a replacement and I ran on as sub for my big brother.'

Brown's bulk (by then he was over 17 stone), scrummage and lineout capabilities and overall aggression made him a natural choice for the successful Lions tour of 1971 – the first and, so far, last to win a Test series in New Zealand – although he failed to displace the great Welsh lock Delme Thomas until the third Test at Wellington on 31 July.

Says Gordon: 'I had the greatest respect for Delme. He was like King Kong, biceps the size of my thigh. He and Willie John McBride, the other second-row, were like twin brothers. They went around together all the time.

'But I got in and on the eve of the match I was rooming with Willie John. I knew he had had a voice in selection and I was babbling away, "Willie John, I'm going to play the biggest game of my life . . . Willie John, I am going to give 200 per cent tomorrow." And of course he's just sat there in his chair, puffing on his pipe and saying nothing.

'"Willie John," I said, "I will repay the faith the selectors have shown in me."

'Suddenly, without even looking up, he spoke: "Well, I know who I wanted."

'To this day I don't know what the big bastard meant.'

Such was Brown's lineout dominance in the third Test that the All Blacks laid special plans for the Scot in the Fourth at Eden Park, Auckland. Andy Haden has written in his autobiography of a special training session, organised with his fellow lock Peter Whiting, which involved various nefarious schemes to neutralise Brown – at one time even including Haden talking in a broad Scottish accent.

In the end, their tactics were somewhat less complicated. Brown recalls, 'At the first lineout Jazz Muller, the prop, grabbed me and Whiting thumped me.' Brown went off with a knee injury later in the match, but the 14–14 draw secured the series for the Lions.

Ligament, knee and tendon problems cut huge swathes into Brown's Scotland career over the next three years, but he was still an automatic choice to partner McBride in the Lions' second row in South Africa in 1974. This Test series was savage, with Brown in the thick of much of the action – although fellow tourist Ian McLauchlan rated him disparagingly in the pugilism stakes: 'A hard rugby player, but he couldnae punch his way out of a wet bag'. Brown, in fact, broke his thumb when he threw a badly timed punch in the third Test.

This was the tour of the famous, and possibly apochryphal, 99 call when McBride would order his team-mates to 'get their retaliation in first' on uttering the magic numbers. McLauchlan insists the 99 story was 'a load of shite', but there is little doubt that the Lions, in those days of non-neutral referees, were determined to protect themselves at all costs.

'The referees were giving us no protection whatsoever,' says Brown. 'In the third Test at Port Elizabeth the Boks had brought in some heavies to try and sort us out, the main one being Moaner Van Heerden. Willie John had singled him out and warned that he would have a go, somewhere in their own half, early on. The nearest Lion would then wade in and give Van Heerden a doing. Sure enough, after ten minutes, Van Heerden belted Bobby Windsor for no reason whatsoever and I was the nearest man; that's how I broke my thumb.'

Broon's various on-field Donnybrooks – his Scotland career was ended by a 12-week suspension for retaliating to a vicious stamping incident in a Glasgow District game in December 1976 – have been detailed in his book *Broon frae Troon*. Most good judges, however, would say there is still a chapter or two to write.

In his decade as one of the world's leading locks, Brown had faced many uncompromising opponents: Whiting and Colin Meads of New Zealand; Benoît Dauga of France; McBride of Ireland; Thomas of Wales; and Chris Ralston of England. But none was as fearsome as the one that crept up behind the unsuspecting Scot late in 1999. 'I had these symptoms of a groin strain that wouldn't go away,' he says. 'I went to a physio and after a few visits he said, "There's something wrong because normally you're a quick healer and this won't go away." In the end, the doctor told me, "Gordon, you've got an aggressive lymphoma."

'"What the hell's that?" I said.

'"Cancer," he told me. Cancer! I thought, "That's something you die of" – this was something totally different.'

The diagnosis was non-Hodgkin's lymphoma and the chemotherapy began in February 2000. By May, and the time of this interview, the tumour had receded slightly and Brown was winning his biggest fight, although he would be the first to admit that there's still a long way to go.

Most of his friends had told me that, in a battle between the tumour and Gordon Brown, Mr Non-Hodgkin and his lymphoma would come a poor second best. When I tell him this, a wee crack appears in the happy-go-lucky facade.

'I've been lucky,' he says. 'Normally you only find out what people think of you when you actually die. I've found out and I'm still here. The number of people who have rung me up and said, "We love you, Broonie."'

It is these occasional bouts of introspection that cause concern in close friends like former Scotland team-mate John Frame; but Gordon Brown's wife Linda has never allowed him to lapse into self-pity. At the height of the chemotherapy treatment, when the suffering was at its worst, Brown was slumped in his chair at home in Troon feeling, he admits, very sorry for himself.

'You're not doing very well, are you?' said Linda.

'Lin, my body aches and I feel sick. I've got sores in my mouth and what feels like thrush in my throat. I feel bloody awful.'

To which Mrs Brown replied, 'Welcome to PMT.'

The burly, obdurate Glaswegian swears he will take the identity of his assailant to the grave with him. 'Only one other person knew, and that was Doug Smith, the manager, and he's dead now,' says Sandy Carmichael. Touring matches against the New Zealand province of Canterbury have often been lacerated by intimidation and violence. Canterbury players liked to perceive these games as extra-mural Tests and some of the most notable – and notorious – All Black hard men were blooded there.

Nothing before or since, however, has come close to matching the sheer brutality of the British Lions game in Christchurch in 1971.

Because it was also looked on by the Lions management as the fifth 'Test' of that tour, Smith and his selection team of coach Carwyn James and captain John Dawes had chosen what was generally considered the team that would contest the actual first Test against the All Blacks in Dunedin a week later. This included the first-choice props of Carmichael and the Connacht and Ireland forward Ray McLoughlin. The Lions had cut an unbeaten swathe through their provincial matches until then, with notable wins against Otago and the New Zealand Maoris and an eye-opening 47–9 victory over Wellington. The invincibility of New Zealand rugby was under threat. The Lions were no longer perceived as underdogs. But Canterbury were ready to adjust the odds.

Says Carmichael, 'They decided to to target me and Ray. Basically, up to then he and I had screwed to the ground anything of size and strength in New Zealand. They had forgotten about front-row play. They hadn't a clue.'

The violence wasn't long in coming. Ten minutes into the game a flurry of punches at a lineout shattered the cheekbone of the Scotland tight-head. Just to make sure, when the Scot next went to ground he was kicked in the head. 'You can see it on film. There's a ruck and I go to ground and someone kicks me in the face. I didn't realise at the time my cheekbone was broken and after some treatment they sent me out again.' The attack had been subtly done.

According to fellow Lions tourist Gordon Brown, 'Sandy's opposite number just hit him in every scrum, but Willie John McBride to this day swears he never saw a punch go in.' McLoughlin, however, broke his thumb attempting to retaliate and, like Carmichael, his tour was over.

Carmichael never uttered a word of complaint at the time. 'Some saw that as a fault in Sandy,' says Ian McLauchlan (who was to achieve instant fame as the Lions' Mighty Mouse when he took over the number 1 loose-head spot from McLoughlin). 'Others saw it as an attribute. Speaking personally, I would never have let that happen to me.'

Carmichael claims, however, he has managed to extract his own form of revenge. 'Because I never complained then or since, it will always hang over them. If I had shown my distaste it would all have blown over,' he insists. 'Even now, some 25 years later, if there's a tour match against Canterbury some New Zealand journalist will ring me up and ask about it. They are still saying they never did it and that the referee had never said, "I'll referee the game and you can do what you f*****g like." Which he did.

'Funnily enough, I went back to Canterbury in 1975 with Scotland and I arrived with a big black eye after getting a whack in training. Of course, they thought I had painted it on deliberately. They can ask anything they like about that match and they will still get nothing.

'One night at Ian McLauchlan's house Alex Wyllie [the Canterbury flanker and captain] was there and he said to McLauch, "Sandy's never said a word about it. I hope he doesn't think it was me." Even Grizzly was worried that I thought it was him.'

It remains, one senses, one of the regrets of Carmichael's life that the Canterbury incident overshadowed all the achievements of a career that earned him 50 Scotland caps and a reputation as one of the best props of the '70s – a player who can look back on six wins out of eleven games against England, but a man who was a lot more than a damaging scrummager. At West of Scotland – his one senior club for 32 years as player and coach – Carmichael and Gordon Brown perfected the lineout peel, where Brown would tap the ball down and Carmichael would take it on the burst in the scrum-half position and charge into midfield.

Says Brown, 'We were playing once against Jordanhill, a brutal, brutal game. With five minutes to go we did the peel. I knocked the ball down to him and he ran through the stand-off, then the inside-centre. The back-rows are hanging onto him, there's five guys on him and he just carried on, running through the full-back for the winning try. I swear the crowd behind the dead-ball area parted. They thought he was going to carry on through them.'

Born in Newton Mearns on the south side of Glasgow on 2 February 1944, Carmichael – like many rugby players from the West of Scotland, such as McHarg, McLauchlan and the Browns – had a soccer background. His grandfather was Alec Bennett who played for both sides of the Old Firm and won 11 caps for Scotland. Carmichael's formidable strength came from his schoolboy days as a shot putter and, later, from Highland Games during the summer.

'Big men should always play football before they play rugby,' he says. 'Rugby doesn't teach co-ordination of the body. McLauch and I used to joke about second-row forwards, the lowest form of human life. I'd say to him, "They can't even clap their hands together," and he would reply, "No, Sandy, you're wrong: they can't clap their hands AND nod their heads at the same time."

'I've seen some second-rows couldn't put one foot in front of another, but all the greats played football.

'As for strength training, the first time I ever touched weights was in 1969, before the tour of Argentina. The joke was that Broonie started with the bar and then put the collar on. But that year was the start for me. With McLauch, Big Al [McHarg], Broonie: that front four were together for most of my 11 years of rugby for Scotland. I went through six hookers and it has always been a test to name them all – a competition for a fleecy jacket or something. People got five but never got them all. They always missed out Derek Deans of Hawick. We had a very light pack, but technically very good. McLauch would struggle to get 15 stone, I was about 15.7, Big Al was about 14.3 with his wet socks on. I wished he weighed then what he weighs now, but seriously, he pushed well above his weight.

'When I arrived at West of Scotland Peter Brown would be out there on the pitch in the shadows in the darkness, on his own, playing right foot against left. He was like that. A total eccentric. McLauch and I met up in 1962 at West. Jordanhill had thrown him out for holding some sort of immoral party in his digs and I've played with him or against him ever since. He's a grumpy wee bastard, but we are great mates. We've fought too many wars together not to be friends.

'Those games against France, they were wars of attrition. You had to forget about ethics, you just had to be totally damaging. One game in Paris, McLauch was playing against Gerard Cholley, who they were trying on the tight-head at that time, and Ian came over and said, "That big bastard is tearing my eyes out." Cholley, a boxer, was gouging McLauch in every scrum.

'I asked him what he had done in return and McLauch said, "Well, I whapped him and that didn't even make him blink."

'"Have you headbutted him?"

'"Yes, that did NO good at all."

'"I'll tell you what we'll do. At the next scrum we'll hook the ball and take a quick step back, they'll fall to the floor and you can kick his head in."

'So that's what happened and next minute Cholley's getting to his feet scratching his head and looking puzzled and McLauch is hopping round in agony. He'd kicked him so hard the nail came off his big toe. Cholley, it didn't even dent him.

'The strongest prop I ever played against was Ray McLoughlin. He made a comeback in 1971 to try and get in the Lions team, but he had come back as a loose-head, having once been a tight-head. I was 27, he was maybe 33 or 34 and someone said before the game, "You'll have no problem. He's an old man, you'll screw the arse off him." The first scrum, I thought, "This is not funny." He played loose-head, all right, but with his feet in the tight-head position – totally the wrong angle. It was the only time in my career when I thought I might come off the floor and in fact I spent all the 80 minutes trying to stay on the ground.'

As with so many others in the front-row union, McLoughlin and Carmichael became bosom buddies. Some of the friendships formed on his two Lions tours of 1971 and '74 were less predictable.

'You learn a lot about life on those tours,' he says. 'Both times I was looking forward to the trip, but a bit worried about some of these English people we had to talk to. Bob Hiller, I thought he was a stuffy-nosed bastard. John Spencer and David Duckham called themselves God One and God Two. Then I found out Hiller had the driest sense of humour of anyone I had ever met, Duckham was a gentleman and Spencer – well, Spencer was just mad. I remember sitting in my room with Duckham after the Canterbury game in '71 and he said to me, "Sandy, we will just sit here and have a drink until whatever time you have to go out and meet the press, or whatever, and when you do go out I'll be there with you." He and I have become very close friends. We invited Duckham and his wife up to a do once: he thought it was a Lions reunion for '71, but it was to commemorate Scotland beating England twice in a week. He took it all very well.'

Carmichael has needed all his courage and humour over the last few years. Three hip replacements and arthritis in an ankle necessitate the use of a stick to walk any distance. He is in pain most of the time: 'It's all right when I'm sat here talking to you, but it will start as soon as I stand up and start moving about.' The spirit is undamaged, however, as he demonstrates by insisting on hobbling back up the two flights of stairs to his office at the Glasgow plant-hire firm where he works, to retrieve my notebook. He has also remained undiminished in other fields.

There is a son of 29 and a daughter of 26 from Sandy's first marriage. But Alison, the second Mrs Carmichael, is expecting the couple's second child in late 2000. Carmichael will be 56 then. Of his youngest son he says, wrily, 'He's only two, but I can't catch him now.'

Alison, as Alison Brand, played as a prop in the first Scotland women's international – against Ireland in February 1993 – thus prompting the ultimate pub quiz question: *Name the two Scotland tight-heads who married each other.*

4. DAVID LESLIE

It's almost a decade since David Leslie made a tackle in anger, but the competitiveness that made him one of the most outstanding back-row forwards in the history of Scottish rugby and player of the Grand Slam year of 1984 by a considerable margin has never been subdued.

At his immaculate house in the seaside town of Broughty Ferry, a bare half-mile from his architect's business close to the shore, there is a warm welcome from his wife, Pamela, and Dalmatian pup, Maverick. There is home-made soup and fresh salmon from Loch Fyne and an explanation: 'When I heard you were coming to interview me for this book I was determined that my hospitality would be better than anyone else's.' Now that is undying competitiveness.

Pamela swears with a smile that the occasional nocturnal digs in the ribs are merely her husband reliving past Five Nations battles. The man himself admits, 'It doesn't go away very easily. I just wish I could still be doing it.'

Leslie's often manic commitment to the Scotland cause is legendary. His pre-match psyching-up sessions and total disregard for his own safety during a match are still spoken of with awe . . . and, it must be said, the occasional smile. The descriptions of Leslie in his days in the maroon-and-white of Gala or the blue of Scotland invariably come couched in martial terms. He is always the 'man who would be first over the top in the trenches', or the 'man you would pick to make a tackle for your life'. Roger Baird, the wing who played in the same Grand Slam-winning side of 1984 calls him 'David Lloyd George Leslie' and, asked to pencil in the first names in his imaginary Scotland all-star team, Jim Telfer names Andy Irvine first and David Leslie a close second – making a nonsense of a rumoured aversion to players who went to fee-paying schools.

Meeting Leslie for the first time, and seeing at first hand the occasional glimpses of that old intensity as he recalls distant battles, the words of

Wellington in describing his troops at Waterloo spring instantly to mind: 'I don't know what effect these men will have on the enemy, but by God they frighten me.'

Leslie himself is conscious of all this. 'I think, and I hope, it's because they respect me,' he says. 'I know I used to get steamed up before a game, but I felt I had to mentally prepare myself. When they were introducing us to royalty before a game, I just wanted whoever it was to get lost so I could get on with it. I used these images to build up my confidence. Being Scottish and playing rugby is not easy. You have to make small resources go a long way. It was how you saw youself and how others and the opposition saw you. They all thought I was nuts going through this routine of imagining a pass, scoring a try or making a tackle – and then, of course, all the sports psychologists came in, asking players to do exactly the same thing, and they realised I wasn't so daft after all.'

The springs of Leslie's competitiveness can be traced to his upbringing in a family of two brothers and two sisters in Dundee: 'We all fought for the last strawberry. None of us liked coming second. It was my brother Roger who introduced me to rugby. Roger is a much harder character than me. I certainly wouldn't take him on in a square go.'

Educated at Dundee High School and Glenalmond – the establishment responsible for that other highly motivated Scotland player, David Sole, as well as John Frame and Rob Wainwright – Leslie qualified as an architect from Dundee University. It was while playing rugby for lowly Dundee HSFP that he caught the eye of the national selectors and the Scotland B coach Jim Telfer. Leslie's speed to the breakdown, his aggression and fearsome rucking were the epitome of back-row play to Telfer. In 1975, against Ireland, Leslie became the first (and so far last) Scotland player to be capped from Division 4. His arrival in the Scotland set-up raised a few eyebrows. Some saw him as something of a public-school dandy and one international room-mate remembers arriving back to find Leslie in bed – with gloves on. Everyone's perception changed, however, as soon as he pulled on a dark-blue jersey.

As with so many other players, the shrewd Telfer proved adroit at bringing out the best a newcomer, particularly one as enthusiastic, ambitious and determined as David Leslie. There were other factors in the new player/coach relationship, too.

'My father died in 1969 when I was 17,' says Leslie. 'You could say that from then on I was looking for a father figure and some sort of approval from someone. I think Jim sensed this when I first came under his wing with Scotland. He is a fundamentalist and I hope he saw the same determination and commitment in me that there has always been in him. I think he admired my attitude to the game.

'But I soon realised that I would have to learn a different culture in international rugby. I had to learn how to cheat, which rather went against my upbringing and the sort of sporting ethos taught at Glenalmond. I had to learn how to play the offside lines, pull the opposition into rucks, using the studs to ruck them off the ball. But it was sink or swim and, as I said, I didn't like coming second.

'I won my first few caps while still at Dundee HSFP, but round about 1976 there was some pressure from the Scotland selectors to play Division 1 rugby. They wanted me in a more competitive situation and I had three years at West of Scotland before the firm moved me to Galashiels and I started playing for Gala. Borders rugby was something else again. Gala v. Hawick: there'd be 6,000–7,000 people there and it was very compelling stuff, possibly more pressurised at times than internationals. There was abrasiveness and abusiveness in about equal measure.'

Any player as headstrong and as fearless as Leslie is always eventually going to suffer injury. Between 1977 and 1980 his Scotland appearances were limited to two games – against New Zealand and England – before a bad leg break in a Gala club game early in 1982 seemed to have ended his career permanently.

At the time Leslie was close to 30 and said publicly that he would welcome the time off to spend with his family. It was a statement that may have cost him a place on the disastrous 1983 Lions tour to New Zealand. However, as with Colin Deans, Jim Calder, Roy Laidlaw, John Rutherford and Telfer himself, that tour (and in this case Leslie's absence from it) proved a catalyst for the Grand Slam of 1984. When the international season opened that season against Wales, there were an awful lot of Scots with something to prove. Looking back now, for many the sight of Leslie – hands reversed on hips and elbows forward in that characteristic pose, as he waited for a long Deans throw to the tail of a lineout, or with arms raised in celebration for one of Scotland's eight tries that year – remains a defining memory.

In Wales Leslie cleaned out the new Welsh back-row golden boy Richard Moriarty and gave the scoring pass for Iain Paxton's try. Against England at Murrayfield he played a major role in Euan Kennedy's try, an effort straight out of the Telfer textbook on power forward play: a hoisted ball from Laidlaw, Jim Calder picking up, Alan Tomes driving, Leslie and the pack clearing English bodies and the ball presented on a plate for Rutherford to put his centre in under the posts. It was an archetypal

Scottish try, the recollection of which even today brings an enthusiatic, proprietal glint to the eye of Telfer.

At Lansdowne Road, the penalty try conceded by the Irish captain Willie Duggan should rightly have been credited to Leslie when he was impeded by the Irishman diving in from the side when he was about to touch down after a Scotland scrum wheel. It was also, it should perhaps be said, a grasping Leslie hand on the Irish blindside's jersey that gave Laidlaw the space to score his second try from a scrum close to the line.

Finally, there was France at Murrayfield, where a Leslie collision with France scrum-half Jerome Gallion was seen by many as the turning-point of the game. There were some mutterings from the French later after their try-scorer was carted off, but Leslie insists today, 'It was totally accidental. That wasn't my style of play. And anyway, Pierre Berbizier wasn't a bad replacement, was he?' Iain Paxton, Scotland's number 8 in that game, confirms: 'David was just totally committed to the tackle. All he was seeing was the ball and Gallion to an extent was doing the same. The bigger man won.'

Ironically, it was one of the few occasions when Jean-Luc Joinel beat Leslie to a Deans throw at the end of a lineout that gave Scotland the Grand Slam-winning try – the French flanker tapping down straight to Calder. Leslie's career was replete, the triumph sweetened by the thought that his family, including his two-year-old son, were in the Murrayfield crowd to see his moment of immortality.

However he was quickly to find that, even for a man sharing in Scotland's first Grand Slam in six decades, glory can be fleeting.

'Our first child died at birth and when our son Roderick arrived we cherished him. Not indulged him, just cherished him that little bit more. I had often thought that the son who did not survive hadn't had chances and one had been granted chances. It was disrespectful in many ways not to make the most of those chances. Anyway, Pamela and my brother Roger took Roderick along to Murrayfield for the game against France and I have to admit I was a bit worried in case he was frightened by the crowd or that he might be a nuisance.

'Neither of these things, as it turned out. As the Murrayfield cacophony rose and we got closer to the first Grand Slam in 60 years, my two-year-old son was asleep in his mother's arms. Later, Roger brought him into the dressing-room and there was Roderick with what I thought were the shining eyes of an adoring child looking up at his hero of a father.

'Then he said, "Daddy, Daddy, weren't the bagpipes wonderful?"'

Ian McLauchlan is noted, notorious even, for not beating about the bush. Asked to name the best Scotland front row of his time, he has no hesitation: 'Me, me and me. I thought I was pretty good.' Well, who is going to argue with a former prop who won 43 Scotland caps – the last coming at the age of 37 – and in eight British Lions Tests finished on the losing side only once? A man of whom his Scotland front-row colleague Sandy Carmichael once told the '71 tour manager Doug Smith, 'His heart is bigger than his body'? Particularly at 7.30 a.m. in McLauchlan's large Gothic pile on Edinburgh's upmarket Kaimes Road on a day when the Mighty Mouse of legend is more like a 58-year-old bear with a sore head?

'Career? I was born in Tarbolton in Ayrshire, went to Ayr Academy, then Jordanhill College, taught for a few years and then started up my own business.'

It was then that the words of Gordon Brown came drifting back: 'I always had a picture of McLauchlan on my mantlepiece to keep my kids back from the fire.'

However, for his trenchant opinions on the game, and its proponents past and present, it's well worth meeting McLauchlan more than halfway. He preferred, for example, Dick Milliken to fellow Ulsterman Mike Gibson as a Lions player and tourist. Like Sandy Carmichael and Gordon Brown, he formed lifelong friendships with the so-called stuffy-nosed Englishmen David Duckham and John Spencer. And he'd much rather talk about soccer – Kilmarnock and Rangers in particular – than rugby.

And McLauchlan's bark turns out to be far worse than his bite.

The strength that made McLauchlan one of the greatest of post-war props was partly hereditary: 'My father was a miner and a very strong man,' he says. 'But I also worked on the local farms in the summers from the age of 13 – no shite about how old you were, then. I was always a good trainer.

'At Ayr Academy we'd have these cross country runs where you'd set off on Thursday and come back Sunday morning. I started in the second row there and also played wing-forward and centre and full-back. I liked to be involved all the time. When I went to Jordanhill to do PE in 1961 I started on the weights and I was one of the few guys who trained every day. It was there that I came under the influence of Bill Dickinson, who was a superb athletics coach as well as rugby coach. He was years ahead of his time.

'Bill once wrote a paper for the SRU stating that every position should have specific training. He worked out that, say, a second-row would go through a match 30 per cent at a jog, 30 per cent at two-thirds pace and 40 per cent at full pace. Of course, they thought he was barmy. Then when the All Blacks started it with Jim Blair, who was a student of Bill Dickinson's, the SRU thought it was wonderful. If you want to be truthful about it, Bill was totally self-centred. He committed himself solely to what he was interested in – and that was rugby. He got guys who had never played rugby in their lives and turned them into exceedingly good players. At Jordanhill he built a really good side out of nothing. He was very slightly built and blind as a bat, but he got what he wanted.

'In those days Jordanhill had to scrabble around for fixtures. We would play Melrose and beat them and they never played us again. Said they didn't like our style of play. My attitude is that if someone beats you, you want to get back at them; but that's their attitude. I played for Glasgow district from the day I went to college and had a Scotland trial at 21. I got capped at 26. Dickinson said he had a fall-out with a couple of selectors and that kept me out. But better late than never. I laugh at people now who say I was a bit small to play. I was 17 stone. Sandy Carmichael was lighter than me.

'The first cap was against England in 1969. They had Piggy Powell and Keith Fairbrother in the other front row. We lost 8–3, but I always felt we had a good side at that time. There were superstars who went unrecognised, like Jock Turner, who was always a very under-rated player – in Scotland he was a fantastic rugby player. He could kick and pass, he was a huge tackler and he had a tremendous vision in the game But he never got recognised. I'm not saying Jock was a great trainer, but he was a great player to play with, and a bad player to play against. We also trained very hard – me, Sandy, Colin Deans, Alan Tomes. Gordon Brown didn't train much, but his brother Peter was very conscientious. It's a fallacy to say the game is any different now. Sandy Carmichael, Gordon

Brown and Alan Tomes would walk into any team now. The game changes and you change with it.

'In 1971 they picked me for the Lions tour. Carwyn James (the coach) was a really terrific guy. I have great memories of him. Like Bill Dickinson, Carwyn wanted his own players, but there was a five-man or six-man selection team in Wales at the time and they didn't want Carwyn.

'In Canterbury I was on the subs' bench when Sandy came off injured. I was ready to go on, but Sandy wanted to go back on. Like a lot of things in New Zealand then, if you didn't retaliate they just kept on going. They'd made that clear from day one. But travelling 12,000 miles to get the shit kicked out of you is not my idea of fun. Sandy never retaliated. Some saw it as a flaw in his character, others saw it as a great strength; but he was just a rugby player, he wasn't a boxer.

'Ray [McLoughlin] wasn't really a puncher either. Some people said he hadn't broken a bone at all, that he was sent home under false pretences. Apart from [Mike] Gibson, I got on with everyone. Gibson as a player was all right with good players. But he kept one of the best players in the country, the guy who won the Canterbury game, out of the team: Arthur Lewis. I'd rather have played with him. The friendships of '71 and '74 are a phenomenon of rugby; the wives get on, too. It's like meeting family. The boys are really close. It's like Jordanhill College, where a guy in our year arranges reunions. There are 40 guys in a year and 12 turn up, always the same 12 – and if you look back, it's the guys who went out for a drink together, who went canoeing on Loch Lomond together. The other guys, some of them stayed at home, some were non-drinkers and some anti-social bastards. It depends on what your make-up is and what the group of guys are about.

'It was [Lions manager] Doug Smith called me Mighty Mouse. They thought I was too small and they found out to their cost I wasn't. I still get on with Alex Wyllie – whom some thought of as the big bad guy of New Zealand rugby – and [Alex] Sutherland. Wyllie stayed over here once and I think there would always be a huge gap in your life if, in what is a hard physical game, you couldn't meet the guys you'd played against in the street after the game. A lot of guys don't drink now, which is maybe not a bad thing, but I'll just have a cup of tea with them. It's too dangerous to have serious enemies.

'I was on two successful Lions sides. It was a progression. A lot of guys from '68 were the nucleus of '71, and '71 for '74. John Dawes broke the chain in '77. Touring with the Lions is a difficult thing. It's like football over here. Alistair McColst couldn't walk down Princes Street and not be molested by people. Well, it's like that in New Zealand and South Africa. Because of the nature of some of the journalists – who are not really sports journalists following the tour – they are looking for any sort of transgression. Even at play you can't relax. Take David Duckham, one of the kindest, nicest guys you would ever meet in your entire life, a real English gentleman and I say that as a great compliment. In 1971 one of the New Zealand journalists wrote that he was an archetypal Englishman, aloof and stand-offish. But he was anything but. He was totally different. He was tall, blond and handsome but at that time very shy. How can someone write that?

'Take the time when I was writing my book. There's a guy called Herbert Waddell, a legend in Scottish rugby. Now Waddell wasn't everyone's cup of tea, but he changed seats on a flight from London to Glasgow and he said to me, "Never write anything in a book you wouldn't want the fellow's children to read." And there were two or three things I'd put in the book and I changed them because of that. If you say that someone is a selfish horrible bastard, the boy's kids might think, "My dad's a shit because it says so in a book." Ten years down the line your opinions might change. You can tell a joke at a dinner and then deny you ever said it, but if you write it you cannot deny it. In the heat of the moment players can say anything, you come off the field and your level of sanity is nowhere. Writing it is different.

'They called '74 a forwards thing. Rubbish. Tommy Grace scored 14 tries, J.J. Williams 13 tries, Andy Irvine 11. It was classic rugby. The coach, Syd Millar, had said he didn't want any miss moves, criss-cross in the middle of the field: he just wanted the ball out to the wings. JJ was absolutely on fire, as was Billy Steele earlier in the tour before he got injured. Billy was one of these guys – against three men in a five-yard area he'd beat all three of them. Give him the ball on halfway with no one in front of him and tell him to run it in, he couldn't do it. He'd always get caught, he just wasn't quick enough. But Billy was the Dancer. And JJ – give him the ball anywhere and he always wanted to score. He was lightning fast, by far the fastest man I've ever played against.

'That 99 thing was absolute crap. The guy who said "Get your retaliation in first" was Dod Burrell, way before any of these Lions tours. Dickinson always said there was nothing ever achieved in anger so you had to be furiously calm. All these guys who ran in swinging punches never hurt anyone. It was the guy who waited and picked his moment who did the damage. Nobody ever saw them. You see guys going windmilling in, it's a waste of time. Gordon Brown was never a puncher; it was the other guys who hung about who did serious damage. Ninety-nine per cent of rugby players you could say to them, "Give me one there [on the chin]" and they couldn't put you on your arse. David Leslie never threw a punch in his life, Sandy never threw a punch, Mervyn Davies never threw a punch; but by Christ, when Mervyn Davies tackled you, you knew you had been hit by something. Like a bus.

'Fergus Slattery was never a puncher, but pick a guy you would want behind you in the scrum, on the flank, and Fergus would come very, very close to the top. Dickie Milliken was a nice guy, but hard as nails. He backed off nothing. That type of guy, very quiet. I used to say to the kids at school, "Never ever assume that the guy you see walking down Sauchiehall Street in a pinstripe suit and with a briefcase under his arm is a big shite because some of them I know personally are not."

'My last game for Scotland was against New Zealand in 1979. After that, I kind of vaguely remember a club game and at one point I thought, "I can't be bothered with this any more." So that was it. No regrets at all. I was 38 when I packed it in. I did some marathon running and got into that. I talked to some guys and they asked what I wanted to do. I said, "Under four hours." They told me how to do it and I did it. It was just another challenge. I played charity football, but gave it up because I found I was still very competitive and I thought, "What's the point?" The red mist comes down and I'm going to get hurt or I'm going to hurt someone. I have a business which is multi-faceted, doing corporate hospitality, event management, things like that. I represented the whole Scotland squad when they went semi-professional; but I also do consultancy work for the SRU, so there was a conflict of interest.

'I never think about rugby at all. I couldn't tell you the score of 90 per cent of the games I played in. But I still go to rugby, I've got a lot of friends in rugby, and I enjoy rugby. It's a great sport and I'd like to see a lot of younger guys committing themselves to the professional game.'

Farnham lies on the border between the English home counties of Hampshire and Surrey. There are colonial-style office blocks and shops, pseudo-cobbled streets and pastry shops that call themselves boulangeries. But there are also the Friday night meetings between the local youth and the squaddies from nearby Aldershot which may explain the plastic glasses in the bars, bouncers on pub doors and broken mirrors in the gents. Farnham, in fact, is the heart of middle-England and a more unlikely place to find one of the great stalwarts of Scotland's Grand Slam year of 1990 would be difficult to find. Like any Scot in exile, Derek White, who works as a financial adviser in Farnham, has to take some occasional stick – particularly about Scotland's sporting prowess – but the Calcutta Cup defeat of England in 2000 offered him some welcome one-upmanship in the office bantering stakes. 'There were some interesting parallels with 1990,' says White. 'It was quite a pleasure coming into work.'

With those raving extroverts Finlay Calder and John Jeffrey as his most regular breakaway partners in the decade he played for Scotland from 1982, it is hardly surprising White has maintained a low profile. Quiet and unassuming by nature, he could however play the heavy when he needed to, according to Calder. He also, insists Jeffrey, possesses a devastatingly dry sense of humour. Jeffrey recalls a moment in the Grand Slam decider against England at Murrayfield in 1990, when early on the England prop Jeff Probyn stepped all over David Sole after a scrum had collapsed. 'Derek was in straight away, swinging a punch,' says Jeffrey. 'Unfortunately he missed and whapped me instead. "Oops, wrong Jeffrey", he said. 'Not a bad crack in the heat of combat. But Derek was never afraid of getting stuck in. He wasn't a dirty player, but if there was something to be sorted out, Derek would get involved.'

Like the Calders and the 1990 Grand Slam lock Chris Gray, White comes from Haddington in East Lothian. He was born there in January 1958 but, unlike the Calders, there was little rugby background in the family.

'My brother Alastair played for the local team, but that was it. I was tall and skinny, but did a lot of swimming when I was younger, which filled me out a bit. I started playing at Dunbar, then moved on to Haddington. We got relegated twice and eventually a guy I worked with from Galashiels suggested I joined them. They had a really strong pack. There was Bobby Cunningham, Kenny Lawrie, Jim Aitken, Tom Smith, Gordon Dickson and David Leslie – maybe six or seven caps in the pack. For the first year I basically sat on the bench. I was about 22 and left when I was 29. Games with Hawick in those days could be quite brutal, but you tended to learn very quickly. I remember playing against Alan Tomes: that was my introduction to the dark arts of rugby and I ended up getting stitched up a few times. I used to hate him, but then I toured with him and found out what a great guy he was.

'I had ten years with Scotland, starting in 1982 against France. I was rooming with David Johnston. He was zonked out and got up at about 10.30 in the morning. I'd been up at 3.30 getting the papers. It was just nerves. After that I was a lot calmer about it. My second game was against Wales and I was stunned by Cardiff Arms Park, the waves of noise. They had all the possession, but kept making mistakes. Yes, I remember Jim Calder's try. Obviously Iain Paxton was there, because he wasn't fast enough getting across the pitch to cover! The same with Tomes and Jim. I was away corner-flagging, of course.

'Jim Telfer was coach and he used to be really, really hard on me in particular. I read somewhere recently that he said that's how he got the best out of me. But he bullied me. We used to have these team meetings where he would pick on me. I'm quite laid back and quiet and maybe that brought out the worst in him. Usually the pack was there and John Jeffrey, Finlay and myself – the back row – would all sit together, never realising he was focusing on us 100 per cent. After that we split up and sat in different parts of the room, but that didn't work either because then he would have a meeting with just the three of us.

'We had a good back-row understanding, with a few notable exceptions that Telfer reminded us of ad nauseam. Against Ireland, once, Brendan Mullin came back on a switch and basically ran through all three of us. Telfer used that a lot after that. He is so enthusiastic, but he sometimes goes right over the top. I recall him telling me once, "Your body doesn't belong to you, it belongs to Scotland, go out there and sacrifice it." But I think his approach was the best. On the '89 Lions tour Roger Uttley was forwards coach and the English guys were obviously used to something different. Roger would say something like "Come on, we'll try that one more time" and Dean Richards or someone would say, "Nah, we've done enough" and that was it. Nobody would ever dare say that to Telfer.

'When I moved down to London Scottish, it was a bit of a culture shock going from the Borders to a city club. There were different challenges, different teams. London Scottish were in Division One then, it was a higher standard than Scotland and they played a different style. The forwards were much quicker. The move resurrected my career and the other thing that helped was Margot Wells. She made a hell of a difference to the team in things like strength endurance work. We were always very fit, powerful and dynamic. She was another one gave me a hard time, but she's very good.

'The timetable in those days was: play for the club on Saturday; away up to Scotland on Saturday night; a training session on Sunday; fly home Sunday night; and return to Scotland on Tuesday, staying there until the game on Saturday, then heading back home on Sunday. You were more or less a full-time rugby player. I can't see, either, that they train any harder now than we did, because there is only so much you can do. I'd like to have tried full-time pro for four or five years. But what do you do when you stop?

'I toured with the Lions in 1989 and that was like being a full-time player. It was pretty intense. But it was great fun and good playing with other nations. It helped the next year because we had nine Scots in Australia. Teams like England have a sort of mystique about them, but then you spend six weeks away with them and you see things differently. We knew from training, for example, that they weren't as fit as the Scottish lads.

'In 1990 Scotland weren't playing that well. France we beat convincingly, but they had Carminati — a nasty piece of work, he was — sent off. Wales was tight and Ireland tight, so it was probably the right way to do it. England had been running in 20 or 30 points a game and we hadn't reached our potential.

'I scored two tries against Ireland. Sean Lineen took a great angle off Chalmers, I think, and cut back in. JJ was standing offside as usual: he got stopped just short of the line and popped it up to me. The second I was quite pleased with, a pick-up from number 8, and I just got in at the corner. I used to work a lot with Kenny Milne the hooker and he would strike it hard – the ball wouldn't hit the ground and come straight to me. Because it's so quick their flanker is usually still pushing and you can get beyond him and onto the stand-off. The Irish thought it was a double movement, but the referee, Clive Norling, said, "No, it was immediate." A lot of refs would have given it as a double movement. I was sat with Clive at a dinner a few years later and he said, "If it wasn't for me, Scotland wouldn't have won the Grand Slam!"

'I had a great time with JJ and Fin, particularly in 1990. We were 100 per cent committed on the pitch, but we also had a lot of fun. JJ and Fin were having a go at Micky Skinner in the Grand Slam game. He didn't know what was going on, he didn't know what to do. "It's not supposed to be like this," he was thinking. Mike Teague [the England number 8] told a story about Skinner going round before the game telling everyone it was going to be so easy, and Teague had said, "I don't know, I think they might be a bit fired up for this." Early on, we took a quick tap and Fin ran it. Skinner got a big hit in, but Fin stayed on his feet and the pack piled in and drove them back about 15 yards. Skinner was lying at the bottom of the ruck when Teague said to him, "Still think this is going to be easy?"

'Once at Murrayfield against Wales, Fin was at the back of the lineout alongside Mark Jones, who was the great white hope of Welsh rugby at the time but then went to rugby league. The Welsh were gasping and Fin turned to him and said, "Great fun, this, isn't it?" I did my knee ligaments in during the Grand Slam game; Skinner landed on my leg. It was a big disappointment, but just one of those things. Derek Turnbull came on and did a great job. It didn't stop the celebrations. I was still dancing at 3.30 in the morning. The unsung hero in that game was Paul Burnell. I was at his testimonial dinner when Kenny Milne stood up and said there was a time in that match when we were under tremendous pressure and if it hadn't been for Paul we wouldn't have won that match. He never gets recognised for it.

'I think I still share the record of Scottish forward tries with JJ. Number 11 came in January 1992, after JJ had retired. It was a pushover try, against England of all teams. They were stunned. Normally you go down and get settled, it's nice and easy, the ball comes in and you push. We had what I think we called the Australian Call where, as soon as you hit, the ball comes in and you start driving straight away. Before they knew it, they were five yards beyond their own line. JJ was sitting up in the commentary box and I could see him as I was running back and I was dying for him to turn round.

'I retired the same season as David Sole. I was 34 and could have gone on for another season, but I had a wife, I'd started a family and I had a career. The last game at Murrayfield, I made a fantastic tackle on Franck Mesnel, which was as good as scoring a try. It was a great feeling because it was at full stretch and I also hit him pretty hard and he lost the ball. It was a nice way to go out.

'I played for London Scottish the following season, then gave up for six months. It was then that a Scots guy living in Guildford rang me up and asked if I wanted to coach the local team, Old Guildfordians. I did that for a couple of years, then moved on to Marlow and I've been there ever since. I think I've retired now. About three months ago I had a shoulder injury and it's still giving me bother now. I played the last four seasons and was happy with the first three, but not so much with the last one. I get a good response as coach. If you have played at a higher level they do actually listen to you.

'I have to say I don't take an awful lot from Jim Telfer. I wouldn't like to put anybody through what he put me through. I once tried on Marlow the SAS speech he used in Wales in 1982. It didn't work.'

'You've really f****d up.' John Jeffrey's first greeting was a bracing introduction to his legendary candour. Like every farmer, Jeffrey's life is governed by the progress of the sun across the sky and I was 42 minutes late; he already had more pressing matters. This was my third attempt at a rendezvous, the others being aborted by matters like calving and the planting of seed potatoes on the Jeffrey farmstead. But at least I had earned a muddy-pawed welcome from his ancient mongrel, Smudge, and Jeffrey himself could not maintain his bad humour for long. The door was opened.

With only six farm staff, Jeffrey works 1,800 acres just outside Kelso. There are 1,000 acres of cereals, 150 acres of seed potatoes (part of a large co-operative), 100 pedigree cows (mainly Charolais) and 150 grey-faced ewes.

Jeffrey was born there in March 1959 and, apart from schooldays at Merchiston Castle School in Edinburgh and two spells at Newcastle University, has never moved away. He lives alone, his parents having moved out into Kelso, and he has never married – 'No one would have me. Far too many sensible females around.'

When Jeffrey played and toured with Scotland he could afford time off work, an impossibility now, he says. 'When I played, Father was still very active on the farm and the farming business was very healthy. We made a lot of good money and I could afford time off. I couldn't do that now. Farming is in a bad state and losing a lot of money. Anyway, you couldn't be an international rugby player now and do a job at the same time.'

Unlike many in the Borders, Jeffrey does not come from a rugby background, although 'Mum and Dad became great followers when I played for Kelso and Scotland.

'I played for Kelso Harlequins Under-18 side before I went to

Newcastle University to study agriculture. I got thrown out after a year for failing my exams – too much rugby and socialising. But I went back eventually and got a degree. I actually played for English Universities when we hammered Scottish Universities at Durham and even scored a try. I have always waited for that to be produced in the papers before an England–Scotland game, but the media boys missed out on that one. I was really surprised. Something else people probably don't know, but which I always tell kids, is that I only got two 1st XV games for Merchiston Castle. It caused some grief to me at the time but it just shows there is always hope even if you are not in the school 1st XV. I was a late developer. Roger Baird was in the year before me all the way through school – at St Mary's in Melrose, and Merchiston – but he overtook me at rugby because he was really a star in his days there.

'At Kelso I played behind a huge front five who just dominated things and made it easy for us to pussyfoot around, scoring tries and doing the glory stuff. Ian Forsyth, Gary Callander, Jim Newton, Cammy Lowther and Jim Hewitt. There have been 14 internationalists in 120 years at Kelso and there were six that year. The back row was me, Eric Paxton and Michael Minto. As a flanker you do learn to bend the rules, but you have to learn to take advantage of your opposite number. Fin and I have always been told we were never onside but we never got lagged for offside. The laws of rugby are fairly flexible, it's never black and white where the offside line is, and you have to push the referee. Sure we'd kill the ball, too, if it meant saving a try. I would go over the ball and get kicked to pieces – I've no problem with that. Sometimes my back would look like a game of noughts and crosses.

'Fin was a great talker, I hardly said anything! Fin was always having a go at wee Andy Robinson. With Ackford and Dooley in the England lineout we knew we'd never win the ball, so we would just throw the ball long to Fin at the back every time and he'd be saying to Robinson, "Here it comes again, Andy, are you ready?" – then, whoosh, away he'd go.

'Once there was a picture of Robinson in the programme with a caption saying something like "Andy Robinson will be covering every blade of grass at Twickenham today" and Fin would turn to him at the lineout and say, "Look, there's another blade of grass you've missed." I think Fin, Derek and myself got very close to the world record for a back row playing together. Derek was a very laid-back sort of guy, but with an amazingly droll sense of humour.

'The one big difference between me and Derek and Fin is that they love whisky and I can't stand the stuff. One time we were staying at Gleneagles and someone came to speak to us and it was awful boring. But Fin and Derek had managed to acquire a bottle of whisky and were sat at the back drinking out of it all the way through. By the end of the evening they were absolutely plastered, like a couple of schoolboys pissed at the back of the hall. The next day we were doing fitness tests: you should have been doing 15 or 16 lengths, but Fin pulled out after three and Derek after four, and of course Jim Telfer was going mental. The back row was his pride and joy and here they were, pulling out. It was unheard of.

'Derek was a very talented player, but Telfer really had it in for him, which was good because it meant Fin and I missed a lot of it. The first game of the Grand Slam year against Ireland, Derek was just lambasted by Jim and he told me, "This is too much. I'm here to play rugby for fun. I'll just quit." And then, of course, he scored two tries and came off the pitch saying, "Great game, this!"

'I was never blessed with speed. In fact, I was slow for a wing-forward, but I had good speed endurance – I had what they call a big engine. I also think I was good at anticipating what the fly-half was going to do, whether he was going to kick or pass, and I would try and position myself. Obviously, if you got it wrong you would end up on the wrong side of the pitch looking a bloody fool and you'd get a good swearing off Jim Telfer for that. I scored 11 tries for Scotland, but I should have been way ahead, the number of times I dropped the ball with the line beckoning! In 1988 at Murrayfield we were all over the Welsh. Just before half-time a big chance opened up. Fin went through and it was two to one, but I was thinking what I was going to do over the line – a triple Salko with pike and triple twist – and dropped the ball. Just then the half-time whistle went. The boys went into the huddle and wouldn't let me in.

'But try records, cap records don't mean a thing to me. Derek, Fin and myself would just laugh. When they announced the team at Murrayfield we'd say to each other, "In again. Fooled them all again." Sometimes we wouldn't get away with it. After Mullin's try for Ireland in 1989 Telfer really tore into us: "You are f*****g useless. I made you what you are and I can go and pick another three off the streets and make them good players if you lot don't pull your socks up."

'In 1986 I was picked to go with the Lions to South Africa, but it was cancelled because of the political situation with apartheid. I had set my sights on going, but I ended up with one game in Cardiff. Three days in

Cardiff instead of three months in South Africa. I got all the kit, the Lions blazer and all that, but I never felt I was a Lion.

'When I was picked to go in '89, that was really something special. I was disappointed not to get in the Tests. Beforehand, Phil Matthews was favourite for the blindside spot, but he wasn't picked, so it was myself and Mike Teague. I thought I would walk into the team. I did play the opening game and in my second game in Melbourne against Australia B I scored two tries, but Mike Teague got in and he played exceptionally well. In fact I think he was man of the series. So that was a major disappointment to me. But of course in the first Test match Teague was injured and they picked Derek White at wing-forward and kept Dean Richards at number 8. Finlay takes great pleasure in telling me that it was a split vote and he had the casting vote and dropped me. He still takes great delight in calling me a Wednesday Lion. I never played in the Saturday team. Cardiff '86 was a Wednesday as well. He thinks I have a huge chip on my shoulder about it. No bloody wonder, the number of times he mentions it.

'It was a dirty tour in '89 – obscene, brutal. New South Wales started it and every game was the same. But after that first game we just said, "Bugger it, we're not going to take this." They meted it out and we made a conscious decision we were going to give it back. There was a lot of bad feeling after the games as well. But I thrived on touring and I think I would have thrived on being a professional rugby player.

'I decided to retire after the 1991 World Cup game where, of course, we got none other than England in the semi-final. That was a dreadful game, a poor quality game. They were just after revenge for the year before and there is little doubt that Gavin [Hastings] cost us that match. There is no doubt, either, that they knew our tactics. I am convinced of that. We always did a certain move off the back of the scrum, but this time we said we'd do something totally different, went left instead of right, and they were waiting for us. They knew somehow or other – someone had told them what we were going to do. They had been spying on us, or something. But all's fair in love and war.

'When I retired I told very few people about it. I had actually been dropped five times in my Scotland career, so it wasn't a case of saying I will retire on such and such a date, because I might have been dropped before then. So I said I would retire after the World Cup and the whole team knew that. Against New Zealand in 1990 Fin had always said to me, "Right, if we beat the All Blacks, we'll retire together." We were beating them in the second Test – Gav cost us that as well – but we lost in the end, so carried on playing.

'So I went on and in 1991 led the team out for the last time at Murrayfield, against England. Folk couldn't understand why I was doing it. It was a very in-house thing: Finlay was going to retire AGAIN and I was going to join him. It was a very emotional occasion. David Sole had asked me to say a few words to the team in the build-up, but I didn't do it very well, I was too emotional. Rugby had been my life. It had ruled my life to the detriment of everything else. It has taken precedence over everything. I just couldn't find the right words.'

8. ROGER BAIRD

In his self-effacing way Roger Baird has modified an old joke at his own expense. Something like this: 'The salvage teams had finally managed to get the *Marie Rose* to the surface and were busily going through the artefacts of Henry VIII's treasure ship when they came across a mummified corpse. Carefully unwrapping the remains, they were astonished to find signs of life and as the last ancient piece of linen was taken off the cadaver, it sat up and uttered its first words in four centuries: "Has Roger Baird scored a try for Scotland yet?"'

If John Jeffrey was the Great White Shark, Iain Milne the Bear and Ian McLauchlan Mighty Mouse, Baird's name always comes with the addendum 'who never scored a try for Scotland'. Not that it bothers him greatly. Baird still won 27 Scotland caps; was one of the few successes of the 1983 British Lions tour, where he played in all four Tests; and is still remembered as one of the country's most exciting attacking wings. What is more, he plainly had a great time throughout.

Baird turned 40 in April 2000 but, to the intense annoyance of all his contemporaries, he looks exactly as he did in his playing days – no trace of grey in the distinctive jet-black hair – and with a boyish enthusiasm that can be infectious. Married to the former BBC journalist Louise Welsh (who 'as well as lecturing me also lectures at Napier and Strathclyde University'), he also has a son, Jonathan, who is nearly 12 ('he plays second row, so there's a few questions there') and a daughter, Alexandra, who is nearly ten. As with a surprisingly high number of former Scotland internationals, Baird is director of a grain merchants in East Lothian, but is still involved in rugby. He helps Roy Laidlaw and David Leslie with the Scotland Under-21 side.

Baird, like John Jeffrey, was born in Kelso and went to St Mary's prep school in Melrose. 'I used to watch Creamy play there, so you could say I've gone through my career with Jim Telfer – to my cost, at times. He will delight in telling you I am a public schoolboy. I went to Merchiston in Edinburgh, but I started with Kelso Harlequins during the holidays. That was a taster into what rugby was about. It was hard. My father had played for Watsonians and Kelso and South and had a trial, so he was pretty chuffed when I got there. When I was a boy I could always tell when he was at a game because I could smell his pipe tobacco. When I was 17 there were a lot of young guys coming together at Kelso. This was the start of the great sevens era. There were three of us in that side only 17, but we won the Melrose Sevens in 1978. Kelso had never won it before and it was a huge thing for the town.

'Sevens is a great thing to develop skills. Rugby is not about contact, it's about beating people, hitting gaps, and sevens is great for that. At Kelso we embarked on a great ten years of rugby. We won two championships and the Melrose Sevens a number of times. There was also a South of Scotland side and it's sad to see that gone now. You'd play for your club and then the South, with 14 or 15 internationalists in the same team. Sides like Wellington came over – we'd beat them and we beat Australia. They were phenomenal games and, of course, in those days rugby was still very sociable. We had some great laughs. We probably drank far too much, but you just ran it off next day.

'It was through sevens that I came to notice, going to Hong Kong with the first Scottish side in 1981. I was 20 at the time and we got to the final against Fiji. Just after that I was picked to go to New Zealand. That was a bloody hard tour, with Telfer in charge. I was really wet behind the ears. I remember the first game we played was against King Country and in the team talk Telfer turned round to me and said, "You, Baird, you're up against a f★★★★★g convict today", and I think he had been one, too. I had played for the B team before that and Telfer was coach of the B team, so I've come all the way through with him.

'My first international honours were against France, in Orléac in the Massif Central, and I was late going into lunch on the day of the game. There was one seat left and of course it was beside Telfer. I was 19 and thought, "You will have to bring all this expensive education you've had to bear." So I said to Jim, "You know, Jim, as a coach, do you get nervous before games?" He just grunted. Then, we were sitting in the changing-room before the match and at that stage – he's got a wee bit quieter nowadays, but then he was mental – he was whipping everyone up to a crescendo, slapping second-rows in the face and you thought the room was going to burst. He was going through a few things, building everything up and suddenly he said, "I was sitting having my lunch today and that wee baa–aastard from Kelso, he says, *Do I get nervous? Do I get f*****g nervous?*" That was my first taste of Jim Telfer as a coach.

'In December 1981 I was picked ahead of the old flying buffalo Bruce Hay on the left wing for the game against Australia. It was nearly snowed off, but we played and won. My first introduction was a pass from Andy Irvine that must have gone about six feet over my head in our own 22. Three years later, when they came back in '84, the Australians were all-conquering. They had Mark Ella at stand-off and Lloyd Walker, who were awesome, and they gave us a real shagging.

'I'd got to know their full-back Roger Gould before that. He was about six foot four and sixteen stone and after the game I remember walking with my wife (who was my girlfriend at the time) and Gould through the railway station from the North British Hotel to Buster Brown's night club. Three youths stopped us as we walked across. They recognised me and recognised him and they stopped me and said, "You were f*****g rubbish today." I'm not normally aggressive, because I'm too small, but of course I had a few beers in me and said, "Come here and say that."

'So they came over and repeated it: "You were f*****g rubbish today."

'So I said, "Come on, try and hit me," and one duly did. He landed one on me and I stood there holding my face when suddenly this huge fist came over from the back and Roger Gould hit this guy right in his nose. That was the end of it – they scuttled away, with one holding his nose and me left holding my nose.

'The milestone in Scottish rugby, as a lot of people will tell you, was in 1982. We beat France at home. This was my first Five Nations game at home and I was marking Philippe Sella, who was playing on the wing. We lost to Ireland, who were going for the Triple Crown even though Duggan, Slattery and Keane had been out for their customary eight pints on Friday night. We drew 9–9 with England, thanks to the after-shave drinker Colin Smart giving away a penalty which Andy Irvine kicked.

'Then we went to Wales and everything clicked. It started with a great try from Jim Calder and it just went on from there. At half-time all the young guys were really excited because we were out of sight and Jim Renwick said to us, "Look, boys, calm down. We've still got a game on." They came back at us a bit, but we won easily in the end. A lot of people don't know that was Jim Renwick's 40th cap and his first win away from home. The Jim Calder try was just one of those things. There was a lot of loose kicking and they kicked over to our right-hand side; Bill

Cuthbertson got hold of it there and I said, "Give it to me" and the f★★★★★g clown just kicked it and of course missed touch. At that stage they had men up. The worst thing Gareth Davies could have done was kick and it just sat up. A lot of people said, "Oh, you were very brave running it from there" – but actually it was the only way to go and it just opened up.

'There were so many good things from so many people that day and it kind of galvanised us. David Johnston scored a fantastic try and it was one of his great games. He ran round Ray Gravell and he tackled Gravell all day. Gravell ran and ran at him and David tackled his socks off.

'In 1983, I remember, in France the fists flew in the first two minutes and when the dust cleared Jim Aitken and the Bear were rolling on the ground in agony. I thought, "What the hell is going on?" But as it happened the Bear had run into Jim Aitken.

'At this time I couldn't get away from Telfer and when they picked me for the '83 Lions he was coach, of course. I loved it, it was fantastic and I think I played as good rugby as I ever played. I was fit, fast and strong. We lost the Test series 4–0. We could have won one – possibly two – but they murdered us in the last Test. At one time Stu Wilson came on a short ball and I tackled him, but got my head in the wrong place and got knocked out. Stu Wilson said later he thought he'd killed me. He didn't dare come into the dressing-room and have a look afterwards. I was being stretchered off the pitch when Peter Winterbottom turned to Roy Laidlaw and said, "The lucky bastard." They still had a bit of pain to take.

'To be honest, the guy who should have gone on that tour was David Leslie. It might have been different if he had gone. They took John O'Driscoll, who wasn't the player he had been. Whether he'd peaked, or what, I don't know. There was some bad selection. They waited for people like Maurice Colclough because Bill Beaumont had said he was one of the first they had to take. A load of shite. There was a slight Irish mafia. Willie John McBride, the manager, had said the captain's place was paramount; so we had Ciaran Fitzgerald playing all four Tests and Colin Deans, the best hooker in world, sat on the bench. John Rutherford was at the peak of his powers and should have been in. As a captain, Ciaran just didn't do it. He is now coach of the Irish Under-21s and when our kids played them this season I spoke to him more than I did the whole of the tour in 1983. Maybe he felt he had to be aloof, but it's all about communication.

'I have one regret about the Grand Slam year of 1984. In the France game I got caught by Serge Blanco and lost the vision in one eye. In a way I'm sorry I didn't go off, because it would have meant Andy Irvine would have got on. If I could turn the clock back I would have come off.

'The best rugby I was ever involved in was during 1986, when we only lost against Wales because Paul Thorburn kept kicking those huge goals. It was Ian McGeechan's first season coaching. I got more ball that year than I had ever had and it was only a matter of time before the winger started dotting down tries. That had become a bit of a monkey on my back, to be honest. But I never seemed to get the run-ins other wings did. Maybe it was just me. But then I succumbed to a lot of injury problems. Iwan Tukalo got in, then I got back and in '87 I went to the World Cup, though didn't play at all. It was a pretty horrendous time as an amateur to go away for a month in your holiday and not get a game, so I was pretty down about that.

'I played my last game in 1988, against Ireland. We were beaten over there. There were two tries scored on the left-hand side and it was deemed I was responsible. But I had a lot of problems with an Achilles and I started losing pace. I definitely lost yards. But I couldn't complain – I had a great run.

'I've been privileged to play with and against a lot of great characters. I remember Jim Renwick's 50th cap at Murrayfield. Coming off the pitch, he was surrounded by the press and they said something like "Well, Jim, that's your 50th cap. You played a whole decade, so what's the biggest change you've seen in that time?" Quick as a flash, Renwick said, "Well, the biggest change I ever saw was Alan Tomes changing his shorts, the smallest change I ever saw was Andy Irvine changing his mind and the most amazing change I've ever seen was Alastair Cranston changing a fiver." Just off the cuff, like that.

'Another time, we went into an Edinburgh pub after a game. There was a boy in there with a trumpet and Renwick got hold of it and brought the house down. He'd been in the Salvation Army!

'In 1986 John Beattie hated Maurice Colclough from the Lions tour and various other things. There was a plan: at the first lineout, Beattie was going to come up and mark Colclough at 2 or 4, wherever he was jumping; Colin Deans was to throw the ball long and, while everyone was watching the ball, Beattie was going to smack Colclough. That was the plan, anyway, but the game went on and there was never a lineout. Eventually we had a drop-out and Beattie just ran and clobbered someone; we immediately got penalised and they kicked a penalty!

'The same year we went to Romania and it was after one of the international dinners where Gavin Hastings had hit the head sponsor with a roll or something. Dod Burrell was the manager. Before the dinner in Bucharest, Dod got us all together and said, "Right, tonight you will be on your best behaviour. The behaviour in recent weeks at dinners has been appalling. I don't want anything like that tonight."

'Well, the dinner was bloody awful. No food, no drink or anything. We left by 8.30 and went back to the hotel and luckily they had a fair bit of refreshment there. From then on things got totally out of control. I remember the Bear dancing about for ten minutes with the hotel manager and there was a bit of damage done to the hotel. They weren't going to let us go and they gave us a huge bill, they were so desperate for western currency.

'We were sitting on the bus. The Bear had been sick into a carrier bag and it was one of those with holes in it and it was dripping all over the place. Renwick said, "Someone fart and let some fresh air in." It was chaos. Then Dod, who had been ill and was walking on a zimmer frame, came on the bus and he was absolutely fuming. You could hear a pin drop. He was actually shaking on his zimmer and then he started: "You've let your toons doon, you've let yourselves doon, but most of all you've let your country doon."

'At that moment Roy Laidlaw piped up, "Aye, but Dod, at least we behaved at the dinner!"

'The next game we beat England 33–6 at Murrayfield. The champagne after the game was flowing. The boys were ecstatic. But Dod stood up again and said, "Boys, before we go to the dinner I want you to remember that you have beaten a proud people today and I want you to be magnanimous in victory. No gloating. Today you have beaten a very proud nation."

'And Roy said, "Aye, 50 million of the bastards!"'

Of all the Scotland players nurtured into world class by Scottish rugby's Professor Frankenstein, Jim Telfer, his universally acknowledged greatest 'creation' is Iain Paxton – the man from Dunfermline without a rugby background, who matured into a number 8 that even the All Blacks admired. Paxton in full flight was an awesome sight and while Telfer has always been reluctant to single out players for anything resembling praise, he says unreservedly of his favourite Fifer, 'What Iain had was natural running ability. What he lacked was probably hardness, but he was very willing and very brave – very good ingredients to become a very good player. I don't think he's a natural rugby player as such, but he was very athletic. The basis of a good rucking game is you must have athletes who can get from A to B quickly and he was also a number 8 and asked to lift ball from the scrum and get away from the scrum. He was also good in the lineout because he was so athletic. But it was his attitude that was so good, he would soak up information. He really wanted to learn.'

These days Paxton is a sales consultant for Scottish Mutual, based in the West End of Edinburgh, and his large frame can regularly be spotted marching, arms swinging, down Shandwick Place. He, too, has remained in the game. He coaches Boroughmuir, who a week after this interview won the BT Cellnet Cup at Murrayfield and promotion to the First Division. It had been a long road from football-mad Fife, where he had been born in December 1957.

'My father was a policeman, so I led a pretty nomadic existence as a boy, moving around Fife to various places. I went to Kirkcaldy High School, where there was compulsory rugby. If it hadn't been for that I might never have played the game, because I was more interested in football and basketball and I still support Raith Rovers for my pains. When I started basketball rugby slipped away and it was only because the history teacher, Bob Hutchison, got me in at Glenrothes that I dropped basketball. At the time I was being asked over to Edinburgh to play for Polonia, but the travelling was a bit much because I couldn't drive at the time.

'One of my earliest rugby memories was of locking horns with the Calders in an Under-16 sevens tournament at the end of a season. We went down, played Stew-Mel and lost in injury time. I started to enjoy the rugby and the decision had to be made. I hadn't much of a grounding in rugby, but I still maintain that basketball was a great help in terms of hand–eye co-ordination and jumping.

'I managed to get into Glenrothes 1st XV and then Midlands District Union while still at school. At that stage I didn't have anything but a quiet dream – I just enjoyed playing – but after five years with Glenrothes and winning all the respective leagues they were in, I started getting noticed and got an international trial at 21. I played number 8. But I wanted to stay at Glenrothes to finish my electronics apprenticeship. Then, about '78, John Beattie came in and those twelve months just galloped past. He came right through, played for Scotland B then got capped that season. It was always a big incentive to know John Beattie was there as number one – that's how it was portrayed. I got dropped in 1983 for John, but we were two different types of player. I would try and run through space, he would try and run through people. I think it finished his career trying to be too aggressive.

'It was in 1980–81 that I decided to move to Selkirk. I had trained with Heriot's for a week, but John Beattie was there at the same time! Heriot's had this policy about ten-per cent intake and the only way they were going to accept me was if I filled in the wee form as a second-row. However I put my foot down: I wanted to play number 8.

'John Rutherford had rung me up and I went down to Selkirk. Iwan Tukalo came down; Gordon Hunter was an up-and-coming scrum-half. At that time, pretty much most of them were from Selkirk but it was me and the seven dwarfs there for most of my career. Anyone over six foot was welcome. If there had been a league for Under-six foot, Selkirk would have won it.

'In 1978 I played against the All Blacks up in Aberdeen and I had a reasonable sort of game. That year North and Midlands beat the South, too, and I got my Scotland trial. I played ten times against the All Blacks, altogether, but I watch Super 12 on TV these days and wonder why I ever played rugby.

'When the Scotland tour of New Zealand came round in 1981 I was fourth-choice number 8 for that trip. John Beattie was ahead of me; so was Peter Lillington from Durham University, but he called off because of final exams. Derek White came in ahead of me, but then Beattie tried to run through Iain Milne at the final training session and I got the phone call from John Rutherford. It was a bit of a shock.

'Touring was brilliant. There was never a Scotsman in our era who didn't enjoy touring. There was always good camaraderie, even if results were bad, and we always managed to get some good results. In 1980–81 there was a nucleus of guys coming together, all in their early twenties. But 1981 was a huge learning curve. Guys you'd read about, you learned more about them. Tomes and Renwick with their Hawick wit and humour. Bruce Hay. There were foundations for a reasonably healthy period for Scottish rugby.

'Some didn't enjoy Telfer's approach, but I did. He maybe overdid it at times. In the second Test in Auckland, we got back to 19–15 and it looked as though Jim Calder had scored a try in corner, but it was disallowed and they just cut loose. Bruce Robertson, the centre, he may have scored one and he was making these tremendous runs up the middle. Our legs had just gone. We'd left them on the training ground – Jim put us through the mill too soon after getting off the plane. But I learned a lot from him. He took me aside and gauged me over the first ten days to see if I was going to produce the goods. Then at Masterton he took me aside and said, "I am going to give you a hard time and sometimes you will think I'm a right bastard or worse; but I wouldn't do it unless I thought there was something at the end of that." I always respected that. Derek White, I don't think he has a lot of time for Jim. He gave him a hard time.

'Jim gave me a hard time, too, but to me it was water off a duck's back. I had a total lack of rugby background, which wasn't a bad thing at times. We played Canterbury, but I had honestly no conception of who I was playing against as such – no idea they were one of the top provincial sides in New Zealand. And we beat them, one of our good results.

'I look back to Cardiff in 1982 and that Jim Calder try and still wonder if one day I will actually make the line. I was starting to track back when Roger did the unthinkable and I turned round to support him. The man who doesn't get enough kudos is Alan Tomes, who backed me up. That killed the bogey, really, and we started winning away from home. I was lucky enough to play in the side that won in Australia and then we won at Twickenham. Things were on the up.

'There were ten Scots on the '83 Lions tour and that was a big factor in the Grand Slam a year later. That tour gave me huge confidence. There is usually in security and uncertainty in any Scots camp, especially against Wales and England, but when training with these guys on tour you see they are fallible. There was also disenchantment with the way Jim Telfer was perceived by some of the players. Graham Price had been a good player, but the Bear should have been in. Jim, I think, was too much of a diplomat. His hands were tied.

'Looking back now, if we hadn't won the game against Canterbury I think Ciaran would have dropped himself. I was well aware of the campaign to get rid of Fitzgerald, but the Irish closed ranks when the pressure came on. The tour party didn't fall apart, but there was a division. Training with Colin Deans, he would have every throw spot on. You would be out for an hour in training with Ciaran to get three throws. He wasn't a great captain. I remember a boat trip in the first week and he just went and sat on his own in the corner. It's not all going to be sweetness and light on tour – there are going to be bad moments and that's when you need a captain to dig deeper to pull the best out of the squad.

'By the time the last Test came round in Auckland the All Blacks had worked out one or two of our players. They'd decided they were not of the required standard and they were probably right. I remember standing in the changing-room before we went out and there were English guys selling their Lions blazers and tour kit. The negotiations were going on well into the last hour leading up to that game. They were selling it to some of the tour parties out following the Lions. That was another thing that really stuck in the gullet. There were some people on that tour I had no respect for. They didn't bring anything to the party, considering what an honour it's supposed to be. It certainly sparked some of the Scottish guys in 1984.

'I played in the Whites in the trial that season. So did David Leslie. Looking back now it may have been a ploy, but it certainly worked, because we both got in the senior side. Jim Aitken, the captain, was a good organiser. He made sure players were looked after. He was loud and abrasive and he sized up how to treat different guys. Technically, you couldn't say he was the best prop around, but he was in the right place at the right time.

'In the last game, the French game, there was a whole load of things going on. I didn't see much but I heard it. I heard the Bear squealing, I could hear his cries of anguish. He never retaliated: he just got angry and did it in the scrum.

'My last cap was against Australia in 1988. It was Gary Armstrong's first international. I had trained quite hard the previous summer and was reasonably fit, but it didn't happen. I didn't see eye-to-eye with Dunc Paterson over a couple of things. I don't feel bitter now, but I did at the time. In 1990 I was at Murrayfield after the Grand Slam game and when I went to the bar afterwards, Dunc Paterson was there with a couple of other selectors and they just cut me dead, just ignored me. I'm still baffled. I had been there supporting Scotland and going through all the emotions of the guys on the terraces. It was the lowest moment of my career. You give your all and they ignore you, although Bob Munro did apologise later. Getting dropped is bad enough, but that Saturday night was far worse.

'And yet I've had more good memories out of rugby than a lot of guys and I would never go back. It's all a long time ago now, but I've still got the scrapbooks and still got all the posters signed. We moved house last August and they were all sitting in tea chests in the loft and instead of packing cases you're spending time looking through scrapbooks.

'Rugby is not a bad way to grow up when you think about it.'

If he had arrived dressed as Santa Claus it would still be impossible not to recognise Peter Brown. The uncoordinated gait, coat-hanger shoulders and clenched-teeth grin remain unmistakable. There is also that famous disregard for what many would consider normal convention. Finlay Calder forewarned me: 'Peter Brown is the most eccentric character in Scottish rugby.' I knew that, from watching his esoteric goalkicking for Scotland down the years – almost like taking a soccer penalty-kick, a sight never seen before or since. But nothing could possibly have prepared me for that first meeting.

For our appointment in Melrose (Brown works as an accountant in Galashiels during the week and returns home to Dunbar for the weekends) I have been double-booked at an upmarket eaterie with four accountants from Albania who are on some sort of exchange visit. One is a ravishing, but somewhat surly brunette; one of the others a disconcerting Charles Aznavour lookalike. None of them speaks English. This does not stop Brown from quoting Burns at them and setting them impossible conundrums. The brunette, along with the flowers on the table, offers a photo opportunity our host cannot spurn and there's a promise to initiate them into the mysteries of Scottish malt whisky later in the evening.

The tape recorder is placed on a side plate and the interview has to be fitted in around the main course. Brown takes this all in his stride, as if it were totally normal procedure.

'I was fortunate in my rugby career because at Marr College the master who took rugby there would say, "Right, boys, go out and enjoy yourselves." Every single game since then I've made a lot of mistakes. I've lobbed the ball across the field to the opposition, I have headed the ball to the opposition – oh yes, I often headed the rugby ball – but you see, I was brought up as a soccer player. Gordon and I never saw a rugby ball until we were 13. Kids should get a football first. It has got a predictable bounce.

'When Jim Telfer was captain of Scotland in 1969, I played for South against the Springboks, that terrible tour with all the protestors. This was the first time I had ever played in a side that was properly prepared to take on a touring side. Telfer as captain had us down at Kelso every Wednesday night for ten weeks before the match. We kept chipping the ball over the top, rucking, driving, we were really focused. But it was also the only time I ever ignored him. One night he said, "We'll do another five minutes," and that was after doing the last five minutes, and I said, "Goodnight Jim," turned and walked off the field. I knew I was making a statement. In the Saturday team talk before we went out, he turned to me and said, "Brown, I don't want you to be the big f*****g lassie you usually are."

'If Jim had a fault, it was that his team talks were so negative. I mean, they were fabulous stuff, the passion would come out, but it was all about how to hold the opposition. My attitude was to say, "You're the best, go out and show them that." In the game against the Springboks I played probably the best game I ever played – and also made my reputation in the Borders. Tommy Bedford, their captain that day, nearly kicked my head off when I went down for the ball; at the lineout immediately afterwards he decided to have a keek round the maul to see what was happening. My fist couldn't have travelled more than two feet, nobody saw it and nobody knew who had done it. He was out cold. I was worried for him, but he was all right.

'After Ireland they dropped Jim, I got in at number 8 and they made Frank Laidlaw the captain against England in March 1970. I talked Frank into letting me kick off. A second-row forward kicked off an international! But I'd reasoned that I needed a kick on the field – you weren't allowed to go out and practise beforehand – and I actually converted the kick-off. I aimed at the posts as a practice kick, knowing it didn't matter if it went dead because we wanted to start in their half. We had planned it all beforehand. The referee that day [Meirion Joseph of Wales] was notorious for penalising right away. England dropped out into touch, there was a lineout, the English were penalised and 90 seconds later I was kicking the penalty. Fabulous. Of course the pressure was on me to kick the goal, but I loved that.

'The SRU were incredibly tight in those days. I have a letter inviting me to play against New Zealand in 1971. I knew I was selected when I tore open the envelope and two complimentary stand tickets fell out. I found out I was captain of Scotland because a note squiggled in the margin – you had to turn it round to see – said, "You will captain the side." The greatest day of my rugby life and that's how I found out.

'Mike Campbell-Lamerton tells this wonderful story of a game against France when his shirt was ripped to shreds: he ran round the rest of the match bare-shouldered with what was left of his shirt tied round his middle. For the next international, against Wales, he got the usual invitation to play in a letter, which added, "Please bring jersey number 4 which you wore against France." He wrote back saying his jersey was destroyed against France. He's still got the reply today from John Law, the SRU Secretary, saying, "Please send jersey for inspection."

'We went to Australia in 1970 – a disaster of a tour. They were changing captain and after the second trial I found myself captain and I wanted it. I was the total opposite to Telfer. I began my team talk, "I am a chartered accountant" – and they all looked at me and went, "Oh, God!" They all liked me, but wondered what I would be like as a captain – "I'm a chartered accountant and I am used to balance sheets and balance sheets are made up of assets and liabilities and all I can see are assets." I wasn't bullshitting. You went through the team and there was Colin Telfer at stand-off, Duncy Paterson at scrum-half, John Frame, Chris Rea in the centre, Ian Smith who at the time was full-back. Everybody could play. The front row was Ian McLauchlan, Frank Laidlaw was still in the team and Sandy Carmichael too. McHarg and Gordon were the second row.

'"Now, can anyone tell me what our liabilities are?" And I told them: we didn't play with enough confidence. I actually took the first Scottish team talk with no selectors present. The minute you started talking about playing rough or taking the opposition out, the Chairman of Selectors would say, "No, no, chaps we're not having any of that, none of that in my Scottish teams." So we started team talks at half past nine before the selectors arrived at half past ten and we practised illegal lifting at lineouts, taking out the opposition, blocking at kick-offs, everything they wouldn't let us do. We decided we would never come off the field and complain about what the referee had allowed the opposition to do.

'Then I asked the boys if there were any moves they did with their club sides and Ian McLauchlan came up with the tap penalty. So we introduced the tap penalty to international rugby against Wales in 1971. That was the day Scotland found themselves – a fabulous performance. But Taylor made the best conversion since St Paul's to convert Gareth Davies's try. People say. "You'd have won if you'd kicked that conversion" and I say, "What about the five that I kicked?" Seven minutes into the game we were awarded a penalty just outside our own 22 and we ran it – the first time any international team had ever done that – and Framey got tackled into touch just short of their 22. It was after that that Bill Dickinson came in as adviser.

'In 1973 I lost the captaincy, but we beat Ireland and went to England for the Triple Crown. That's a story in itself, because in the lead-up to that game six Scottish forwards had painkilling injections. McLauchlan had a broken leg. I played left-hand second-row behind him and in the team talk he said, "It will be OK."

'When Alastair McHarg and I played second-row for Scotland I wasn't 16 stone and he wasn't 15 stone, but we were both athletes first, long rangy types and we did the training. I ran 800 metres from the age of 14; I did 880 yards on grass in 2 minutes dead at 18. I was a genuine half-miler and I learned to do the interval training which a lot of them do now. I have to confess Alastair and I cheated a bit. We had rugby league heel studs in the soles of our boots, so what we lacked in poundage we really dug down with those studs. We got criticised because we were out in the open a lot: they thought we couldn't possibly be doing the work in the tight. But, famously, we played for the Baa Baas against Leicester. John Reason had written [in the *Daily Telegraph*], "Baa Baas pick powder-puff second row." And we scored a pushover try against Leicester that night. I remember Big McHarg saying, "We're going for this." It's amazing what you can do if you've got the technique.

'I never appreciated how good I was until I stopped playing and started to coach. I remember coaching Tom Smith, the basketball player, and tried to get him to deflect the ball to the outside shoulder of his scrum-half. That first year I came in for Scotland, Eck Hastie and David Chisholm were in at half-back. Chisholm liked the ball short and fast and Hastie said to me, "Peter, instead of catching the ball and giving it to me there, can you just flick it off the top? Don't give it to my chest, just give it to me so I can flick it on to Chisholm." And I did that. It was when I tried to coach Tom Smith to do the same thing I realised I had natural hand–eye co-ordination. It came from my father, who had the most wonderful hand–eye co-ordination I have ever seen. He was a scratch golfer for 20 years and is still a bandit off 19 and he's 84. I play off 11 and I formally protest about Gordon. In ten years at Royal Troon he has never submitted one card and they allow him to play off 17.

'I could also jump. I could jump up and just touch a rugby crossbar with the tips of my fingers. The story about Gordon and the hand reaching the gutter at the family home. Is he still claiming he touched it? He never, ever bloody did it. It's a lie. He cannot produce a witness and I won't take his word for it.

'I played against some great jumpers. Delme Thomas was the softest, gentlest giant I ever played against. I played in a Scotland–Ireland joint team against Wales and England, to celebrate something or other, and we all stayed together on the Friday night in the same hotel. At about 9.30, after the meal, I was sat next to Delme and he said, "Fancy a walk?" We went out and walked for a couple of hours round London and he told me about his family in the valleys and how he hated Clive Rowlands [the Wales coach] screaming at him. He said, "I don't need anyone screaming at me." I made a friend for life. Delme was a fabulous, natural jumper. I remember once at Murrayfield going against him and just nicking the ball in front of him to my scrum-half. I fell on the ground and he grunted, "Aagh." In other words, "Good one," but also, "I'll get you the next time." We used to help each other up. So within the terror of internationals I was playing against a pal. We never gave any quarter but am I ever going to stand on his head or tear the jersey off his back? No bloody way. You have to be fabulously stupid to do that.

'My main claim to rugby these days is that I'm the old fart in the stand doing the Citing Commission. I spent 16 years on the bench here as a magistrate. In the World Cup each country had to nominate a past eminent player with experience of the bench and they decided they wanted me. I did three in the World Cup and was match commissioner for the European Cup and Six Nations this year. You watch the game and you pick out incidents that the referee has missed and that should be drawn to his attention. If they're bad enough you can cite them. In the Heineken European Cup, if anyone is sent off you can convene a court within two hours and sentence them. They can appeal and the appeal is heard the following Thursday in Dublin. You need someone with legal training to make sure the procedures are carried out correctly. I enjoyed it.

'I was in Rome, match commissioner for Italy against England, which was a very aggressive game. John Spencer was the match commissioner/old player for England and he said to me after the game, "Broonie, a couple of things there you must be looking at?"

'And I said, "Yes."

'"Are you going to cite?"

'You're not supposed to talk to anyone for 48 hours and I just winked at him and he said, "The English hooker?"

'The press missed it, I didn't miss it, Spencer didn't miss it. It was touch and go and I went over it with the referee and, given the toughness of the game, we decided not to cite the player. Now he doesn't know, and the English coach doesn't know, how close he came. But I would like him to know that we spotted him.

'I told you about Tommy Bedford, didn't I? I've been there, seen it, done it. The most difficult one in the World Cup was the South African centre [Brendan] Ventner, who maintained he couldn't help trampling on the head of the guy whose head he trampled on. When we gave him his three-week sentence, his reaction could not have been more severe if we had said "You will be taken out, tied to a post and shot dead." I have never seen a guy so devastated.

'I don't believe in the sin-bin. I refereed for eight years and I never once walked a player ten yards back for speaking to me. I was on the discipline panel for the Spanish last year. The English referee yellow-carded a Spaniard and as he turned away the Spaniard made this rude gesture and the referee changed it to a red card. His counsel made the point to us later: "Would it be an absolutely correct defence if the referee *was* a wanker?"'

And so it went on – a flood of outrageous stories, most of them unprintable, some of them possibly litigious, all of them hilarious. As I headed out into the Melrose night P. C. Brown was settling the bill and the Albanians, surly brunette and all, were giving every indication of being about to burst into a chorus of 'Annie Laurie'. All in all, probably the most entertaining evening of my life.

11. BRUCE HAY

Bruce Hay's whole-hearted commitment to both his clubs, Liberton and Boroughmuir, as well as his 23 Scotland caps and two British Lions tours, have left him with the nose of a none-too-successful middleweight boxer – a battered profile that has prompted more than a few wisecracks over the years. Even a royal one. But Prince Philip, the king of the public gaffes, did get more than he bargained for from the former coal board apprentice before the 1979 Five Nations match against England at Twickenham: 'We were lined up and Prince Philip was going down the line asking the usual questions,' recalls Hay. 'Anyway, he got to me, looked me up and down and then asked, "And which lamp-post did you run into then?" And I turned to Jim Renwick, who was stood alongside me, and said, "He's no beauty himself." He heard me and turned round and smiled.'

Perhaps His Royal Highness was fortunate to get away with that. As the Scotland hooker Colin Deans says, 'Maybe we were all lucky we didn't finish up in the Tower of London!'

It is one of the great anachronisms of Scottish rugby that Hay should have thrived in an era when his main rival for the national full-back spot was Andy Irvine. But from the mid-'70s to the early '80s, the Scotland selectors managed to find room for both these wildly different players and personalities: the dashingly svelte public schoolboy and the barrel-chested artisan. Irvine, from his first appearance in December 1972 (against New Zealand) through to the match in June 1975 (again against the All Blacks) enjoyed an unchallenged run in the number 15 jersey until it was deemed that the side would be stronger defensively with Hay there, the Heriot's man moving to the right wing.

The selectors then did a volte-face and decided that Irvine's pace and intrusiveness were a bigger offensive weapon at full-back. So Hay found himself first in the number 14 jersey and then in number 11. As he says now, 'I was the only man ever to play right wing, left wing and full back in one international season!'

Even Hay would admit that as a wing he might give some modern-day props a good run for their money. His interception try against Ireland at Murrayfield in 1981 prompted Jim Renwick – who was backing up when Hay latched onto David Irwin's floated pass and outpaced Tony Ward to the corner – to remark that it was the only international try he had ever seen live and in slow motion. However his unflinching defence and combativeness proved priceless at times to Scotland.

Boroughmuir, too, have reason to be grateful to Hay's continued commitment for over a quarter of a century, as he is still the club's director of rugby. Nor has his diligence to the Scotland cause lapsed, for at the time of writing he is also in charge of the Under-19 squad.

Bruce Hay was born on 23 May 1950 on the south side of Edinburgh. Educated at Liberton High School, he left there at 15 to become an apprentice electrician with the Coal Board. At the same age he joined Liberton, the local rugby club, although there was no history of the sport in the family. His parents came originally from Aberdeen and his granny used to serve the teas at Pittodrie. Hamilton, Hay's middle name, came from the former Aberdeen player, Geordie Hamilton – and before picking up the oval ball at Liberton, Hay was a 'competent' footballer himself.

'I played one game at Liberton and then went into the first team and stayed there for the next seven seasons. I played for Edinburgh in the play-off game against Glasgow when Andy Irvine was unavailable and I got my game. We won, I scored a try and it was recommended I find a senior club. The only feasible one was Boroughmuir. Selkirk were quite keen, but I didn't have a car at the time and was working three shifts in the pit. This was the 1972–73 season and Boroughmuir, I must say, made me very welcome. I have been here in some capacity or other ever since.

'I was coaching here when Sean Lineen arrived for the first time. He'll probably tell you the story about him throwing up on the first night. But I was the one who encouraged him to play for Edinburgh because I was coaching them at the time as well. Sean brought a directness at inside-centre and he has certainly helped Boroughmuir develop. He's still here and I know he's proud to be a part of Boroughmuir. It's very much an open club and we try to keep it that way. We are also lucky to have Iain Paxton now. His first cap for Scotland was my last cap, in New Zealand in '81. I suppose you could say I'm the old man around here!

'I've been lucky. I think I was the only miner from Scotland to get selected for a British Lions tour. So it speaks for itself, I was in a very fortunate position. The pit were very good to me, giving me time off and the manager saying I could have my job back tomorrow. He also said, back then, that there would be no pits left in Scotland in five years. At the time that was very hard to imagine, but he was right. However I still had the trade as an electrician, something else I had in common with Roy Laidlaw and Jim Renwick. Jim, I think, is classed as a hot-wire electrician (he is a lineman).

'You could say I had plenty of aggression, when playing, and was fairly robust. I wasn't slow, although I did struggle pacewise at international level. But I had an eye for the ball, especially the high ball, and that stood me in good stead at full-back.

'I first played against the All Blacks in an Inter-City match in 1971 and the following year I got a trial; but I had to wait until Scotland's 1975 tour of New Zealand for my first cap. I think I lasted 15 minutes when I broke my arm trying to claim a fair catch in the Water Test. I won two caps against Australia, started the Five Nations against France and then got dropped for Andy Irvine and was out for a year and a half! But the Renwicks and Irvines of this world don't come along very often. I was 25 when I got my first cap. Even Roy Laidlaw was on the bench for a long time. You need that maturity, it's hardness really. It's probably harder now for the boys because few of them do any manual work at all. The likes of Roy and myself, Alastair Cranston and Jim Renwick were used to being out and about, working.

'I remember one of the first times with Scotland. David Leslie was my room-mate up at the Braid Hills Hotel and he was there in a locked room in his bed with pyjamas buttoned up to his neck and his leather gloves on. There was a bowl of oranges all cut up by the side of his bed and of course I had been for a pint with Renwick and I was terrified to even speak to him. But I always got on with David – a very committed man, single-minded.

'Being away from home can be difficult. Both Dougie Morgan and I had problems with sleepwalking at one time. My wife would be following me round the room making sure I ended up in the right place and the dog would be following Linda. Once I opened the main door and finished up in the street, I didn't know anything about it. It's something to do with all the travelling: you are moving twice a week, sometimes you never unpack. I think Andy Irvine had the problem, too. Maybe it's because you're hyperactive, all the good food and all that training.

'Most players are lucky to get one tour. I got four – two with the Lions in '77 and '80 and two with Scotland. The Lions tours were the most successful tours up until then, apart from '71 and '74. In 1977 it was 16½ weeks in New Zealand and another week in Fiji, that's a long time away from home. You have your moments on tour, but I like to think I was a good tourist, you just go out with an open mind and enjoy yourself. New Zealand is a great place. The grannies in the street used to know more about the rugby than the spectators here. There were five Scots there in 1977 – Ian McGeechan, Dougie Morgan, Gordon Brown, Andy Irvine and myself. Five of us and sixteen Welshmen on the trip, so you had to share rooms with whoever.

'That stood me in good stead, actually, because I finished up being employed by a Welsh firm and was working with Steve Fenwick, Derek Quinnell and Tommy David. It was a chemical firm based in Cardiff and sales conferences used to be like mini tours. I'm still very friendly with them all. Gerald Davies is another good mate; I think I even managed to tackle him once in an international. I first went down to Wales in 1966–67 and we played this team near Cardiff whose captain that day was Alec Rayer, Mike Rayer's dad. Mike was in my house when he was nine years old and I gave him my first pair of football boots.

'But rugby really is a small world. In 1977 I remember going to a party at Wairapa Bush: it was fancy dress and there was Peter Wheeler, myself and Peter Squires all turning up with our Lions jerseys on and a case of beer. We started drinking away and a boy in a monk's outfit turned round and it was this guy who'd played scrum-half for Boroughmuir four years previously, Graham Anderson.

'I was a bit amazed to be selected for the Lions in the first place, because I was only a reserve for Scotland. But both Jim Renwick and I had been selected for the Barbarians in Northampton before the tour and we knew we were close. Unfortunately Jim – and I don't know how, because he had a great game that day – never got selected. They took Dai Richards and David Burcher of Wales instead. They left Jim Renwick out for them. I was amazed.

'Renwick was a great character, one of these players who could predict what he was going to do and make it happen. I tended to be less instinctive. He'll have told you the tale about the try against Ireland in 1981. The whole story is that the president at the time came in and gave us a bollocking about this behaviour after we scored tries. We had to be straight-faced and cut out the celebrations. After I scored against

Ireland, I was running back and Renwick said, "That's the only try I've seen live and in slow motion." I just smiled . . . to avoid another bollocking.

'We had John Dawes as coach in '77 and Noel Murphy in '80 and I must admit I got on better with John. Noel was very difficult and it didn't help that they had an Irish full-back (Rodney O'Donnell) and he seemed to get away with murder. In Scotland we had Jim Telfer, of course – a different character again. Like a lot of folk, I've had my ups and downs with Jim, but I consider him a good friend. One of the problems in Scotland is that you have to be a major figure before you are accepted by everybody. We tend to put people up there and then knock them away. Jim has done well to last the way he has. He's certainly changed. He's far more approachable than he used to be. Or so they say!

'I've been lucky in every way, not just rugby. Linda and I had a very late child. We had been married 21 years and then had a daughter, Lynsey. Linda had had a miscarriage in the past and we'd more or less given up. Then, lo and behold, during the 1991 World Cup she fell pregnant. My role's reversed, really. At my age now I should be a grandfather rather than a dad. Linda and I were married before I came to Boroughmuir, so we came through the rugby together to a certain extent. Another pleasing thing is the youngsters I see coming through. On the last trip to France with the Under-19s, young Stephen Cranston was with us and of course I played with his dad, Alastair. This has happened a few times.

'My last cap was in New Zealand in 1981, when we were beaten in the second Test at Eden Park. I sat on the bench for a year, which was quite pleasing because I had a good view of Roger Baird's famous break-out at Cardiff in 1982. The late John Bevan and Terry Cobner were sat in front of me and I took great delight in knocking their heads together. You could say I was assisted to retire by Roger. Jim Renwick and I talked a lot about it; one weekend we went to Ireland and we had about 20 minutes to ourselves the whole weekend and I began to realise then I wasn't as keen as I should have been. I had a chance to go to Australia, but I had decided that was it. I'd lost my place to Roger. I used to throw darts at pictures of him after that.

'I played on for Boroughmuir until I was 39, as player-coach. I didn't do much tackling, mind. I've been very, very lucky with injuries. I've got a disfigured nose. Apart from that I had a cracked shoulder joint which, if it goes again, will have to be pinned – but then again, I've no intention of playing rugby again. I still enjoy my rugby and I try not to argue about it in the bar afterwards.

'I'll stay here as long as Boroughmuir want me. But I wouldn't know what to do without training on Tueday and Thursday. It's something I've done all my life.'

The immaculate white bungalow stands high above Jedburgh with a fine panorama south over green rolling farmland towards Melrose and Galashiels. There are two acres or so of field at the back, a couple of ponies and some laughing Armstrong children, Darren and Nicole. And of course the familar four-square figure with the blacksmith's forearms and build of a pocket-sized weight-lifter, looking mightily content as he strolls back to the house. If there is one man who has benefited totally from professional rugby, in terms of lifestyle and security, it must be Gary Armstrong – the former farmhand and lorry driver who now plays for Newcastle Falcons in England's Zurich Premiership.

'I've been very lucky to experience both sides of the coin,' says the scrum-half who for a decade from 1988 became perhaps the key component in Scotland selections. 'I had great times at Riverside Park with Jed, don't get me wrong, and I played for South of Scotland. But if professionalism hadn't come in I'd have been finished, because I needed a new challenge.'

Armstrong, 34 in September 2000 and anticipating 'one, maybe two more years in rugby', uses the word 'lucky' a lot. He was lucky, he says, to play for his home-town club, Jed; even luckier to play for Scotland and the British Lions; and luckier still to be offered a contract by Newcastle's sugar daddy Sir John Hall at the start of the sport's professional era. Armstrong has done well out of rugby, but with retirement not too distant, he insists disarmingly that when his career ends he will simply go back to working on a local farm.

It's hard to reconcile this modest and unassuming man with the combative Scotland half-back who possessed the on-field mean streak of a John Beattie, a Sean Fitzpatrick or a Martin Johnson and who operated like a fourth back-row forward in Scotland colours.

Like his great predecessor at Jed, Roy Laidlaw, Armstrong began his illustrious career in the club's mini-rugby set-up, where his father was a coach.

'When I was five or six I was too young to play, but my brother and myself used to go down with my dad. We used to watch Jed, but we moved around a lot because he was in insurance. We finished up in Coldstream, then Dunfermline, but I was glad to get back to the Borders. Like Roy and a lot of others, I started with Jed Thistle and came right through the grades. As a boy I used to work on a farm: it built me up because the farmer didn't have much machinery and a lot of it was manual, it helped build my strength up for rugby. Folk used to think I'd been doing weights all my life, but I never touched them until I went to Newcastle. It was, of course, an amateur game at the time, so you trained Tuesday and Thursdays and were falling about the streets on Saturday night. It was hard to do any extra because I was working 12-hour shifts and that didn't leave much time for anything else.

'I only got to watch Roy Laidlaw in Scotland internationals, because Jed Thistle played the same day as the seniors and we were all striving to get where he was. He came up to me with a few tips, but basically he told me to play my own game. I must admit I was quite lazy. I wouldn't go away and do extra stuff like the boys nowadays who will practise for hours on end. It's only recently that I started practising my passing and kicking. You have to keep ahead of the young lads.

'The most influential person I had was my dad, Lawrence. He was always pushing and prodding me in the right direction. My mum and all. My brother Kevin and I were always very competitive and when you come from a family like that it's natural you want to do well in whatever you're trying. It's a pity there's not a lot more than that now, because they've brought a lot of foreign players in – the local boys think, "Oh, they've brought someone in to my position" and just drift out of rugby. In the past some clubs have played a foreigner on Saturday and he's just got off the plane on Thursday. It doesn't work, it just upsets the whole club, especially in the Borders where it's a very close-knit community.

'Like Roy, I couldn't pass off both hands when I was an amateur. I can now. I used to pass cack-handed – that or a dive pass. It must have been a Jed thing. It was only when I joined Newcastle that I got to practise passing off my left hand. Any scrum-half nowadays can pass off both hands. Steve Bates, the coach at Newcastle, helped me big time with both hands.

'I played for Scotland B team before I played for the South because Roy was there. But then I went through the same channels. When you get to the Under-21s you don't realise how close you are to a cap and some of the boys now are getting in at 21.

'It's some feeling when you get picked for your country. I was standing waiting for the postman. I played for the South against Australia at Hawick in 1988 and the Scotland side was getting announced the following week. It was on the radio before I got my letter, because the post never arrived until dinner-time where we were. I was working on the farm when it came on the radio; then when I got the letter, away to the phone box to tell my mum and dad. Unbelievable! It's one of these things you can never describe.

'Your first cap, it just flies past. You can sit and watch it on the video afterwards and you think, "God, did this happen or did that happen?" You cannot recall what's been going on in the game. The Friday night before a game, you are thinking, "Am I fit enough, am I good enough?" and then it just passes in a flash. You come off the field and you don't even feel knackered, you're just running on adrenaline all that time.

'It's been a bit of a roller-coaster since then. I was capped against Australia in '88. Craig Chalmers was capped the following year and it has gone from there. I had to learn fast. I remember coming up against Pierre Berbizier in my first game against France in 1989. I was just a young pup at the time and he was pulling my jersey, standing on my toes, standing on my ankles and I thought, "This is unreal." After the game he wouldn't even shake hands because I hadn't won his respect. But the next time I played him I made up for it because everything he did to me I gave him the same back and at the end of the game he came across and shook hands and said, "Well played." That was one of my first lessons. I've done the same to a lot of young boys who came in against me – it just goes on.

'I also got into a fight with Blanco that match and was booed every time I got the ball. Later that night two old ladies came up and set about me with their umbrellas. My toughest opponents ever!

'A year after my first Five Nations season, we were off to Australia on the Lions trip. That was my first major tour, two months with the Lions, what you would call a quick learning curve. There were seven Scots on that trip and we gelled when we came back. We won the Grand Slam and then basically all the players tended to disappear and you started thinking, "Christ, I'm getting old – look at all these young ones coming in!"

'Ian McGeechan was taking over from Jim Telfer when I first got in. Thank God, Jim has mellowed now. When we used to meet up on the

Wednesday in our amateur days it was forwards and scrum-half, and it was a scrumming and lineout session, and – God! – what Jim used to put them though. I've seen us scrumming in a polythene tent when it was rock-hard with frost, or down to the beach because the pitch was unplayable.

'I hit it off with Jim. We're from similar backgrounds. If you want to be the best, and you've got a coach like Jim, you'd hit it off anyway and in 1990–91 everybody we had was striving to be the best. You had your Finlay Calders, your John Jeffreys, your Derek Whites. Everybody was after toppling everybody else and that was a great team spirit we had. Just a couple of months ago we had a reunion and you could feel it again. It was like we'd never been away. In 1990 at Murrayfield I've never experienced an atmosphere like that. The All Blacks game in the World Cup came close, but when Finlay took off at the start and the forwards hit the ruck we knew we weren't going to get beaten. When we got off the bus and dumped the kit all the English players and the wives were on the pitch taking photographs of each other. Everyone was just champing at the bit after that.

'One of the plans had been to have a piper to walk us out, but maybe that would have been a bit over the top. As it was, the crowd responded to the slow march out. It's something that will stick with a lot of people for the rest of their lives.

'I can't remember much about that game except getting a good telling-off from Gavin Hastings in the first half. We tried exactly the same move that we later scored off, but I gave Gavin the ball too early and he got absolutely mangled and he came and gave me a bollocking for cocking up the move. So the second time we tried it I held on and held on and he was lucky to catch the pass. After that try we were never going to get beaten. Scott Hastings made that great tackle on Rory Underwood on the ten-yard line – but looking at the players lining up behind, he wouldn't have scored if he'd got past Scott, everyone was that keen on stopping him.

'Finlay was like a father figure to me. He taught me a lot and I thought he was a right old git at the time because he was always on my back. Looking back, he was trying to make me a better player. That's how it goes on. At Newcastle Doddie Weir is quite hard on Ross Beattie only because Doddie realises his potential and maybe Ross will come back in a few years' time and say, "You were right." That's how I feel with Finlay.

'I've been quite lucky. I've played with a lot of great players, won a Grand Slam, been a British Lion and played rugby professionally. I've been very, very lucky. A lot of boys don't get that. You make your own luck, fair enough, but you also need the rub of the green. I mean, I've had a couple of serious knee injuries – I was out 18 months the second time – but I managed to get back from them and I'm still going. After 1989 I was picked for the Lions in '93, but I had to pull out with a groin strain. There was some daft rumour that I didn't want to tour; but you don't get picked for the Lions and then say, "No, I dinnae want to go."

'Captaining Scotland – I used to think I wouldn't fancy that job, but I think you sort of mature into it. The only thing I had trouble with was the after-dinner speaking. I managed to get through, though. I could manage the press conferences, but there's times when they seem to be chasing you all the time. You just can't get away. You just have to be polite and get on with it. I think my time for retiring was about right before I and the likes of Taity [Alan Tait] started getting some of the stick for the Five Nations defeats. I thought that if I got picked for the World Cup, that would be it.

'Looking back, everything ran like clockwork for me. I couldn't ask for anything better. A Grand Slam, then the last-ever Five Nations championship. I fell asleep watching the Wales–England match in 1999 because I thought England had it in the bag; but I woke up at half-time and Wales were still in it. When Gibbsy [Scott Gibbs] scored, I went through the roof. They'd been trying the same thing the whole game and I just thought, "Oh, no, not again." But then he went through and I went berserk!

'My last match, against New Zealand in the World Cup, was quite emotional. I never told anyone Jim Telfer, Taity and Paul Burnell were all retiring on the same day. When you've been about the boys for 10 to 11 years, it's fitting to be playing against the Blacks in your last game because I still respect them and they have been the outstanding team in my time.

'It was great to beat France in France in my last year, too. That was a great performance, apart from Kenny Logan missing a kick in front of the posts. He said he looked up and saw himself on the screen. What an excuse! It's a wonder he didn't get his brush out and do his hair.

'Then you're finished: you ken you're not going back there. We had our nameplates in our bag and we knew we wouldn't be back in the dressing-room to play for Scotland again. We'd been there a long time – we'd been at the old Murrayfield, then the new Murrayfield and then that was it. But I was lucky enough to be there. I couldn't get any higher than captaining Scotland in the World Cup against the All Blacks in my last match.

'The only pity is, we never won. I was 11 years at that level and enjoyed every minute. But I wonder sometimes now where those 11 years went.'

13. ROB WAINWRIGHT

Handsome, urbane, witty, Rob Wainwright is the sort of man other men should hate on sight. I speak from experience here. A girlfriend, unashamed of her total disdain for spectator sport, developed an inexplicable passion for rugby union after a brief exchange with 'Big Rob' for the press agency at which she worked. Others might hate him on sound. That extraordinary accent, recognisably Scottish but with the elongated English vowels, is an easy target for the jealous who will too easily dub him a priviliged public-school 'hooray'. In fact, most people will tell you Rob Wainwright is a jolly nice chap – and a mean back-row who won 37 international caps, captained his country and won the grudging respect of Jim Telfer despite attending upmarket, fee-paying Glenalmond School and often giving the impression he was only there for the cheer and the beer. He is also a marvellously funny raconteur.

At the time of the interview Wainwright is on a rare trip to Murrayfield, for the Scotland–Barbarians match on 31 May 2000 (he's on the Baa-Baas committee) from the remote island of Coll, west of Mull, where he, his wife Romayne and children Dougie, Natasha, Alexander and Cameron are heavily into the Good Life.

You could say Coll has been a new challenge for the new-age Farmer Wainwright, but he is learning quickly: 'I always had this desire to get some land on the West Coast and this place came up on the island of Coll. It wasn't ideal, but there was a farm with a freehold in a realistic price bracket. It's fantastic, but a simple lesson I learned last week is that when you go away camping and you have just mended the electric fence, turn it on again. That way the bullocks don't all get out and wade through your newly sown barley.'

It was inevitable that the boy Wainwright would take up rugby. His father was a former Blue at Cambridge and a housemaster at

Glenalmond and young Rob's enormous bedroom window at the school looked out over five rugby pitches.

'The family connection was always there. I didn't play until I was nine, first at the local school, then on a sort of reciprocal arrangement to a place called Lathallan, a wee school up near Montrose. My introduction to rugby was there. My first representative game should have been the Under 11½s against someone like Blairmore, but I had a scrap in the changing-rooms three days before. My skipper was saying to me, "Rob, don't get involved, you'll only get hurt and miss the game. Just ignore him" – and I said, "No I won't." So I learned an early lesson because I had my thumb inside my fist when I punched him and of course I missed the game. There's a picture in the family album taken three weeks later of this skinny little boy with the knobbly knees lining up for his first game; it's been continuous since then, really.

'At Glenalmond there was David Sole, David Leslie, Iain Morrison and myself of recent vintage and it will produce more. For me the recipe for getting to the top at anything is determination, self-belief and willpower. We used to have old boys' games. Soley and I would go back and Soley would play in an uncompromising manner against these poor young 18-year-olds.

'But there'd be all these young players there, and they seemed to have it all, yet two years later they would have given up rugby because of other interests, or their careers going in another direction. Really, to get to the top it's patience, self belief and determination that gets you there. The raw material is important, but you have to make the best of what you've got. I remember speaking at a function a couple of years ago when John Jeffrey got involved in some Merchiston Castle old boys' dinner. He introduced me something like, "Our next speaker is one of the least skilful players Scotland has ever seen, but he made up for it with determination, much like myself . . ." And I thought, "Well, he's hit the nail on the head there" – and to be likened to JJ by someone like JJ was an honour in itself!

'I went to medical school at Cambridge University and played for them for six years. I had a couple of elective periods and I went up and worked with a Highland GP to see whether a Highland GP's job was for me (which I found it wasn't, incidentally). While I was up there I met David Sole after a game and he persuaded me to play for Edinburgh Accies. So I was driving all the way down to Edinburgh from Ardnamurchan. It took a while to get used to club rugby because at Cambridge we had a lot of good backs and we played fast and loose against these bulls from Llanelli and clubs like that.

'Accies were my first club, but then when I joined the Army I got moved down to Catterick and was travelling three hours each way to train. Hartlepool had been on at me for a couple of years, so I thought it made sense to play locally – and I'd get a great thrill playing against all these English people and I wouldn't have any trouble getting psyched up for games against them. Then, about a week later, the Army posted me up to Inverness for six months! My argument at Accies had been that I couldn't take the travelling, but then at Fort George, instead of travelling three hours to training, I was travelling six hours. The argument suddenly didn't hold a lot of water. So I had half a season with Hartlepool before deciding to move up to Scotland. It was the start of the professional era and I had the impression Scotland had a bright future in profesional rugby (that might be a bit misplaced, in retrospect).

'I'd had all the fun of amateur rugby, of course, before professionalism. Drink played a large part in the former. After the games in the old days we used to go into the Carlton Highland. Everyone would be shoulder-to-shoulder on the first floor, where the bar was, and there'd be singing and everyone having a good time. But this year I went to Scotland v. France and afterwards, when I went to see the boys in the hotel, there were two people at the bar.

'I have great memories of winning in France in 1995 when we walked into the hotel and they had Moët & Chandon and stuff like this and we said, "We're not drinking this rubbish! Can we please have some of your good champagne? What have you got?"

'"Well, we have the Dom Perignon '87."

'"Fine, bring us a couple of bottles of that and stick it on so-and-so's bill."

'We drank that and I think they ran out of everything in the end. I remember sitting on the sofa next to Doddie Weir. He had passed out and his kilt was riding up, giving all the girls a thrill. I was saying, "God, what a great night. This champagne, I could drink it all my life. What are we on now?"

'I was holding this bottle up and I thought it looked a bit pink, this stuff in the glass, and I remember asking, "What region of champagne is Ashti Shpumante?"

'I think at the end of the night the team manager, Duncy Paterson, had a bill for about £8,000. With all the recent changes, and now they're paying players, the budget's got tight. I believe Arthur Hastie's room bill last year was something pathetic like £500 – I'm sure I put a fair bit of that away and I wasn't even playing! I've had this long-running argument with the SRU: they sent me the bill for that champagne in 1995 because I'd ordered it in the wrong bar at the wrong time.

'When we went to New Zealand in 1996 there were radical changes around. It was just after professionalism started and Jim Telfer said, "Right, we're going to go over there and the All Blacks won't be drinking, so we're no' drinking either." We just laughed because we thought nothing more would come of it. But the next thing, Jim was announcing this at a press conference and then the press were coming out with headlines like "DRY TOUR FOR SCOTLAND".

'Drinking's a major part of touring, of course. It pulls all the boys together. You're stuck in a hotel in the middle of a city and there's not much else to do at night except go out into town and have a meal and a drink. So it was reaching a head in New Zealand. There was a fair bit of tension on the tour. A midweek match was on in Marlborough and it was a day off for those not involved in the game. Jim said, "Right, there are two activities for the non-players. You can either come round the vineyards – with me – or you can go fishing in Marlborough Sound." Two or three of us would have gone fishing, anyway. There weren't many others interested in fishing but the thought of no drinking on a wine tour made everyone keen fishermen all of a sudden. So Jim did the wine tour on his own and the rest of us went fishing. We were met on the boat by this Kiwi guy and the first thing he said was, "Welcome aboard. No doubt you know the Marlborough region is famous for its wine. Well, if you look down there in the cool box you will find one bottle of wine from every vineyard in the area." I don't know if we caught anything but I do know we finished up completely pissed.

'On the way back on the coach we got held up by a road accident and this chap lying there had been pretty banged around. Well, there were three doctors in our group: James Robson, the physio, Jimmy Graham, the official doctor, and myself. As we went past, after this all-day tasting of wine, we started wondering whether we should stop. But we decided the last thing he needed was us tending him in that state.

'I suppose I had a love-hate relationship with Jim Telfer. On the Lions tour of '97, in terms of day-to-day training and getting the forwards prepared, he was fantastic. I did have my differences with him when he was Head Coach of Scotland, because I thought some of his methods for getting the forwards prepared didn't necessarily work in preparing the team. Mellowed? Some days he has done, other days he hasn't. You'll usually know within two seconds of seeing him what sort of mood he's in. He'll either greet you or ignore you completely. I've just had a great chat with him, but other days you'll just get a grunt. We all have our moods. Jim's are just more obvious!

'Of course, in South Africa in '97 we had this film crew trailing around. In the end you just ignored them. Jim would ignore them more than anyone else, which is why some of the more colourful language in the video occurs when he's on it. Jim likes his metaphors, you know, and he was talking about rucking in the first training session. He was saying, "When you go in a ruck you have to be low. You have to be tighter than a nun's" – then he saw the camera – "tighter than a nun's . . . tighter than a nun's . . . drum."

'Then he shooed the camera away and said to us, "You know what I meant, boys!"'

14. ROY LAIDLAW

The definitive Roy Laidlaw–John Rutherford one-two came against Ireland in the Five Nations clash of 1982 in Dublin. When the scrum-half sold one of his trademark dummies from a lineout on halfway, burst past the back row and fed his half-back partner for a run to the posts, such was the speed and precision of the move that not an Irish hand was laid on either. And when Rutherford straightened, both cover and support were left streaming and straining in lanes behind, like the last-furlong cavalry charge of the Ayr Gold Cup. It was a try that had all the ruthless and simple incisiveness of a guillotine blade falling.

The two half-backs produced that level of instinctive rapport for Scotland for a decade from 1979 after the Selkirk stand-off first appeared in Scotland colours. His friend and sparring partner from Jedburgh won his first cap a year later. The quality of that partnership was no fluke. In rugby terms – and in their lives outside that game, for that matter – the pair had been metaphorically joined at the hip. Both were from small Borders clubs; both played together for the South of Scotland; and in tandem for the national side, they formed a then-world record pairing of 35 caps.

Both were also Librans and both fathered three sons – the last of both born ten years apart from the second. Both work with the SRU – Rutherford is backs coach to the senior side and Laidlaw is in charge of the age group teams. They even wrote a book together and were banned from rugby by their current employers. It should also be said that both, in their playing days, sported almost identical dodgy moustaches.

Laidlaw's interest in rugby was kindled by his grandmother, Peggy, a famous Jedburgh character and vociferous rugby fan who actually saw all three Scotland Grand Slams, in 1925, 1984 and 1990.

'I don't come from a sporting background,' he says. 'My mum is a miner's daughter from the West. My dad was a joiner, an only son, but his father played for Langholm and Jed. Peggy was the connection: she was a great character and died two years ago, aged 97. She was widowed when my dad was only four, but she used to talk about the "fitball". She remembered when Jed used to play Langholm and Hawick and she would tell me they didn't have cars in those days. They'd go by horse and cart and the horse had to find its own way home because they'd all be lying drunk in the back.

'Peggy was a great fan and always went to local games. On her 80th birthday Jed were playing West of Scotland at Riverside and she had planned a family get-together – telling stories, singing and a few nips, of course. But with ten minutes to go I got a knock on my face and a cut and I was dazed a bit. I was sitting in the changing-room when all the players came in. Then I heard this voice: "Where are you aboot, where are you aboot?" and it was my granny coming down into the changing-room. All she was worried about was if I was coming to the party.

'She gave me a rugby ball that had fallen off the back of a lorry, or something, although I was introduced to rugby by the primary school teacher, Rod Sharp. He used to take us up to the local park after school. We would play the other local schools and you became attuned to the game. We used to go and watch Jed play. The other lads wanted to play football, I just wanted to play rugby.

'Another influence was George Forbes, Papa Forbes as we called him. He would take us walks on Sunday and stop every so often and tell us about the game, or explain something about it. From Jed you progressed into the South team. Jed were quite small and it was a big step. The South had all these internationals and it was great for a young player from a small town coming into that environment. I think I played 69 times for the Borders and we hardly ever lost a district game. That's where the partnership with John started, of course, and we've had some happy memories together. We both grew up as runners, we loved to run with the ball in our hands – which is just as well, because neither of us could pass off our left hands. We fooled the selectors for years.

'Nowadays you wouldn't get away with it because the technical skills of the players are much higher. There is less space and more emphasis on defence. So although John and I were talented individuals, we had big technical weaknesses which we covered up. We can both spin-pass now, but it's only come in the last few years with going to coaching sessions. John's kicking was his big weakness, but he worked on that and he got help with it. A lot of it is natural ability but the process of when to use it is something that only comes with experience. My ability to accelerate and get away from players was one of my strengths. Poor Ireland got the brunt of it, but they were easy to bribe – I'd just line up a couple of pints of Guinness after the game for them!

'I scored six of my seven international tries against Ireland. I wished it had been England or France. But I've actually got a worse record against Ireland in terms of wins than I have against England or France. Ireland played a prominent part in my career. My first cap was against the Irish, my first international try was against Ireland and the first time I captained Scotland was against Ireland. They even got me started in '79 when I scored two tries at Lansdowne Road against them for Scotland B. That got me noticed. Alan Lawson and Dougie Morgan, the players in possession, were getting to the end of their careers. John had been capped a year before, although he is younger than me. I was 26 when I got my first cap. My passing let me down a bit.

'I also had some great nights out in Ireland – or rather, I didn't. In '84, when we won the Triple Crown in Dublin, I ended up with a knock on the head and had to spend the night in hospital. I actually have a bill from the hospital – £60 – sent to my house. I was probably only earning about £30 a week as an electrician at the time, but fortunately the SRU sorted it out. An examination and two paracetamols was what I got for my £60. Two years later the same thing happened and I missed the celebrations both times.

'The Irish had some of the greatest characters in the game, of course. In 1979 I was sat on the bench, a fresh-faced boy all starry-eyed taking it all in, and Willie Duggan was sat opposite. Players used to all sit together, then. I said to him, "What are you doing tonight?" and he looked at me and said, "You, if there's nothing else happening." Another time, I played in a charity match in Ireland: no one was taking it very seriously, although with five minutes to kick-off a few of us started stretching off in the changing-room, but Willie was still sat there with his feet up in a chair, smoking a cigarette.

'I got the one Lions tour in '83, although I was 30 at the time. It was a disappointment to go at that age, because to have gone as a youngster in my early 20s would have been fantastic. Jim Telfer nearly quit after that tour, but the reality was New Zealand were a very good team and the Lions weren't particularly well prepared. There were a lot of guys you'd never met before and a coach whom a lot of them didn't know. The backs used to coach themselves a lot of the time. The first Test side had never played together as a a a team and we nearly won it. If we had, New Zealand might have panicked and started making changes. They were criticised, but they stuck with the same team.

'At Dunedin it was bitterly cold and wet. When the All Blacks ran out, they rolled on the ground and I thought, "Jeez, these boys are tough." I discovered later that they had these special vests on. They were ahead of the game and we were just naïve. Alan Hewson, the full-back, even had gloves on. That's the sort of experience you only gain by going out there and playing.

'I played 11 of the first 14 games, as the scrum-halfs were getting injured – Terry Holmes, then Nigel Melville. I had played midweek before the final Test and was feeling quite good; but I'll never forget when we kicked off, they caught the ball and one of their forwards ran right through our forwards. I had to tackle him and then the whole New Zealand pack went over the top, one of them stamping on my ribs as he went past. So it was pretty painful after that.

'The bottom line is, they were better than us. But the experience as a 30-year-old was great and I just wish I'd had that experience earlier. Nigel Melville could whip it away with one hand, but I still passed off my right hand, left to right. Terry Holmes was a very intimidating guy, but he couldn't pass off his left hand either! In any age group now, scrum-halfs have to be able to do that. It's one of the first things they learn. Sometimes you try to learn and then just go back to your old ways. Like Gary Armstrong, a lot of us could have been a lot better without these weaknesses.

'I enjoyed touring, although some places you could say were better than others. Romania was an eye-opener. There were armed guards at the airport, women working in the streets and it was grey – a really grey place. In one hotel there was mould growing on the wall. The food was awful. Jim Aitken had diarrhoea and he came down once and said, "Boys, I feel so bad, I think I'm in love with my wife."

'We went back there in '86, which was quite an eventful trip. It was the year the Hastings boys came on the scene. They were up to all sorts of capers. I think Gavin, who had just won his first cap, threw a stuffed tomato that hit the chief executive of the Royal Bank at some after-match dinner in Edinburgh. That didn't go down too well and I remember Dod Burrell, who was president at the time, coming down to the next squad session and saying, "Right, boys, I want a word with you. I don't know who it was, but one of you bastards threw a stuffed tomato and it hit the chief executive of the Royal Bank of Scotland just when we were negotiating a new £100,000 contract. So that got us off to a f★★★★★g good start." That same year – and I'm not saying it was anything to do with the Hastings – the after-match dinners seemed to deteriorate.

There was a lot of drinking and I believe that year Gavin took the Calcutta Cup to bed with him and Scott was running round with its top on his head. The same year, one of the Irish players declared it a no-cutlery dinner and the players had to eat their food without forks and knives.

'But we all let Dod down in Romania of course. The Bear was walking round the airport with his poly-bag of sick, but he got on the plane. At one stage he came waltzing down the aisle with the stewardess's pinny on and later there was an announcement from the pilot: "You are now flying over the Alps at 30,000 feet." The next minute the Bear's voice comes over the intercom: "You are now flying over f★★★ all!"

'In the hotel in Romania the Bear had all the waiters doing the song "Head, Shoulders, Knees and Toes" with all the actions. They were all frightened not to do it. The Bear was great. In the World Cup in '87 we were doing a lineout drill in the car park when a bus drove through. We all stood aside to let it past, then the lineout reformed and the Bear said, "Right, boys, tighten it up, you could get a bus through there." As a tight-head he was one of the reasons I scored so many tries. When he was really fired up it was an awesome sight, this big man grunting and hitting the scrum.

'I sensed the end coming at the World Cup in '87. We drew with France, but lost out on the try count. Against the All Blacks we struggled, we were carrying a lot of injuries, and our resources were stretched a bit. I could sense the game changing then, as well. Guys like [All Blacks wing] John Kirwan were interviewed as part of their daily routine. He was training in the morning and then doing PR work the rest of the day. Andy Dalton, the captain, didn't play but he was still appearing on TV adverts. You could see professionalism was going to come after that. Colin Deans wrote a book and, like John and me, was banned. We were professionalised. Our book was fun, but probably cost us money at the end of the day. I think it paid for a family holiday – but that was it.

'But by then I was having problems with an Achilles tendon and couldn't train at all. I would just play and then recover. I got back into full training, but I was playing catch-up and Gary Armstrong was coming on the scene. He actually played in the South game and we played against each other in the trial – two scrum-halfs from the same club. I remember him catching me at the back of the first scrum and there was a big cheer from the crowd and I caught him at the back of the next scrum. He was coming onto the scene, an exciting young player, but somehow I got selected. It was a season too many. Not only was I playing catch–up with my fitness, but John wasn't there, so I had to get used to a new partner at half-back. There were two or three around at the time: guys like Andrew Ker, Richard Cramb, Rod Wilson.

'My last game was against England, the day someone said they invented the game then killed it. So it wasn't a great way to go out. But Jed got promoted from Division Two and won the Border League. Then, of course, when I retired Gary came in and that was a great achievement for a small club like Jed. I would sometimes play stand-off to help him. I had done that before and it helps you understand what's required. Gary's son is ages with my youngest and they both play mini-rugby. It's great to see Gary coming down to the club.

'One of the best things about rugby was the mix you got. David Leslie would arrive at training with his gloves on and be sat there reading a book. For someone like me, coming from the Borders and quite a humble background, it was quite something.

'One thing that has never changed is my friendship with John. When he phoned up to say his wife was expecting their third child, I said, "Well, you're never going to believe this, but so's Joy." It was uncanny. There was a ten-year gap between my second and my third son. That's dedication for you!

'We are different, though. When we were playing, John was always described as tall and elegant. "Rutherford just oozes class," Bill McLaren would say, "and as Rutherford puts in a huge touch-finder they'll be cheering down in Selkirk tonight . . ." That sort of thing. And I was always "Laidlaw the little Border terrier". Bill would say, "And it's Scotland's put-in and there's Laidlaw ferreting away at the side of the scrum" or, "Scotland go forward and Laidlaw burrows in like a well-nourished mole . . ."

'When we pass away I think John will be put in a glass case at Murrayfield. And I'll be sent to a taxidermist.'

15. COLIN DEANS

When Colin Deans arrived at Franklin's Gardens in 1994, to help Ian McGeechan with the coaching of the forwards at Northampton Saints, he immediately ran into something of an identity crisis. Although he won 52 Scotland caps, took part in a Grand Slam, captained his country 14 times and went on a British Lions tour, hardly any of the Saints players had heard of him. One of them even went so far as to say, 'Did you play rugby, then?' One night Deans was invited to a Lions reunion where he met the surprised Saints captain Matt Dawson, who said, 'I never knew you were a British Lion.'

Perhaps professional players of today should be given lessons in the history of the sport, as well as passing and handling skills. It might even improve their game.

None of this bothers Deans. In his own quiet way, he believes he has won the respect of the current Saints professionals. Certainly the club's achievement in winning the Heineken European Cup in May 2000 could be put down to Deans's work with the front five, who dominated Munster in that Twickenham final.

The Deans rugby work ethic – he was undoubtedly one of the most dedicated trainers the game has seen – was best seen on the fractious British Lions tour of 1983. There, despite being universally regarded as twice the player as the incumbent hooker and captain, Ciaran Fitzgerald, he never won a Test place. Deans simply tried harder and harder; and although his rewards did not arrive on that tour, a year down the line he was a key part of the Scottish 1984 Grand Slam side and he later became captain of Scotland.

Deans is an amiably friendly and quiet-spoken man, but the 1983 experience has clearly left its scars. His autobiography, *You're a Hooker, Then* (which landed him a five-year ban from the SRU) was a light, feelgood documentary of an honest rugby player, but the chapter on his

Lions tour is darkened by bitterness. Now separated from his first wife, Val, and curiously ambivalent about any loyalties to his home town of Hawick, Deans has his own foil laminates business in Kettering. Yet many of his ambitions lie in rugby.

'My career was controversial in specific parts, but I was also wanting to promote the sport with my book and the SRU took the view that I was out to rip the sport apart. I was banned for five years. They barred me from a game which was to open the Hawick floodlights – that was around 1988, a Hawick Legends side against a Scottish Classics side. The SRU told Alastair Cranston, who was overseeing the whole thing, that if I played, action would be taken against all the players, the touch judges and the referee and also against the club. This was because I was professional. But all I really wanted to do was put my life in print and take the book off the shelf one day and give it to my grandchildren. It took me about two years, I handwrote the whole thing and it was an opportunity to say my piece – particularly about the 1983 Lions tour.

'In '83 they picked the players who were supposed to be good. Players were picked on past reputations. Colclough was big and bulky, but soft underneath when the crunch came. I firmly believe that if the nine Scots on that tour had played in the last Test we wouldn't have been hammered by thirty-odd points. We knew Jim [Telfer], we were fit and we were prepared to push ourselves to the limit. Some of the other players were not. To train as hard as we did, it was a shock to them. There were occasions when I trained three times a day.

'On the last day all the Scots got together and were talking and we decided that we were as good as any of them. I get so annoyed at Northampton, where I'm involved now, that some of these players get dropped and go away and sulk and take the huff. But they should do their talking on the pitch, get as fit as possible and then produce the goods on the pitch. That is what I tried to do.

'In 1983 David Leslie was left behind, which was sad. I think if he had gone he would have pushed Peter Winterbottom; I think he would have been in the Tests. You need someone with that mental toughness. I felt sorry for Jim Telfer. He was there for one purpose only. Willie John McBride was manager on the tour and Willie John was living off the '74 Lions. The captain was Irish, too, of course. I will never know till the day I die, but I think Jim wanted me in the team. I was man of the match against Canterbury and even David Irwin, the Irish centre, came up to me and said, "Well played. You have to get picked after that."

'And of course, when the announcement of the team is made,

everyone's looking at you and that's it. Nothing I got Jim on his own, afterwards, and he just said he couldn't say anything. I respect him for that, I suppose. On the Lions tour of '67 I believe Jim approached the captain Mike Campbell-Lamerton and told him someone else was playing better and Campbell-Lamerton did step down from the Test side. In '83 there were some references to that happening with Ciaran Fitzgerald. But ten years on – and this is hindsight – I should have helped the guy. In the end he just withdrew into his own shell. To me he was the wrong captain. I'd have picked Peter Wheeler [the England hooker], which would have made life interesting. But perhaps they learned a lesson. It certainly wouldn't happen now.

'Iain Milne also suffered with the selection on that tour. The Bear, of course, is huge, but he's big boned! What would he be like if he did weights? Over the years he was a joy to play with. He just gave you that sure-fire feeling that the right-hand side of that scrum was going nowhere. You can look at people in the street and know what role in life people are made for. You know the Bear is a prop. New Zealand were laughing their socks off in '83 when they knew the Bear wasn't being picked for the Tests because we were just ripping teams apart in midweek.

'The Grand Slam game in particular owes a lot to Iain because the first half was all France, France, France and you had to admire them. But when Jim Calder scored the try we got on top of them and you knew we were getting to them because they were beating the hell out of the Bear. The worst thing they could do to him was hit him, though, because he just ground them into the dust. The lift that gave to me was incredible. You just felt them go. It was like their last breath. We could have played till twelve o'clock that night – we were running on adrenaline and they were a broken team.

'When I was a kid, playing for Hawick was the be all and end all. I hope it is now, too, because my son Roddy is playing there. If you're born in Hawick you're born with a rugby ball. My father played and Bill McLaren is more Hawick rugby than the Hawick rugby team. Norman Mair, the journalist, said I would never make it. I was twelve stone four. He always referred to me as 'the slight but swift Deans'. That was his way of saying I was too light.

'I had a few knocks like that. There was a guy called Ernie Murray – Cammie's father. He was a PE teacher at Hawick. One day at training he told me and Raymond Corbett, a great mate of mine, "You two away and play football – you'll never make rugby players." Ernie has regretted that line ever since. Cammie and my son Roddy were in physio not so long ago and Cammie said, "My father will never forget telling your dad he would never play rugby!"

'I was always ambitious. I remember playing against West of Scotland. We had this player factfile and there was a space for your ambitions. I put "to play for Scotland and the British Lions" and everyone laughed at me. I thought, "Why are they laughing at me?" That was my ambition. Things like that stick in your memory. You make sure you go ahead and do it.

'After I retired in 1987 I coached some of the Hawick junior side and then stepped up to the big team. That only lasted about six months because my marriage broke up. When I moved down here I was sitting in a hotel four nights a week getting fat, basically. I wanted to get back into rugby. Geech [Ian McGeechan] had just moved down to Northampton and I rang him up to ask if there were any junior sides he knew which I could get involved in. He just said, "Never mind junior sides, just come down here."

'That was five years ago. I coached the development side, did the Under-21s, did the Seconds and then got involved with the first team. In 1987, when I finally quit playing, I could have gone on for another couple of years, but my body was telling me I'd had enough. Nowadays it's run until you drop, but at least you can make enough to be secure for life, which is great. I don't feel jealous of the guys at Northampton. Well, maybe I do, because I wish I was doing it. It has changed, now, in that you don't pick your best team, you pick a team to play another team. That's where the squad comes in. Some players don't understand that they are not *dropped*, they are just not required for this particular match.

'They call me forwards coach but – ach – you can't coach someone like Pat Lam, Tim Rodber or Budge Pountney, so I think I'm mainly responsible for the front five. I hope they respect me now, but when I arrived they didn't know who I was. I recall the second-team prop coming down from Sale, saying, "Did you play rugby, then?"

'"Yes, I played."

'"Who for?"

'"Oh, a little club in Scotland."

'"Did you play for anyone else?"

'"Aye, representative rugby."

'"Oh, who with?"

'"Scotland."

'"Oh, right. You played for Scotland? How many caps?"

'"Fifty-two."

'"Fifty-two? Anybody else?"

'"The British Lions. I captained them."

'When the 1997 Lions had a reunion at the Lancaster Gate Hotel, I was fortunate to be invited down as a guest as a past Lions captain – the only Lions skipper never to leave these shores, in 1986, when we played an International Board side. I went down, booked into the hotel and went across to Hyde Park to look at Princess Diana's memorial. Coming back, I was just crossing the road and there was Daws [Saints and Lions scrum-half Matt Dawson] sitting there in a sports car. He couldn't understand why I was walking across the road in London. Then, at the reception, I was there in my full Highland regalia and Daws came in and said, "Did you play for the Lions, then?" Tim Rodber was the same. It's been nice, because I've said nothing and it's only this season people have picked up on it.

'If I didn't work for myself I wouldn't have the time for rugby. But I would like to get involved in coaching. I'd honestly like to go back to Scotland to take a super-district, because they need someone who can teach them bloody rugby.

'I don't miss Hawick. Twenty years ago I would never have dreamed of leaving Hawick, or even Scotland; but there is more to life than the Borders, there's more to life than Scotland, or even Britain. I was lucky in that I was born in the right family, although my upbringing was limited. We learned that when you've got something you tend to look after it. I've been very, very lucky. If I died tomorrow I'd die a happy man.'

Married to a bonnie New Zealand girl, Bid, with a baby daughter, Rosie, and living in the sumptuous pre-Alp town of Grenoble in France surrounded by magnificent limestone scenery, everything in the garden of Tony Stanger is lovely. On the face of it. The only problem is the rugby. Grenoble are a forward-oriented side and the ball seldom gets past the inside-centre. Wings are almost superfluous and yet, bizarrely, Stanger has been criticised for not scoring tries. It is obvious, even during a brief hour-long conversation, that his days there are numbered.★

Stanger is waiting with his training gear at the Café de la Gare, a strangely isolated figure. Like many English speakers living abroad, he is almost demonstrably grateful to chatter away in his native tongue. The arms, shoulders and chest bear testimony to the daily Grenoble weights regime and he is probably a couple of stones heavier than a decade ago; but otherwise little has changed about the Hawick lad who tore up the Murrayfield wing like a runaway steam engine in March 1990, and into legend.

It's undoubtedly true that Stanger would prefer to be remembered for something other than that try. There are the 52 Scotland caps, the 24 tries – he is joint Scotland record-holder with Ian Smith – and the 1989 hat-trick in only his second international. He agrees: 'There are other things. A pass here, or a tackle there, something you can be particularly proud of because you know it has taken a really good decision under pressure to do the right thing. Little things people don't notice.'

Growing up in rugby-mad Hawick, Stanger's sporting future was mapped out, particularly with Bill McLaren and Mae Sinclair as the local

---

★ Tony Stanger returned to Britain and signed a contract for Leeds Tykes in September 2000, ending his contract with Grenoble 'by mutual consent'. A son, George, named after Tony's late father, was born in August the same year in Borders General Hospital.

primary school teachers. 'Mae was one of the few women involved in rugby and, along with Bill, she used to have everything organised,' recalls Stanger. 'I was one of five boys. My father, George, had been a sprinter and there was the influence of Hawick rugby from day one. At school during the winter there was rugby or nothing. I'd play for the school in the morning, then Hawick Wanderers in the afternoon. That was hard work and I remember my mum used to have to dry my boots with the hair-dryer ready for the afternoon match.

'In my last year at school I started with the Hawick Linden junior team, so this time it was school in the morning and then playing, aged 17, against grown men in the afternoon. As a back you could probably get away with that. I played rugby because everybody played rugby in Hawick. It was a real focus of your physical education from a very young age. It was a sport for the big fat guy and the tall skinny guy, although things have changed now. Back then, you could have fun with your mates no matter what the standard. That's why you would play twice a day, even though it was no joke in a Scottish winter.

'I just missed Jim Renwick when he was retiring, but we had Alistair Campbell, Colin Deans, Gerry McGuinness, Alan Tomes – he played a long time into my career. Some great players and great characters. It was good, as a young player, because I was quite quiet and shy, but they would crack jokes with you and make you feel at home. With four junior teams and the one senior side it was a great structure, but sometimes I had to pinch myself to make sure it wasn't a dream. My first season, they won the championship and that was the last time they won it. It was a good life experience as well as a sporting experience.

'I played centre all my career until my first game for Hawick. That was on a Tuesday night against Gosforth. Then, from Christmas on, I became a regular winger. It was as a winger that I got into the South team.

'The end of 1989 was the first time I toured with Scotland. There had been some talk about it because it was the year of the Lions tour and it was an under-strength Scotland side going to Japan. The three wingers were myself, Matt Duncan and Iwan Tukalo and I was really understudy to those two guys. I played two out of the five games, one on the left wing and one on the right. At the end of 1989 there were two internationals, one against Fiji and one against Romania. I had no thought of playing for the national team but then Bill Lothian from the Edinburgh *Evening News* phoned me at the Royal Bank in Hawick, where I was working at the time, and said, "Congratulations." I genuinely didn't have a clue. It was a bit unfortunate hearing it from a journalist, but I raced out to tell my mum and dad and they were jumping up and down about it.

'Keith Robertson was about to retire, but there was still very strong opposition from Iwan and Matt. In my first match against Fiji I scored two tries and suddenly I was pinching myself and wondering, "What have I done to deserve all this?" I'd come back from Japan determined to play in all the big matches, but maybe Fiji was an ideal introduction. It was daunting for a shy youngster to go into a changing-room and find all these guys like the Hastings brothers and David Sole there. It was like being in a dream. I shared with David Sole the first time. You maybe feel there should be some sort of induction period, but there you are, suddenly sharing with the Scotland captain. They were great, making sure I got an early feel of the ball. To score two tries was just unbelievable. But then I scored three in the next match against Romania, so if it had all finished then it would still have been a great experience.

'My first Five Nations game was in Ireland against Ireland. I played against Keith Crossan, a very underrated player, and he brought me into international rugby with a bump. He was coming in, hitting me hard and he was a handful to defend against. It was a great learning experience in what to expect in international rugby. We played France at Murrayfield and won 21–0, then we went down to Wales the same weekend as England hammered France. We won 13–7, but I remember missing a tackle right out in the open against Arthur Emyr. That stood out like a sore thumb in a game I wasn't particularly involved in.

'All the press were saying later that it was going to be a Grand Slam decider against England, with probably the same Scottish side 'except for Tony Stanger'. It's one thing I have learnt through my career that no matter who is slagging you off, or who is praising you, you have to have this bit of honesty where you can look at yourself and say, "Yes, that wasn't really good enough, I can do better than that." That's what I based all my rugby on. After the game I was really down and Finlay Calder came over and had a word and that was when it really hit home that what I was feeling was being felt by someone else. With two weeks to go to the big game I finally got the letter to say I was in the team, but no one knows how close I came to missing it.

'Hawick had a big club game against Stewart's-Melville the week before. There was no pressure on me to play and a lot of the boys stood down from their club games, but because of what happened in Wales I thought it a good idea to play in a game like that to try getting some confidence back. So I played that game and of course I got injured. I was lying on the ground when Alex Brewster landed on top of me and my collar bone shot out. There was a lot of pain and eventually I came off. A week before the game. They had a look at it at Murrayfield and they weren't 100 per cent sure if I could play. On the Wednesday we all met up at Murrayfield and Roger Baird was there, who had been called in as cover. I was called out to do a rucking session with the forwards on the Wednesday night and they had the bags out and they were smashing into the bags. The shoulder was sore, but I did have the contact session. Then, when I was walking in, Dougie Wyllie was there – the half-backs must have been doing some kicking practice – and Ian McGeechan said, "Do some live tackles on Dougie," which didn't please Dougie. The pain was there but it wasn't restricting me and they decided that night I could play.

'Of course, I woke up next day and it was absolute agony. I never felt it in the game, but one of the sorest motions was to put my hands above my head for that try. Roger Baird doesn't know how close he came to two Grand Slams!

'In that Five Nations – and the tour of New Zealand afterwards – it was almost like a mini-career. In your first two games everything is going well for you, then you come into the Five Nations and realise what rugby is all about. You learn about your body, your healing and what your body can do and can't do. It was like a roller-coaster. It was almost like my whole career in one year. In some ways the thought was there that you wished you were 31 instead of 21 and could finish on that sort of high.

'But I wanted to move forward after that and I knew there was a lot more to come. People thought of me as a winger, but by 1994 I had this feeling that I was getting into a home-town comfort zone. I wanted a bit more challenge. I had played in the centre for Hawick and I liked the business of bringing other people into play, so that year I made the decision not to make myself available for Scotland on the wing. I wanted to be considered as a centre. It was something I had to do. As a winger you sometimes feel as if all you do is chase a ball up and down a touch-line and I wanted to contribute more. I played as a one-off on the wing against South Africa, because they had rung up and asked me and I wanted to play against the Springboks, but the same call came later that season and I turned them down. Come the end of that season I was selected as a centre in the World Cup squad. It was the same year I decided that, to give it my best shot, I should give up drink. So alcohol wasn't on the cards and I won't even touch a glass of wine now.

'It is strange how things work out for you. The Scotland tour of South Africa in 1997 was seen as a development tour and initially I wasn't selected. I was heavily involved in exams, anyway. But then Kenny Logan called off and I was called in and managed to swing things round with exams. Moray House were always very good with things like that, but if you are doing a sports course they can hardly stop you going and playing sport. Then amazingly there were a couple of injuries in the Lions squad and I was called in there.

'I remember Scotland were staying at this park out in the bush and there was nothing much to do. One of the activities was to go and visit a steel mine and then we went up the river on a floating piece of wood. Then the Lions arrived later in the week and they had water-skiing, clay pigeon-shooting, things like that. The Lions were obviously more experienced in organising things! I was 30 at the time, a lot older than a lot of the other players there, and I was only there for four or five days. I came in at the end as the last player to be called up, but the Lions still made an effort to make you feel part of this tremendous camaraderie.

'I managed to get in for the second-last match. I haven't looked forward to, and been as relaxed in, any game as much as that one. There was this feeling that you were lucky to be there in the first place and someone cynical could say I was in the right place at the right time. But I feel that if you give everything your best shot it's amazing what turns up for you. I have found that so many times in my life. I went to university, having failed O Grade physics, chemistry and biology, and came out with a degree in sports science. Often the little breaks go your way because you have worked hard. I've found that in life and I've found that in rugby. The rugby has been a real parallel with life. When I was young I was a very quiet, shy lad. Rugby has helped me come out of that.'

Diffident, softly spoken and nervous in strange company to the extent that his hand visibly shakes when he lifts his coffee cup, Ken Scotland has never found it easy to embrace fame. Like Andy Irvine, that other great Heriot's and Scotland attacking full-back, Scotland has always preferred to leave the limelight to others. On the 1959 British Lions tour of New Zealand – the first tour to demonstrate that there were cracks in the All Black armour – that limelight was hogged by the Ireland golden boy Tony O'Reilly, England's wraith-like wing Peter Jackson, Hawick prop Hughie McLeod and the towering Wales lock Rhys Williams; but such was Scotland's influence that he was voted one of the five players of the tour by a discerning New Zealand press.

Before Scotland there had, of course, been full-backs prepared to run at the opposition, but their forays invariably came after fielding a kick and counter-attacking. Scotland was the first to take part in pre planned back moves and New Zealand, who fielded the ponderous but deadly place-kicker Don Clarke in the number 1 shirt, had never seen his like before. Scotland had a curiously peripatetic career as a player, with a host of diverse clubs on his playing CV. However, these days he is happily ensconced as president at his first one, Heriot's, where he is a hugely popular figure on home match days and training nights. He takes in a game – not necessarily a Heriot's one – every week and Andy Irvine says of him, 'Ken is very, very talented and very astute. He was a good selector and although he didn't really coach us, he would always come out with one or two points which were always absolutely spot on. An astute, very observant individual and just a lovely character.'

Scotland, in fact, is the archetypal rugby man. He was born on 29 August 1936 within sight of Heriot's Goldenacre ground on the north side of Edinburgh. 'My father was a Hearts fan,' he says, 'but he was very enthusiastic about my choice of sport from day one. I started watching rugby during the war when they had wartime internationals at Inverleith, but the first big international I saw was at Murrayfield when Scotland played against New Zealand just after the war and from that day on I had this burning ambition to play for Scotland, to join these gladiators on the pitch. I managed three years in the school 1st XV playing stand-off, but the nearer I got to leaving school the more difficult I realised it was going to be. In Scottish school rugby there were a lot of good stand-offs about – Gordon Waddell, Gregor Sharp, Tommy Hall, Ian Laughland, all playing schools rugby in and around the Edinburgh area. The standard was very high.

'When I finally left school I went straight into the Army, into the Signals at Catterick, where they had a first-class fixture list and a reputation as the best centre for rugby or any sport. That was 1955 and in many ways it was good not to go straight into Scottish club rugby because you were being watched every week and people would see your weaknesses as well as your strengths. There were three Scottish trials that year and I played in the first two as stand-off and was dropped for the final trial. But I got called up as reserve full-back – full-back underlined – having played all my rugby as a stand-off. So I got in the first and second trials as full-back and in early 1957 they dropped Robin Charters and brought me in at full-back for the game against France in 1957, my third game in the number 1 jersey. To emphasise how things worked in those days, Micky Grant, who pulled out to let me into the trial, was then selected at stand-off. He was playing for Harlequins at full-back and I was playing for the Army at stand-off and when they put the jerseys on for the final trial I automatically put on number 6 and he put on number 1 and we had to swap over!

'The team talks used to terrify me, because all they discussed was sticking the ball as high up in the air as possible then clobbering the full-back and I could imagine them in the other dressing-room discussing exactly the same thing. It didn't fill you with a lot of confidence. At the time Scotland had had 19 successive defeats from 1951 to 1955 but in '55 the revival started. We beat Ireland and Wales at home and were just beaten at Twickenham for the Triple Crown, although the late Tom Elliot swore to his dying day he had scored a try when the referee was unsighted. I think at the time Hughie Mcleod, myself and Arthur Smith had never won against England. There were some greats around. Jackson and Jeeps for England, Cliff Morgan and Jackie Kyle – who was my hero – for Ireland. But they weren't superhuman, at the end of the day. My main sporting idols were Kyle and Godfrey Evans because I fancied

TOP: The Big Controller: Jim Telfer
ABOVE LEFT: Ten of the best: John Rutherford
ABOVE RIGHT: Thinking man's coach: Ian McGeechan

Telephone: 031-337 2346/7 (Office)
          031-337 4434   (Home)

Telegrams: Scrum, Edinburgh

Murrayfield,
Edinburgh,
EH12 5PJ,

7th December, 1972.

Dear *Peter,*

Scotland v. New Zealand   *You will be Captain.*

You have been chosen to play/~~not as reserve~~ for Scotland against New Zealand at Murrayfield on Saturday 16th December, 1972. Please let me know if you are able to play/attend by returning the attached form in the enclosed envelope **immediately** after stating whether you require accommodation at the Braid Hills and/or North British Hotels. The Committee have ruled that it is unnecessary for those who reside in Edinburgh to stay at the North British Hotel on Saturday night.

Those requiring to travel from England by train overnight may do so at first class fare.

If you are doubtful as to your ability to take your place please indicate so on the form. It is imperative that I should know by not later than mid-day on Wednesday 13th December should you subsequently become unable to play or be in any doubt whatsoever.

Arrangements

Thursday 14th December

Report at Murrayfield by 11.00 a.m. for training session.
A light lunch will be available in the first floor tearoom
(stair 8/9/10) after the training.
Return from Murrayfield to Braid Hills Hotel
Dinner at Braid Hills Hotel   6.30 p.m.
Coach to Kings Theatre (Black and white Minstrels)   8.20 p.m.

Friday 15th December

There will be a public practice at Murrayfield   10.15 a.m. approx.
Coach departs Braid Hills Hotel   9.45 a.m.
Lunch at Braid Hills Hotel   1.00 p.m.
Tea at Hotel   4.30 p.m.
Dinner   6.30 p.m.

Saturday 16th December

Meeting at a time to be arranged by the Captain
Lunch at Braid Hills Hotel   11.45 a.m.
Transport to Murrayfield (all luggage should be taken)   12.45 p.m.
White Jersey No ..8... will be provided
Bring white shorts and plain dark blue stockings
Team photograph   1.55 p.m.
Kick-off   2.15 p.m.
Tea at Murrayfield (in Internationalists' tearoom,
           Stand Section 2)   4.45 p.m.
Dinner at North British Hotel at 7.00 p.m. for   7.30 p.m.
(Dress - Dinner Jacket)
2 Complimentary stand tickets are enclosed
There will be a dance in the North British Hotel
Restaurant from 10.30 p.m. to 1.30 a.m. and each player and
reserve will be issued with two tickets for this dance.
Admission is restricted to players, reserves, Committee Members
and their ladies.

Yours sincerely,

John Law

Your country needs you: Peter Brown's call-up for
Scotland – note the hastily scrawled addendum

ABOVE: Scotland the Brave: Ken
Scotland makes a break

RIGHT: Double trouble: Jim and Finlay
Calder pictured aged six months

BELOW: at Inverleith 42 years later
[Picture: Jeff Connor]

WEE TRACTOR CO.
Used Compact Tractors and Attachments
01786 489565

Power in the pack: Stewart Hamilton (above) and Sandy Carmichael (below) are big in machinery these days [Pictures: Jeff Connor]

ABOVE: Golden boy: The great Andy Irvine

RIGHT: Son of the soil: John Jeffrey with Smudge at home in Kelso
[Picture: Jeff Connor]

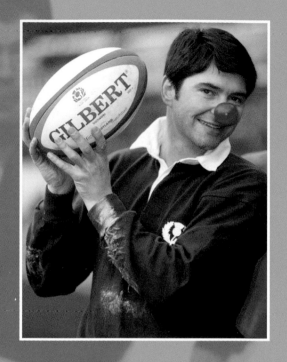

Having a ball: Rugby has always been a game for a laugh to Roger Baird (above) and fellow Scotland wing Iwan Tukalo (below)

ABOVE: Live wire: former
electrician Roy Laidlaw
makes the sparks fly at
Murrayfield these days

RIGHT: Captain Sensible:
Scotland's former 'daft
laddie' Doddie Weir is now
Newcastle skipper

ABOVE: One lovely black eye: Iain Milne shows signs of wear and tear at the 1984 Grand Slam party

BELOW: If looks could kill: David Sole in intimidatory mode

myself as a wicket-keeper on the cricket field. I still see Jackie occasionally.

'From the army I went to Cambridge University. I had had four caps as full-back for Scotland, but didn't get into the university team in my first year. In those days I was a goalkicker, too, kicking with the instep or with the toe – and I could miss equally well with either. Despite all this, the 1959 British Lions took me to New Zealand.

'It's a cliché, but this really was the pinnacle of my career. I did it as a student with nothing else on my mind and I was lapping up the atmosphere of Australia and New Zealand. We were the first tour to fly out, but were still away for five months; the 1950 team took the boat out to South Africa and they must have been away for ever.

'Australia were no pushovers, but of course the centrepiece of the tour was New Zealand. The level of enthusiasm was eye-opening for someone from Edinburgh. Everywhere you went you were a known figure. There were special supplements in the newspapers and photographs everywhere. Playing behind Jeeps, Risman, Jackson, Hewitt, Price and O'Reilly gives you a lot of scope. John Young and Jeff Butterfield, too. From a full-back's point of view, if you gave someone a half-overlap there were plenty of people to finish it off. O'Reilly was blindingly fast. Jackson wasn't, but he was so aware: he beat people without actually doing anything. We used to call him Nikolai the Spy because he had this deadpan face and was ashen-looking all the time and we reckoned he used to mesmerise the opposition into leaving him alone. I could never quite work it out, but Jackson scored some brilliant tries. The backs got the credit, but without the forwards to go along with it you don't get any ball and there were some great forwards.

'We infamously lost the first Test to six penalty goals from Don Clarke and that still rankles. It's still the only time I have seen grown men in tears in a dressing-room. We really did outplay them. At 17–9 up going into the last 15 minutes, one of the penalties at least was fairly technical and another was right over the top of the post and debatable. Four tries to six penalty goals was a bit hard to take. I got a knock on my knee in a midweek game and missed the second Test.

'In the third Test they really gave us a hammering, but we just managed to squeeze through in the final Test and I think that was the greatest test of character of the lot because at the end of five months you are getting fairly weary. But we beat them three tries to two penalty goals and Don Clarke missed a penalty goal late on, with two minutes to go. I remember Jackson caught the ball behind our line and I was in the centre alongside him and for a minute Peter looked as though he was going to set off and run. I for one was shouting at him to touch it down and in fact I was ready to tackle him. It was no time for heroics.

'I am a bit of an expert on O'Reilly because we actually played against each other four times at school when we had a fixture with Old Belvedere in Dublin. He was always a big lad and very dominant as a schoolboy. He was always very ambitious, always very mature as a youngster and very, very bright. He could stand up and entertain in a speech without any preparation and have people rolling about laughing. He is also very loyal to his old friends. On his 50th birthday he invited most of the '59 Lions to his home, Castle Martin, which is beautifully restored and all in the best possible taste; but he also invited ten schoolfriends, so he's very conscious of his roots.

'I still regard everyone on that '59 tour as a personal friend. I don't see much of Hughie now, though. I think he is more interested in his bulldogs. Hughie was the perfect tourist, almost strictly teetotal, first down to meals, first on the bus, first down to training and first to every scrum. He was an example to everyone and a very good ball player to boot.

'After Cambridge I played for London Scottish, Ballymena (including an Ulster Cup final), Leicester and also Aberdeenshire for five or six years. I was based in the Northeast and this is a bit of a commentary on Scottish rugby at the time. I was an international, but I couldn't play for Aberdeen Grammar, who had the best fixture list, because I hadn't been to the school. I couldn't play for the strongest side, Gordonians, because they had all gone to Robert Gordon's. So I had to join one of the open clubs. I was always of the opinion that the only way you could keep playing at a high standard was to have a really hard game every week. I played for Leicester for two seasons and never had a training session with them. I just turned up on a Saturday and played. You couldn't get away with that now. The Army was full-time sport, Cambridge was full-time, too – except this niggle at the back of your mind that you had to get a degree – but I think it would be pretty soul-destroying to have to think about rugby all the time, as they do now.

'I was lucky with injuries. I dislocated a shoulder playing for the Army and there was a doctor playing for the opposition and he put it straight back in. I was once carried off on a stretcher playing against Canterbury – and I was by no means the first player to do that. I was coming into the line outside the outside-centre. I was looking in the way and their winger timed his move far better than my centre timed his pass to me;

as I received the ball it was just like running into a brick wall. I was only bruised and winded, but I thought at the time it was a lot worse than that. In my day, if you were small you could keep out of the way of the big boys. Nowadays all the big lads are running round like the little lads.

'Best players? Jackie Kyle would take some beating, but Mike Gibson and Gareth Edwards were the two outstanding players of my time. But I think ultimately rugby is a team game and you are only as good as the people around you, which is why I am not wildly enthusiastic about man-of-the-match awards. The contemporaries I enjoyed playing with were Arthur Smith, Ian Laughland, Gordon Waddell and Hughie Mcleod but I tend to remember teams rather than individuals. Andy Irvine, more than anyone else, was capable of changing the direction of a game, usually in the direction of his own side. People talked about his lack of basics, but I think he had good basic skills.

'Workwise, I was in construction mainly. Then I worked for the National Trust for Scotland, at Brodick Castle on the Isle of Arran for five years, then in the Borders. I am now more or less retired, though I potter about and keep myself out of mischief. My three sons all played rugby but unfortunately lightning seems not to have struck twice in the same place. In fact, the youngest boy is far more interested in the fortunes of Aberdeen Football Club.'

Jim Calder and his brother Finlay are twins, with all the affiliate blood ties that 20 August 1957 gave them. 'We are 42,' says Jim in response to the interviewer's traditional opening question. Both went to Stewart-Melville School in Edinburgh, both played in the back row for Scotland – Jim gaining 27 caps, Finlay 34 – and both were British Lions. After a few minutes in the company of both, too, there is an instinctive feeling that these are men you would trust with your life.

But really, that is where the similarities end. The Calders are not identical twins for a start – elder brother Gavin bears more of a resemblance to Jim than Fin – and while fidgeting, hyperactive Finlay seems unable to sit still for longer than a few seconds, with his sharp mind jumping from subject to subject, Jim is deliberate and more focused. Fin always seems to be on the way somewhere; Jim has already arrived. Says Fin, 'Jim as a person is far more single-minded than I am. You would imagine that two out of the same pod would have a similar intellect. Maybe we are, but one thing's for sure: if he set his mind to do something, he would just get on and do it.'

Their differing personalities also reflect the way they went about their business on the rugby field – Jim unobtrusive, workmanlike and almost unnoticed on the blindside, Fin far more extrovert with his chit-chat, opposition wind-ups and that distinctive windmilling running style. They would have made a great international back-row team, but in fact Fin's Scotland career began when Jim's ended and it is Finlay who now comes to the public mind when the name Calder is mentioned. Jim was once the more famous one and he laughs now: 'All my friends know when to go out and buy me a card because Fin's name appears in the paper in the "Today's Birthdays" section!'

Jim Calder played his last game for Scotland 15 years ago, but still suffers happily from what he calls the 'rugby sickness'. On Sundays he can be found with a bunch of fellow enthusiasts on the Stewart's-Melville School playing fields at Inverleith on the north side of Edinburgh, coaching the Stew-Mel Lions, a 200-strong kids' rugby club with ages ranging from five to fifteen. Jim's 12-year-old son, Lewis, is there every weekend and sometimes Fin finds time out from coaching Gala to join in. At one time Stew-Mel had three sets of brothers in the 1st XV: the four Calders and Alex and David Brewster in the pack and Simon, Julian and Andy Scott in the backs. There is still a comforting family feeling about Inverleith.

Jim Calder had various jobs in corporate business and worked as a sales and marketing director before jointly setting up a successful recruitment agency in Edinburgh. Fin and John were once in the grain business and farming is the brothers' heritage.

'Dad was an agricultural auctioneer in Haddington and our mum was a farmer's daughter,' says Jim. 'There was a plot of land and a field in front of the house. You can't get much better than that. Our dad, Robin, was keen on rugby, but always quite gentle with the support. He was a huge man, 6ft 4in. and 19 stone. John is 6ft 3in. and the tallest; Fin and Gavin 6ft 2in. and I'm 6ft, which is a bit of a bone of contention. It was always Fin and myself against our older brothers. Dad was quite clever at winding us up. He'd say to me, "Isn't Fin fantastic?" which would get me going, and to John he'd say, "Didn't Jim play well?" As far as motivation goes, he was actually ahead of his time.

'We went to Melville College, where none of us ever got to being a back. In the last year at school I toyed with the idea of scrum-half, because I was small for a flanker, but I stuck there in the end. We had a bit of a thing about the Borders in those days. There was a feeling that with an average 12 out of 15 from the Borders in the Scotland team, captained and coached by a Borderer, and with the chairman of selectors from the Borders, we had to try that bit harder. At Stew-Mel we had four Calders and two Brewsters in the forwards. The Brewsters were powerful farmers and mean with it. The tradition was that a city team would go down to the Borders and have hell kicked out of them, but we turned the tables. There was no mucking around with us. Stew-Mel were respected.

'Fin and I played left and right and there was always this big unspoken rivalry. Early on, I captained the school team and was vice-captain of Scottish schoolboys. I knew Fin was very, very good but he didn't seem to have that push. He went to Melrose and came under Jim Telfer and by his late 20s was becoming a really good player. But I got in the

Scotland squad first and I think he thought he wasn't going to make it. I remember one really nasty rainy Wednesday night we were out training, just running, and halfway round I kept going and left him behind. He arrived five minutes later and I turned to him and basically called him useless. "What do you mean?" he said.

'"Look, I was dying back there, too, but I kept going and you just gave up." I can still see his face now. That was a turning-point for Fin. A week later, doing the same training, we got halfway round and he just took off. From then on he developed real confidence in himself. It was strange being the same age and yet we seemed to play in different eras. I got in the Lions' 1983 trip and he had to wait until 1989.

'A lot has been said about New Zealand in 1983. All I will add is that, in the best team, Iain Milne and Colin Deans would have been in the front row. But the manager Willie John McBride was Irish and the captain Ciaran Fitzgerald was Irish and Telfer, the Scottish coach, was sat in the middle. A lot of the issues were Ollie Campbell or John Rutherford, Deans or Ciaran Fitzgerald, Calder or John O'Driscoll – it was a bit disheartening.

'Telfer said to me on the bus part-way though the tour, "Jim, do you think if we got a few people together we could do what we did in '66?" That was when they ousted Mike Campbell-Lamerton as captain. It was what everyone wanted. I wasn't in the Test team and I think he was just testing my reaction. If Syd Millar had been there I'm convinced it would have been a better tour, because Willie John McBride isn't quite the guy everyone portrays him to be. It was an aged Graham Price keeping the Bear out. But a lot of players, John O'Driscoll, Maurice Colclough and even John Carleton, their best days were behind them. We never picked our best team. Ollie wasn't a robust guy and most people would have had John at stand-off. I got in for the third Test and broke my thumb, so I had two weeks just waiting for the tour to end. But I watched the fourth Test, where we were absolutely murdered, and it was obvious that it was embarrassing to some of us and not so embarrassing to some others. You realised then that you got a sense of purpose when you knew you understood the following season's opposition.

'In 1984, playing against Colclough – who shouldn't even have gone on tour because he had been injured – we knew that if we put John Beattie up front against him it would make him wonder, because there certainly wasn't much love lost there. The Colclough–Beattie thing goes back a long way, so we shoved Beattie up to number 2 in the lineout just to intimidate him. The feeling was that Colclough was not popular.

A lot of the English guys were all right – Alan Tomes on his Lions tour said the best ones were English – but Colclough was just dismissive and arrogant. I can remember coming back though Heathrow and he was shouting at the top of his voice, "We're the worst Lions ever."

'I really felt for Colin Deans on that tour. I have never seen anyone train like him before or since. We'd train in the morning and he would go out on his own in the afternoon. I remember running with him at Christchurch. John Beattie was there too. It was a rainy day and I thought I'd better start working hard. John gave up, but Colin just kept running and running and running. It was the most incredible thing I'd ever been involved in. He kept turning round and saying, "Come on, where are you?"

'That Colclough thing at the airport, the next time you go out you remember things like that. The hurt of defeat has to be there because you can always learn from that. I think a few of the Scottish players of today have lost that. Kenny Logan, for example. I have always liked Kenny, but we were out in Est Est Est [an Edinburgh restaurant] on a Saturday night last year and he was there. We had just been hammered by France at home and he should really have been at the official function, but there he was with a load of guys in dinner suits in this restaurant, not embarrassed at all, and I just find that difficult to understand. After a defeat I would go and hide away. You know that at some stage you are going to have to face the music through your coach, through your family, the fans or at work – but you wouldn't go out celebrating. There's a lot of showbiz about it now. I think Alan Tait found that quite hard to handle when he came back into union.

'Our family farming background should have gone down well with Jim Telfer, but there was that fee-paying thing. Mike Biggar, David Sole and David Leslie were probably the hardest guys he'd ever dealt with, but they were from the top end of the public-school set-up. Stew-Mel were not quite up there! It was such an experience for me to come under someone like Telfer, because everything was really nice at Stewart's-Melville and suddenly there's Telfer. He would call me Calder. It was "Jim", "Peter", "David", then "Calder". He would say to me, "Look, in a way I feel sorry for you guys in the back row because I know your game inside out. I may not know as much about props, second-rows or centres, but I know your game and I'll be watching you."

'That might explain the strength of Scotland's back-rows down the years. Jim would say to Derek White, "You have far more ability than I ever had, but I'm not convinced you are any better, because you don't apply it." This is Derek at 23, 24, a different player from three or four years later. Jim was a dangerous man because you would say something innocuous and he would just turn it. He did have a hold on us and it's a fact that Scotland would not have won Grand Slams without him. It just wouldn't have happened. I remember in the early '80s, when Scotland and Ally MacLeod had that disaster in the World Cup. He hadn't even looked at the opposition, never looked at a video or anything. He was full-time. But Telfer had a job as a headmaster and was Scotland rugby coach and yet you would arrive at 9.30 on Monday morning and he'd have all the videos ready, he'd know exactly where to stop it, he'd have everything analysed and there was no time wasted.

'One criticism I would have of Jim is that he's too dogmatic. He shouldn't be doing the job he's doing – he should be forwards coach and for as long as he's alive he will be the best in Scotland by a considerable margin. He shouldn't be wasting his time doing other things. If he was coaching forwards every day of his life, Scotland would always be better. He is a brooding presence at these SRU committee meetings, it's just not his scene. He should be involved with the Under-21s, the Scotland B or even Edinburgh Reivers. The people at Murrayfield are petrified of him. When I was setting up the mini section at Stew-Mel, I phoned the SRU to ask for a dozen rugby balls and I was told I'd have to wait for Jim to get back from New Zealand for a decision.

'The worst feeling in your rugby career is when you get dropped. Anyone will tell you that. It's horrible. It happened to me twice. I was dropped in '85 before the England game, but two years later I got in the trials again, this time for the Reds and scored two tries. Fin had got injured before the Scotland–England game and it looked as though I was going to get back in. It was between me and Derek White and Derek was away skiing, so Fin was convinced I'd be back. Then the game was cancelled because of snow! I was sitting at home looking at Ceefax and I could hardly believe it.

'In '87 I was in the squad for the World Cup, but I hated the business of standing around on the Sunday having been in the team. There's very few players get to go out on their own terms. Fin did that, I didn't. When I was dropped at the age of 27, he came in at 27 and it was difficult sitting there in the changing-room together when they announced the top team.

I remember sitting there with my brother after the '86 trial. I'm sure Telfer did it it deliberately when he announced the team. He went from 15 to 9, named all the backs. Then he started on the front row, through the second row to number 8 and finally number 7 ..."Calder Fr, Finlay Calder."

'So that was it. I shook Fin's hand, but really I just wanted to get away. But there have only been three Scotland Grand Slams in history and the Calders were involved in two of them. So that's not bad.'

The Glenalmond School governors eventually had to cancel indefinitely the annual Old Boys v. 1st XV match. There were, apparently, problems with insurance caused by David Michael Barclay Sole's reappearance on the Perthshire playing fields of his Alma Mater every 12 months and his inability to offer less than wholehearted commitment and aggression to any game of rugby. Sole, in fact, was treating the 18-year-olds ranged against him like the men in white jerseys he famously faced on 17 March 1990 and, by all accounts, there were battered teenage bodies everywhere. The school's rugby hopefuls of an earlier vintage had had to contend with another old boy, David Leslie, and his philosophy about so-called 'friendlies'. Rugby's rites of passage must have been painful at Glenalmond, but Sole justifies all this with a knowing smile: 'You have to keep these young whippersnappers in their place!'

Sole's occasional smiles are welcome because, like Leslie, he can be, well, a bit daunting at times. Certainly I recall that frowning concentration and beetle-browed countenance from a thousand video replays, particularly of Murrayfield 1990, when Sole slow-marched his side out into history.

The famous headband is gone (although he still favours short-sleeved shirts) and he certainly looks fit enough to do some damage on a rugby field still, a reminder here that Scotland's Grand Slam captain of ten years ago retired at the age of 30. He puts his fine physical condition down to the gymnasium provided by his employers, United Distillers, at their large headquarters in central London, where we meet in the staff lounge bar. He works there as the exotically titled Global Category Manager for Commodities and Neutral Spirits, managing a budget of £150 million a year.

'It was a bit daunting moving down here,' says Sole, 'but we might attempt to go back to Scotland at some stage in the future. My wife misses Edinburgh. Since retiring from rugby I've been promoted every couple of years. I've been with them ten years. When I joined, I had just been awarded the captaincy of Scotland, so they didn't know what they were taking on at the time. They were enormously supportive over the piece when I was working. At first, they only used me as a guy who would take a bottle of Bell's or a bottle of Johnnie Walker around and say, "Look, I am a wonderful guy and I work for this company" – that sort of thing. But they also used me in a very nice way, like meeting some of their key customers at things like the Bell's Scottish Open. From a career perspective, it's very hard to try juggling a business career, a family and international sport. To reconcile all three is very difficult. One of the reasons I retired when I did was to devote more time to my career and my family.'

Like Rob Wainwright, Sole's accent is famously Anglo-Scottish posh and he also went to one of Jim Telfer's beloved fee-paying schools. But any doubts Telfer may have had about Sole when he appeared on the international scene were quickly swept aside:'I think I earned Jim Telfer's respect the way I approached my rugby and my training and quite often you get the hardest players from fee-paying schools. It's possibly because you are sent away from your mother's bosom at an early age and have to stand up for yourself.'

'When I was coaching for a while I always said the most important part of the body was the two inches above the eyes. If you get that right, you can do anything. If you have the attitude right you can go a long, long way. I remember Richard Hill, the English scrum half: I went to university with him and going to the gym he would be working on his pass for an hour. Twenty balls off one hand, twenty off the other. He didn't have the same talent as even some of the guys at university, but that dedication won him a lot of England caps and the captaincy. Just a terrific attitude. If you can have that attitude it will stand you in very good stead in anything you do.

'When you look through that Grand Slam side of 1990, there were a lot of strong personalities. The Hastings brothers, they could be going out to play the best XV in the world and still be convinced they were going to win. Exceptional self-belief. Derek White, Gary Armstrong and Kenny Milne were much more introverted, but if you were picking one guy to go over the top you would pick Gary Armstrong. He would put his body on the line for the cause – a phenomenal player with incredible courage.

'We had very young and very inexperienced players like Gary, and

Craig Chalmers, and a lot of experience in other areas. My job was pretty easy because we had so many leaders in that team – Fin [Calder] and John Jeffrey, the Hastings brothers, all leaders in different ways. 'The blend of that 1990 Scottish back row was tremendous, all different skills, and it was when you put them all together that you had one of the best back rows ever to play for Scotland. I don't think Jim Telfer ever got the very best out of Derek White.

So for me to do a tub-thumping speech or bang my head against the wall wasn't appropriate. It wasn't me and anyway we had plenty of other guys to do that. Perhaps my style suited those particular individuals. You don't need to say anything to Gavin and Scott, whereas someone like Kenny, perhaps, you have to build up. You have to recognise that different things motivate different people. Mind you, if you can't get wound up playing England for a Grand Slam, there's not much hope for you.

'I learned a lot about many things from former Scotland captains. I first started with Colin Deans as captain in 1986 and through to the World Cup. He was another dedicated, brilliant player. I took over from Fin and carried on from there, for some unaccountable reason. Fin was a different sort of captain, more gung-ho. But I think he would be the first to acknowledge that he had strong leaders about him, too.

'I think the English are arrogant without even knowing it. I see it coming in and out on the train. It must be wonderful to have this wonderful self-belief. The Scots tend to be down on themselves and self-deprecating. When we achieve something we tend to be very modest about things.

'There was a lot of pressure on Fin in the '89 Lions tour; there was a lot of pressure on us all. We lost the first Test, which wasn't in the script at all because the idea was to go through unbeaten. We went down to Canberra to play ACT and were 18–4 down after 20 minutes. Their fans were going berserk and there was this ridiculous song playing and you were thinking, "Jesus, where's the plane? Take me home." To be honest, I think one or two players had their bags packed and were booked on that plane, because their minds weren't on the job.

'We actually turned that Test round and it may have been something to do with the fact that we fielded an all-Scottish back row for the only time on that tour: JJ, Derek and myself! We won, but it was looking decidedly pear-shaped at one time in that match. But we'd had our backs to the wall and showed the character to fight back, so that was a big turning-point on that tour. Of course we had been lambasted in the UK press as well as the Australian press, so that helped as well.

'So on to the Battle of Ballymore where there was an awful lot of pressure. When we walked out in front of the stand on the way from the dressing-room they were giving us dog's abuse. Talk about red mist! At the first scrum Nick Farr-Jones went to put the ball in, Robert Jones stepped on his toes and it all just blew up. There were a couple of other incidents and I'm sure that nowadays a couple of guys would have been cited. In those days you got away with it. Then we get lambasted as "British Thugby Players", but there is an element of whinge about Australians when they are losing. Doing them over physically really brought that whingeing to the fore.

'The third Test was a cracking game. It was only 19–18, but it was one of those games you knew you were going to win. The '89 Lions live in the shadows of a lot of other tour teams, but we should stand up alongside the '71, '74 and '97 Lions as a really good side. Don't forget the Australians went on to win the World Cup two years later.

'People will always remember that Scotland team for that 1990 Grand Slam, but we played far better rugby in the tour of New Zealand that year and should have beaten the All Blacks in their own backyard. As it happened, we became only the third team ever in history to tour New Zealand and be unbeaten in the provincial games. One of the others was Wales, who I think played two games – hardly a significant tour of the provinces!

'In the first Test we gave the New Zealanders too much respect. I remember phoning my wife Jane after the game and she said, "I knew you were going to lose." She said she could see it in some of the boys' expressions as we faced the haka. I related that story to the guys and told them, "Sure, respect them, but don't fear them." In the second Test we outscored them two tries to one and lost to two daft decisions from referee Derek Bevan when Grant Fox kicked the goals. I think we earned their respect in that match.

'If we had won that Test it would have signed and sealed the credentials of what was one of the greatest sides ever to represent Scotland. Two years after that I quit. It was a long, long year that year. In August we went off to Romania, then played the Barbarians, then had the World Cup. Then it was the Five Nations and then off to Australia, where we got absolutely railroaded – whoever agreed to that itinerary should have been strung up. After the World Cup I was under a fair bit of pressure because we had lost three games (two to England and one to New Zealand) and I began to think, "I'm not enjoying this any more. I'm not enjoying the training, I'm not enjoying the international rugby."

There was the potential to go on for one more season, because there was the possibility of getting the captaincy of the Lions tour. But I realised that if I did go on I would be doing it for ego. It would be self-indulgence rather than enjoying what I was doing. Whether it was the monotony, or the fact that a lot of the guys had retired, I don't know. I just knew it was no fun. It had become a burden.

'I have a huge amount of passion for Scottish rugby and that is maybe why I make outspoken remarks about it. I love what it has given me and I'm very grateful for what it has given me: the friendships, the memories, the experiences. You can't buy something like that.

Family has in some ways taken over from that. We have had Christopher and Tom since Gemma and Jamie. It's funny – everyone asked, when we were expecting a third, if that was a mistake, but no. The fourth wasn't entirely planned, but we wouldn't be without any of them. They fight like cats and dogs but they are great company. A lot of our lives revolves round them now. You become like glorified taxi-drivers ferrying them to and from school and birthday parties. Jamie is a real sports enthusiast, he would quite happily play sport all the time. But it's daunting for children following in their father's footsteps. Jamie will always be *my son*, especially in Scotland. He is totally different physically, though: he's tall, he's got strong legs and has his mother's build. He is actually very talented and plays in the centre, scoring lots of tries. Even in the hotbed of England, he wants to play for Scotland. He was grinning like the Cheshire Cat going back to school after the Calcutta Cup match.

The great thing about rugby for me is that it brings together diverse characters. The one thing that unifies you is that stupid sport you play. Chasing some bloody pig's bladder round the park. In the era that I played, the values it brought were phenomenal: the sense of fair play and the integrity, and then when you put it in a Scottish dimension, the sense of passion you have representing your country.

'The closest thing to picking up a gun and dying for your country is putting on a blue shirt with a thistle on it and going out to play against whoever it is in front of 60,000 Scots. It's the most wonderful, wonderful feeling and a wonderful, wonderful privilege to do so. I never allow myself to forget that.'

20. ALASTAIR McHARG

The king in exile sits in his large office in Farnborough, Hampshire, a bit heavier than in his days as one of the lightest locks ever to push for Scotland. The distinctive black, curly hair has long given way to wavy silver and he walks with a pronouced limp. But even 400 miles from home, Alastair McHarg remains as patriotic a Scot as ever walked the earth. There is a copy of the *Collected Works of Burns* on his desk and when his three daughters were due, his wife was rushed back north of the border, heavily in labour at the time. As David Sole puts it, 'You tend to become even more patriotic when you are living away from home.'

McHarg, who turned 56 in June 2000 and runs a company dealing in tractor spares, made his home in England back in 1970 and for many years – odd to think of, this, in these days of the Leslie brothers and assorted kilted Kiwis and Springboks – was barely tolerated in Scotland colours. He was a sort of necessary evil, selected only because his country could not do without his athleticism, a mean streak nurtured in Irvine, Ayrshire and that amazing mobility that some put down to looseness.

'If you played for the Exiles, London Scottish, you were looked on as English,' he recalls, 'which was quite hurtful. Imagine listening and reading about the English side and how good they were. How many times you turned up to play against England just to make the numbers up and come away with the spoils? And it was never-ending. But there was still this feeling that we were all English when in fact you are more Scottish than ever. You go to your Burns Night, you address the haggis and you express your Scottishness. You become more conscious of your roots, particularly as you get older.

'The attitude then was that you were a traitor. I would rather see 15 Scottish-born players lose than a New Zealand 2nd XV win in Scotland colours. I wouldn't go down the road to watch them. The identity is the issue. You have a pride in your culture, your history, your roots, it's where you come from, it's your background, it's your mother, father, grandfather – the whole thing. All of that is represented by your national side.

'Say I have, somewhere in my family, a great-great-grandfather from Argentina and I am invited to go and play for Argentina in Buenos Aires, with a blue-and-white Puma jersey on and listening to the Argentine national anthem. Do I consider myself an Argentinian? Of course I don't. I am basically a Jock travelling for money and that is what these guys are doing. They couldn't cut the ice wherever they came from, so they decided to try somewhere else.

'I remember playing a match with the Scottish Exiles against London Scottish some years ago and we had a guy from Coventry playing in the Exiles side. We were in the dressing-room at Richmond before the game and this guy, in his Midlands accent, shouts, "Come on, guys, let's get stuck into these f*****g Jocks!"

'My kids were sent home to be born in Scotland. They are Scottish. These guys whose granny once spent a long weekend in Sauchiehall Street can stand there and sing "Flower of Scotland" as long as they like, but it falls on stony ground with me.

'I am proud of what Scotland have achieved. Jim Telfer would always say we are a nation of 5 million people with only 20,000 rugby players and to achieve our level of success over the years is incredible. Rugby is not the national sport in Scotland, so in many ways the only ones in Scotland who took up rugby were the ones who couldn't play football. And I was one of them. When I was in primary school I used to go and watch my brother play at Irvine Royal Academy. I would go in the school coach and I just couldn't wait to get to the senior school and play rugby. The games master had a problem getting guys to play rugby, so when he heard my brother played, he just put me down for rugby too. Irvine Royal Academy sounds very posh, but it's actually a comprehensive. I had problems, healthwise – pneumonia which turned into asthma – and I was actually in bed for six months. I never thought I would play sport at any level because of my chest problems. I used to wake up in the morning wheezing and my parents would send me up to Glasgow for homeopathic treatement, so I'm lucky, really, to have been able to play at all.

'I was scrum-half at first and in those days the flankers could come round the scrum and bury the scrum-half. The physical gap between someone of 15 – me – and 18-year-olds was enormous and our hooker could never work out why he was never winning strikes. I was putting the ball in squint. To the opposition!

'In my day Scotland had very lightweight packs. When I was first capped in 1968 I was about 15 stone with wet socks on, which nowadays, of course, is the size of a midget back-row forward. When I was playing against the England side you had guys like Peter Larter, who was probably 17 stone and a bit, Nigel Horton, 17 stone, Chris Ralston, maybe 16½, and the Welsh guys, Delme Thomas and Allan Martin — all about the same size — so you were giving away a couple of stone against the opposition.

'But what were you selected for? Winning the ball in the middle of the lineout. Jumping was a skill. On TV nowadays they say, "What a wonderful leap by Dallaglio" and of course he hasn't leapt at all, he's just been lifted. That skill isn't there any more. Or maybe there's a skill in lifting! But in the days I played, you were talking about individual skills and how you were able to manoeuvre the ball back using your inside arm to get leverage. That was banned when they cottoned on you could hold the other man down, so then you started using the outside arm to hold him down and win the ball because that was your job.

'I was lucky in the '70s because I played behind Sandy Carmichael who was undoubtedly one of the best scrummaging forwards I ever played with — just outstanding, solid as a rock, so it was relatively easy to sit in behind him and use your 15-stone weight to its maximum. If you scrummaged technically correctly — and the whole scrum is based on your tight-head prop, anyway — you should do all right.

'Ian McLauchlan on the other side would scrummage low. Low scrummaging was introduced into the game in the late '60s by Jordanhill College and Bill Dickinson. Guys like Struan McCallum and Ronnie Boyd and McLauchlan were the front row for Jordanhill and Boyd the hooker never hooked: he just put his head down and headed the ball back. In those days you could scrummage any height you wanted to. In '71 with the Lions, McLauchlan was scrummaging against a big Maori guy in the Tests and this guy had his bloody pilot's licence, he needed a parachute by the end of the game, he ended up that high in the air. We had a great front five, as good as any in the Five Nations.

'Sandy Carmichael was a baby, really. He had a torrid time in his early matches against Ray McLoughlin of Ireland. I shared a room with Gordon Brown at the Braid Hills Hotel and it was about one in the morning on the day of the match. The bloody door opened, I saw this massive frame in the door and it was Sandy. He said, "I cannae get to sleep." I said, "Great, now I cannae get to sleep either." He was so worried about playing against McLoughlin. But he had no reason to be worried, because although he'd had a tough time the year before, he actually had an outstanding game at tight-head that day and any bogey was well and truly laid.

'He was a pussy-cat compared with McLauchlan. Hugh Young of the *Daily Record* phoned up his wife one Saturday afternoon on match day and told her, "Mrs McLauchlan, I've got some bad news for you. Ian has broken an arm." And she said, "Whose arm has he broken?"

'Guys like Broonie were very positive, although not in an aggressive way. They were a good bunch of guys, no real lunatics among them. Peter Brown would be called a mild eccentric, but he also gave a lot of confidence to the others when he took over the captaincy. Totally positive. When you went out with guys like Jock Turner, John Frame, Ian McGeechan and Jim Renwick, you always felt you would do well. In my first game in '68, I won the first couple of lineouts and thought, "That will keep me in the side." But then as that side developed, it never crossed my mind that I would be dropped. It was almost like a club side, the same bunch of guys with a high number of caps.

'Other than a defeat by Wales in 1971 and then 1977, Scotland hardly lost a game at Murrayfield other than to touring sides. I remember Dickinson saying to us, "Do you realise schoolkids have come along here, maybe at the age of ten, to watch you play and then they've left school at sixteen and only seen you lose once? We coincided with a great Welsh side, but the difference between the two of us was the half-back partnership.

'I don't feel we were inferior to any Welsh side up front. In the centre we had Renwick and McGeechan, who were as good as any of them. They had Gerald Davies on the wing, of course, but the partnership of Gareth Edwards and Barry John at half-back to me was the difference. If Scotland had those two it would have been the other way round. Maybe J.P.R. Williams, too. We had a lot of problems at full-back. We had Ian Smith there. He scored a couple of tries, but he was playing for London Scottish Third team at the time. He was a dentist in the Army. Gordon McDonald was first-team full-back, Jim Wilson [Stewart's brother] was second choice and Smithy was in the Thirds. I think his only claim to fame, apart from his two tries, was that he was the only bloke I ever saw who could touch the end of his nose with his tongue.

'When he played at full-back in the '71 game against Wales, it was in the last two or three minutes and the defence was this: if J.P.R. Williams came into the line on the 25, our winger Ally Biggar was to come in and take JPR, leaving Smithy to take the wing. In the lineout Peter Brown came up to jump against Delme Thomas and told me to go back to the number 8 position. Delme won the ball and I was running across the park at number 8 and I can see it: Williams was coming in and I screamed for Biggsy to stay out, because if he came in and Gerald Davies got the ball, it was curtains. Gerald was ten yards in from touch and Smithy dived but never even touched him. If Biggsy had stood out, Williams would have been tackled in the centre and it would have been a different game. As it was, we lost 19–18.

'After that we had to play Smithy in the first team at London Scottish and he used to take the kicks and I remember one when he kicked the ground first and the ball went about 15 yards along the floor. So we did have a problem at full-back.

'Then Andy Irvine and Bruce Hay came in. Andy actually cost us more games than he won for us, but the press only remember the games he won. There was some suggestion he should have taken a bucket on the pitch to catch the ball. In fact, when I used to come across him when he was coaching Heriot's, I would say, "Got your bucket, Andy?" Same with Gregor Townsend – he has been forgiven so many times.

'When we played, I always tried to think of something no one had ever thought of before. Going back to '62 at Irvine Academy, we had a fitness trainer who took us on the park to give us warm-ups. We adopted eight-man scrummaging, heading the ball back in the set scrum. When the opposition dropped out and we caught the ball midway between the 22 and the 10-yard line, we would mark and have a drop at goal. I think there is still a bit of room for novelty in the games and I find it a tad boring now. It's developing into rugby league. In the lineout, unless you are a total wally, you are going to win 95 per cent of ball. In our day it was 65 per cent. Now it's just repetitive possession. I don't view that with the same enthusiasm. You think about why the game is there. It's to allow guys of the stature of Ian McLauchlan and Peter Stagg to play in the same side – 5ft 0in. and 6ft 10in.

'I used to have these battles with Chris Ralston, who was the most awkward, gangling jumper ever. It used to annoy me, because I would play against him for London Scottish v. Richmond, Surrey v. Middlesex, Scotland v. England – and I used to think, "Not bloody Ralston again" and of course he would be thinking exactly the same thing about bloody McHarg again. One London Scottish–Richmond game, I think we managed to win two or three lineouts between us in the whole game.

The referee was a guy called George Crawford and he said that because we were always jumping against each other, arms entwined and climbing all over each other, he was just going to let us get on with it and we just nullified each other while the number 6 or someone was winning all the ball. One could never get on top of the other one because of the skills and techniques we had. Now a lineout is just a way of restarting the game.

'There was a lot of rough stuff, too. Nigel Horton was in his second international for England and we were playing them at Twickenham: it was decided that we were going to give him a good sounding in the first lineout. Broonie was going to get underneath him and I was going to smack him, or maybe it was the other way round. Anyway, the first lineout was in the England 22 and I thought, "Let's go for the ball instead." As I went for it, Horton smacked me! So much for this experienced international playing against a new boy. Then one time against Moseley, down at Richmond, it was ludicrous. We were just stood in the lineout kicking each other, just swapping boots. Then I went down on the ball and as I came up the sun was over the stand and all I could see was this massive frame. He would have scalped me with his feet and I dropped the ball and just punched this figure. Penalty against me. And, you know, it wasn't even Nigel Horton I'd hit, it was the other second-row. The ref warned me that if I did it again I would be sent off. In the bath after the game I explained that I thought it was Nigel Horton and he replied, "Well, if it had been Nigel Horton I wouldn't have penalised you."

'It's not just internationals, either. Going back to Irvine Academy, we were playing Kilmarnock Seconds and it was one of the dirtiest games I could remember. As we were clapping them in after the game, one of our guys tripped one of theirs up and there was a fight in the tunnel. Then there was a fight in the dressing-rooms and then another fight in the bath.

'You could say it's a man's game.'

There always seems to be an air of mischief about Keith Robertson, whether tormenting his opponents (and occasionally team-mates) on the field with his eccentric running in the centre or on the wing, or metamorphosing into the major thorn in the side of the SRU when they first brought professionalism into the game. When he turned to coaching after retirement, his post-match analyses at Melrose, and later Musselburgh where he coaches now, would usually disintegrate swiftly into a diatribe against the sport's governing body.

His playing career was also touched by controversy. It ended in 1989 with a 'rebel' tour of South Africa which left him for a while Scotland's public enemy number 1 – in the eyes of *The Sun* at least – and he left Melrose in acrimonious circumstances after confrontations with some of the senior players at the Greenyards. When the Grand Slam party of 1984 were invited to meet the Queen at Holyrood and Her Majesty asked Robertson what he did for a living, he replied, truthfully but not very tactfully, 'I'm one of your three million unemployed.'

But while Andy Irvine considered him 'not the most generous of players' – meaning you didn't often get a pass – Colin Deans insists that 'Keith Robertson oozed confidence. He could do anything, step off either foot, kick, tackle. Anything. If he played now, they would probably put a stone on him, but I think he would survive.'

Robertson himself disagrees: 'These days I don't think I could play, because you have to have a certain physique, you have to knock people back and stop them getting over the gain line. I got to 12 stone at my heaviest. I got dietary help and worked on a strict diet for a year, but my metabolism wouldn't retain it. Even now I probably eat more than the average 15-stone person.'

Even as a child, Robertson was often not allowed to play rugby because of his diminutiveness. But it didn't stop him winning 44 caps for Scotland.

Robertson was born on 5 December 1954, in the Borders village of St Boswells near Melrose. His father was a bus driver and his mother came from London: 'I qualify for England and of course I thought long and hard about playing for them. About a second. In fact, not even that!

'I first went to the Crichton Tournament at seven and that was it for me. I loved everything about it. David Chisholm was the local hero in St Boswells. Some of us had even seen him on TV. The first time I played I wanted to run at the opposition, I wanted to beat them and I wanted to take the mickey out of them. That's the sort of person I was. It was nice to find something you could play that allowed you to make fools of people much bigger than you – as long as you could keep running quickly enough. I loved it from the moment I picked up the ball.

'Melrose was the club from an early age. You were seeing these players from Melrose on TV – Eck Hastie, Chisholm, Frank Laidlaw – and they were coaching the boys at the Greenyards and you had real heroes to look up to from day one. That is something that really sinks in with youngsters. We had a black-and-white TV for so long and they were icons. For them to speak to you was awesome. They were great characters. Eck and Chisholm were almost like the Two Ronnies, they just bounced off each other all the time and were so funny to be with.

'If you were big enough you played from Melrose from about 15. I played scrum-half at the time and I wasn't physically strong enough to compete. When I left school I grew just over six inches in 14–15 months and that transformed me. It gave me pace I didn't have and the strength to compete. At 15, Melrose wouldn't pick me to play for the Colts because they were afraid I would get hurt. So I went away to play for St Boswells seniors, among all the hard nuts, because I was too small!

'As I grew more, I moved out to stand-off and then into the centre. My first game for Melrose was in 1974, against Gala, playing against John Frame at Netherdale. John was maybe 15 stone and if I was 10½ I would have been lucky. I was just short of 20 years old. He was playing for Scotland, but there is no doubt about it, he gave me an easy run that night.* I've mentioned it to him since that I was glad I came across a gentleman that night who knew he had the beating of me and didn't take the mickey. Honestly, I think he could have just blown me away if he had wanted to – I would have tried my damnedest to put him down on the deck, but a 10½-stone weakling doesn't cope very well with a guy like that. Either that, or he was getting older and just couldn't be bothered.

---

* Frame himself denies he would ever have taken it easy on anyone!

'But throughout my career I have always come across bigger guys. The games against Hawick were the funniest, because although I was a big pal of Alastair Cranston – Cranny – he was always wanting to have a go at me. And Jim Renwick was always happy to let him have a go at me. So Jim would give him one or two pop passes and bring him straight onto me. Then of course all of a sudden Jim would say, "Here's a little dummy, Alastair, I'm gone." I would be stood there waiting for Cranston and Jim would be away somewhere else, scoring in the corner. Then you would see the little glint in Renwick's eye when he came back.

'One of the problems Jim Telfer had with Renwick is that he couldn't understand this funny guy laughing and joking with the crowd, totally unfocused and then going on the field and doing all those wonderful things. I think that cost Jim Renwick a few more caps and more British Lions tours. He got stick for it. He was told, "Focus, focus."

'In 1983 against England, John Rutherford had two attempts at drop-goals and both of them were crap and then Jim Renwick had a go from the 10-metre line. It was such an awful kick, the worst I have ever seen, so bad no one even chased it but I almost beat Dusty Hare to the touchdown. To make matters worse, I dropped a goal later on and told him, "That's the way to do it, Jim." I won't tell you what he said back. In the middle of an international you would just get great banter from that guy.

'I played alongside Telfer at Melrose. He actually retired and came back to try to keep us out of relegation. This would be about 1977–78. Jim of course had no time for the Colts, these whippersnappers running around, but I can remember stripping him a few times as a 14-year-old and smiling at him – as long as he was not looking at me. He was such a mean son of a gun, you'd get a wee cuff on the lug to keep you in your place. So we've been hammer and tongs ever since. People think Jim and I don't get on, but I like to think we respect each other. I certainly respect his commitment, enthusiasm and dedication to the game. It may look self-centred but it's because he believes that what he's doing is right for the game.

'The tour to France in 1980 – that's where it all started for Jim Telfer. It was a two-week tour and it was a mixed bunch of experienced players and up-and-coming players like myself. We effectively beat the shit out of each other for that fortnight. We played some very good sides, including the French Barbarians, but it was terrible at times.

'There was one Scottish second-row and I can remember Telfer standing in the team room saying, "Some guys are destined to make it, other guys will do everything they can to make it and other guys will never make it." Then he picked out this forward, stood him up and looked him in the face and started on him: "You are the sort of guy I'm talking about. You've just not got it. These guys out there are going to take the mickey out of you." Then he shoved the player back against the wall – to which this guy just took off and rammed Jim in the ribs. Jim's head hit the hooks on the wall and he was genuinely winded, but he stood up and said, "That's more f*****g like it!"

'Telfer said a similar thing to Jim Calder. He didn't get physical, just told him he was too nice a guy. He probably didn't believe it himself, but he did have this knack of saying the right things to get a performance out of a player. That touring team were ready to die for him by the end. It was also on that tour he decided we weren't going to drink alcohol. He prepared songsheets one night, sat us down and said, "This is the night we enjoy ourselves, we're going to sing a few songs." No one had the guts to tell him, "Jim, I'm sorry, that's not how it works." That was the night he was going to let our hair down.

'That tour was just incredible. We were training twice a day, two physical sessions a day, and we were just knocking hell out of each other. That was Jim Telfer coming on board.

'My first cap was in 1978, against the All Blacks. I had only played twice on the wing before that and I was up against Bryan Williams, which goes back to what I said about facing bigger guys. He was one of the biggest and best in the world at the time. I was shaking in my shoes, not about getting hurt, but about going on the park and getting ripped apart and made a total fool of in front of millions of people.

'What happened was that in the first minute they put up a high ball on top of me and I marked the ball with Williams coming in; as I marked it, Mike Biggar cut across in front of me and just shouldered Williams into touch. Mike just came along and said, "Well done." Thankfully, after that they never put a high ball up. Thankfully, too, it was a pissing wet day and twice the scrum-half gave Williams a chance to run one-on-one at me and both times he dropped the ball! If it had been a dry day I might never have been seen again. Then I had a couple of breaks and effectively that gave me a run in the position.

'Another New Zealand hard nut, Bernie Fraser, became a friend – but on the field, forget it. However, I'd rather face the hard ones than the fast ones. I enjoyed playing in the centre an awful lot more; there again, you came across some big physical guys who would just run straight at you, I didn't mind that so much.

'In 1983 I missed out on the Lions tour, which was very disappointing. Gwyn Evans got the nod as utility back ahead of me, although I was on standby. There again, if there was one Lions trip you wouldn't have wanted to go on, it was probably that one. Jim Telfer came back almost a broken man, very, very depressed.

'But at the first South session when the guys came back, I can remember someone saying, "These English buggers are nothing special at all." At the first Scotland session the feeling was that we could do really well out of the Five Nations. Jim and everyone else knew the opposition and knew all their weaknesses.

'I scored eight tries for Scotland and can only remember four of them. In '85, against England, I scored what I think was the best try of my career, cutting inside Rory Underwood. In 1984 I scored one of the tries in the Triple Crown game against Ireland. When I went over, the ball was under my gut and I got winded: I ended up just lying there with no one taking any notice whatsoever. Everybody was away upfield and I was still sprawled there. I didn't even get on the TV, running back. After that game the Irish players took us to this pub and there was a roped-off area with a banner saying "Scotland's Triple Crown". Just incredible. The Irish had tried their guts out, but the Jocks had won the Triple Crown and they were going to give us a good night.

'My career ended on a controversial note – at least, that's what some called it – when in 1989 I took part in the South African centenary celebrations, the only Scot to do so. The only reason I went was that all the British Lions were wanting £50,000 to go. I was the Scotsman that was putting the Scots athletes at the Commonwealth Games in jeopardy, the person who was supporting the apartheid system, the one whose morality was in his pocket. According to *The Sun*. But it was the end of my career, I'd never been to South Africa and I jumped at the chance. I was reported to be getting £35,000 for going and the only thing I would say for myself is that there's no way I would go to South Africa for as little as £35,000!

'You thought I was going to be serious then, didn't you?

'People say we weren't as committed in the amateur days, but someone should ask my wife Alison and a few others how often they saw us in a ten-year period. It's just amazing there aren't a hell of a lot more divorces.'

When a road accident prevented Max Boyce from appearing to speak at the Musselburgh dinner to launch the Struan Kerr-Liddell appeal* in September 2000, it was Jim Renwick who stepped into the breach. Most good judges thought the replacement did a better job than Boyce could ever have done. But then most of the players who played with and against Renwick over the years would have said that anyway. For delivery, timing and off-the-cuff wit, the man from Hawick would give most professional comics a run for their money, never mind the international midfield defenders he faced over 11 years and 52 caps for Scotland.

Although he would never tell you, and he is mainly remembered as arguably Scotland's finest-ever centre, Renwick is a man of many parts. A fine swimmer in his youth – the sport that helped give him the broad-shouldered, deep-chested physique ideal for centre play – he was also a keen soldier in the Salvation Army and a mean hand with the trumpet. He also took to fatherhood in style: seven at the last count, of various ages from 19 downwards.

'What you see is what you get,' says the former Hawick and Scotland lock Alan Tomes of his great pal. Renwick has never been tempted to leave Hawick: 'I wouldn't move,' he says. 'I'm not very ambitious, I just do my job, my kids are there and I'm just happy.'

He lives in an unpretentious flat on the town's main street. There seem to be children everywhere, but Renwick is totally immune. His stories are delivered with that famous twinkle and in a thick Hawick accent which makes them even more hilarious. Renwick, say his friends, has never had a bad word to say about anyone – and vice-versa – although he can be totally irreverent at times.

---

* Struan Kerr-Liddell, whilst playing for Lismore, became paralysed from the neck down when a scrum collapsed.

As with most youngsters in Hawick, Renwick progressed through the local primary schools and junior sides. 'We milk the system as much as we can. If every town in Scotland of 16,000 produced as many rugby players as we've done over the years, Scottish rugby would be in a healthy state. My first game for Hawick was at 18 and I was capped at 19, so it was pretty quick. I was surrounded by good players and the problem now is that the boys coming in aren't with international players.

'I mind my first game against Melrose. I was a young stand-off and the wing-forward came in and late-tackled us. I went down and Robbie Brydon, who was our captain, came up and said, "Are you OK? Who was it?" I replied the number 7 – not Telfer, by the way – and nothing was said; but at the next ruck everything broke up, the number 7 was left lying and the stretcher came on and off he went. I hadn't seen anything, but that was the way it was done. Quietly and efficiently. As a youngster that gives you a lift, knowing someone is looking after you.

'In Hawick the first words you learn to say as a bairn are "Dirty Gala". I remember one of our players getting battered with an umberella by Arthur Brown's mother at Netherdale. Another time, an English guy came up to referee on an exchange and I was captain. Jim Aitken was captain of Gala. The ref wanted a word with me before the match, "Jim, can you go in the dressing-room and calm your boys down? They look a bit excited." So I went in and there's Derrick Grant and he had a maroon scarf and he was showing the Hawick boys how to ruck over a maroon jersey. Then he turned round and said, "What did the referee say, Jim?"

'"He's an exchange boy up from England, Derrick, and he's quite happy with the rucking laws up here and he doesn't mind if we ruck over Gala." And I just saw the boys' eyes light up in the changing-room. It was hard stuff, all right. Not that I was involved in that. It was the donkeys' job to get the pill for us boys who could play. Derrick was a bit like Jim Telfer, though not as hard.

'Jim Telfer is priceless. We were once having lunch in the Braid Hills Hotel before an international. Normally you can't eat because you are so high, but I went in and there were some fancy prawns and some scampi. Jim was marching up and down, making sure the boys weren't overeating, and he said to me, "Did you get that when you were playing for Hawick?" And I replied, "You cannae get pie and beans in this restaurant, Jim." Then he went over to Alan Tomes, who was tucking into a steak, which is frowned upon before a game. Jim asked him the same question: "Did you get that when you were playing for Hawick?" Alan said, "I'm not playing for Hawick, I'm playing for Scotland."

'That's Jim. He has these little digs at you, but it's just to let you know he's watching you. Before the Welsh match in 1982 in Cardiff, he sent us to bed on the Friday afternoon. I couldn't go to bed on a Friday afternoon, I'd never have slept at night, so some of us nipped out for a game of golf at St Pierre – Andy Irvine, John Rutherford and myself. Of course, Scotland won that game, so ever since then he's sent the boys to sleep on a Friday afternoon. It's ironic that the ones who played quite well that day were away golfing that afternoon and Jim didnae ken.

'I came in in 1972 and we beat England and France, but lost to Wales. No one beat Wales in those days, though. We never went to Ireland because we had a couple of Army boys in the team and they must have got personal letters or something. But I like Ireland. Barney [Hawick forward, now coach, Ian Barnes] and I went over in Tom Kiernan's XV against Syd Millar's in Ballymena: Barney, who speaks broader than me, was in the second row with Moss Keane, who comes from Kerry, and they were jibbering away the whole game to each other and it was only towards the end of the game that I understood what they were saying to each other: they were pushing on the wrong side in the scrum and wanted to swap over. They played the whole game on the wrong side.

'Barney is actually the most capped Scottish player. He got his first cap in 1972 against Wales and then came on as sub against France two years later. The SRU thought it was his first cap and sent him another cap, so he's actually got two caps – twice as many as anyone else, because you only ever get one cap, even if you're capped 50 times. It's not like football where you get one for every game. Actually, I think Barney got pissed at some dinner and told someone, so he's had to send the second one back.

'I scored a try in my first game at Murrayfield. I have a photograph somewhere and I'm scoring in the corner; Eric Grierson, the "neutral" touch judge from Hawick is standing there in his shirt and blazer with his hands up, celebrating. I think they all frowned on that a bit. France weren't that keen on coming to Murrayfield, but they beat us there in 1978 when Heg – Brian Hegarty, he's a Hawick boy – came on after Andy Irvine got crocked. Heg went onto the wing. Jérome Gallion put up the high kick and Heg dropped it behind his own line and they scored. I think Gallion still sends Heg a Christmas card for that.

'The nearest thing to a head-case I've ever seen walking on a rugby pitch is David Leslie. Before a match he was frightening. That's fine if you have to get stuck in and make tackles, but you might have to take a high ball in the first minute, so other guys would need to stay calm and collected. If you looked round the dressing-room before a match, Alan Tomes would be yawning, John Rud and Roy Laidlaw would be passing and doing their thing and Davie would be banging his head off the wall. I was fairly low key. I used to be sick, but if I was a bit worried I reckoned that was better.

'Some boys, if they make a mistake, their game goes downhill. Other boys, it doesn't bother. The likes of Andy Irvine, if he makes a mistake it doesn't bother him – he'll let one try in and go and score two more. That game against France in 1980 at Murrayfield was a classic. I said to him at half-time, "Andy, are you sure you've got your boots on the right feet?" He said, "I just want to go home." I said, "Well, get a bus over there." Yet at the end of the day it changed round and he ran them in.

'David Leslie once asked me to speak after a dinner up in Dundee. The first speaker was to be Gary Player, the second was me, then Ron Yeats, the Liverpool footballer, and then a boy called Richard Noble. Davie phoned me up and asked me to pick Richard Noble up at the Airport. I thought nothing about it and then I read in the paper that someone called Richard Noble has just broken the world land speed record in *Thrust II* or something. And I was thinking it cannae be the same Richard Noble, it's a coincidence. So I rang up Davie and he said, "Aye, it's the same Richard Noble."

'So I said, "Well, I'll tell you, I'm driving a Skoda at the moment. Do you think he'll even get in the car?"

'"You're right," said Davie. "I'll phone him a taxi." It would have taken us a couple of days to get there anyway.

'In 1978 we had six Hawick players on the pitch: Norman Pender, Colin Deans, Hegarty, Tomes, Alastair Cranston and myself. The substitute was Graeme Hogg and he's a Hawick boy, he's my cousin, but he went to play for Boroughmuir. So I said to Bruce Hay, proudly, "That's seven Hawick boys on the pitch." Just then, the ball went down through Graeme's legs and they scored. Bruce said, "Aye, look at that seven b******s frae Hawick" and I said, "Six frae Hawick and one frae Boroughmuir."

'The Lions tour I went on in 1980 was the last of the big tours. It was a funny tour because there was press everywhere. There used to be a bus following you around. Billy Beaumont was captain. He was OK as a leader, but I didn't think he was a good captain technically. It's a long time to be away, two and a half months; but way back in the 1920s, when Doug Davies from Hawick was a Lion, they were away for nearly a year.

They sailed over and travelled everywhere in South Africa by bus. He told me they had to have eight shirts for the boat, but he just took the two and nicked a couple of others.

'In 1980 we had some world-class drinkers, the likes of Colclough and John O'Driscoll – John O'Desperate, we called him. He was quiet as a mouse sober, but a wild man with drink in him. That's the Irish for you. They either drink all the time or not at all. In the Scotland Centenary Game, Scotland-Ireland played England-Wales and I was sharing with Willie John McBride. I'd cracked my cheekbone and was away to my bed early, but around four in the morning the door just came off its hinges and Willie John came in. I said, "What's wrong with the door?"

'"I forgot my key." Then he said, "Do you want some sandwiches?"

'"No thanks."

'"You'll have some sandwiches."

'"Fair enough." He brought in enough sandwiches to feed the Five Thousand and we sat there eating them while he told stories. Then he said, "Do you want something to drink?"

'"No."

'"You'll have something to drink."

'"Aye, I'll have something to drink." Eventually he fell asleep in the chair and I got to my bed – at about six in the morning.

'The 1981 trip to New Zealand finished me with touring. There was too much intense stuff with your man Telfer. They went to Australia the next year and I made myself unavailable. It's funny looking back at some of the things that went on in those days. In '82 Keith Robertson got the flu and they brought in Jim Pollock, lucky Jim. He played a few games and never got beat. I didnae even ken him before the match: when he walked in I thought it was the ball boy.

'I think you play your best internationals at the tail of your career. We had the lull before we came good, but that's Scotland all over and not just in rugby. If I was playing now I'd probably have to play stand-off because I wouldn't have the size to play in the middle. It's like Keith Robertson. There was one game against France and a chicken came on and I turned to Keith and said, "Keith, I thought that was you for a minute."

'I played from '73 to '84 and when I retired they straight away went and won the Grand Slam. Maybe there's a message there somewhere. Serge Blanco once said, "You can either play the piano or you can shift it. And that's rugby. You're either one or the other." To tell the truth, he's not far away either.'

It is 27 April 2000, and Murrayfield is under water. The Water of Leith has burst its banks and the floods have turned the offices of the SRU into an island, fortified by sandbags and without power or telephones. There's no one on reception and without electricity the security system on the main door is redundant. As I walk into the darkened, muddy corridors the thought strikes me that if I were a member of the SAS (Scrap All Superdistricts) I could take out the SRU hierarchy in five minutes flat.

In the gloom the Scotland coach can just be made out at the door of the office of Bill Watson, the Chief Executive. Despite an exaggerated opening and closing of the corridor fire doors, a loud stomping on the carpet and an attack of loud coughing, McGeechan remains oblivious to the intruder. They are discussing the fate of a Scotland player who has displeased the SRU over his non-availability for the coming tour of New Zealand. The player's Scotland future does not sound bright and I move swiftly out of earshot. It's an unexpected and illicit insight into the steel that lies behind the genial exterior of Ian McGeechan, the smiling, quietly spoken Yorkshire-Scot who is arguably the most respected coach in world rugby.

But then you don't win Grand Slams or British Lions test series on smiles and sympathy; and with Jim Telfer retired, someone has to wield the stick. Most of the time, of course, McGeechan prefers the carrot.

Like Telfer's, the office of McGeechan is surprisingly tiny, but then as his tracksuit tells you, he probably doesn't spend much time there. Even in the half-light it's obvious there are no papers on the desk and few files round the wall. Scotland's rugby master plans must be all in McGeechan's head. With two Lions tours as a player, a Grand Slam, Triple Crown and two winning Lions tours as coach, he has clearly found a winning modus operandi.

McGeechan's two most famous tactical victories with Scotland were both against England at Murrayfield – in 1990 and ten years later. It's one of the ironies of the game that he could actually have played for the Auld Enemy: 'I was born in Leeds, although my father was from Glasgow and a regular soldier in the Argylls. My father wasn't nationalistic, but most of my relatives are in Scotland. Funnily enough, I was approached by England for a trial a year before I got a Scottish one in 1968. I turned them down in the hope that I might get a Scottish one. Quite right, too! My family are soccer players. I'm the black sheep. Dad went to Queen Victoria School, Dunblane, who provide the pipe band at Murrayfield internationals, of course. In my first international, the Pipe Major actually knew my father from the war.

'I played first for West Park School in Leeds. Then six of us went from the school to Headingley and I managed to get in the first team there in 1965. I was actually far more serious at cricket: I played for Yorkshire Seconds and in the local leagues. Chris Old bowled at the other end in a Yorkshire Schools game.

'From the start there was an interest in sport in the family. Mum was a high-jumper and I played as much sport as I could, as often as I could. I went to Carnegie PE College to train as a teacher, which suited me, and in the year I went into teaching I got my first trial for Scotland. One of these upstarts from the south! With my name and everything, there were a few questions asked and it went on from there.

'In the first trial I was at stand-off and I remember being against Jim Telfer. He was captain of the other team. He and Rodger Arneil were chasing me around the field all day. I didn't realise at the time that you were allowed to stay in a hotel. I stayed in Glasgow with family and came over on the train in the morning, played the trial, then caught the train back. Like Jim, my career has been dominated by the All Blacks. I remember watching Whineray's 1963 sides when they played in the north of England and I even did a dissertation at Carnegie on the '67 tourists and got a credit for it. It was a chance to look hard at that team and learn.

'My first cap was against New Zealand and so far I have been out there about nine times. I actually played them three times in four weeks – for Rest of Scotland, the North of England and then the first Test. People thought I was crazy, but even then there was a special relationship. They do have an influence on you. I always said New Zealanders were Scots who learned to win. It's down to attitude, system and knowledge. Even an average player in New Zealand understands the game. I always think of New Zealand with the standards I try to set.

'During the first World Cup in New Zealand in 1987, Derrick Grant and I were in Wellington before the Zimbabwe game. We had drawn the first match with France. We went into Wellington for a coffee and there was a middle-aged woman sitting there with her shopping at the table next to us. She recognised us, which made quite a change, and for the next half-hour we just had a conversation about the game against France. She was saying how well she thought the front row had played, thought Iain Milne had put so much pressure on them the hooker couldn't lift his feet, thought we should have done more through the back row . . . On and on it went. So you end up thinking, "Goodness knows what knowledge the coaches have!"

'Another major influence was Ian McLauchlan, who became captain in my first season. I just thought his presence, what he said and how he managed were superb. Gerald Davies used to say he wished he'd been a fly on the wall in Ian's team talks before we went out to beat Wales in '73. A lot of that victory was down to the sheer power of the Mouse's leadership.

'I reckon conservatively I was sixth choice: when I came in there was a whole list of stand-off/centres who were either retired or injured. I got the nod, played against the All Blacks and France at stand-off and then Colin Telfer was fit again and I assumed I would get dropped. After the French game Jim Renwick and Alastair Cranston, who played in the centre, thought that would happen too. So they took me out for a good night and we got onto whisky and cokes this night in Paris. In the end Scotland moved me to centre and I actually never got dropped in seven years. That was the confidence boost to me because I thought, "They actually want me in this team." I never looked back. After that selection I just felt different. Andy Irvine, who at 21 was the new golden boy of Scottish rugby, came in at the same time as me and for a time Andy and I played the same games for Scotland and the Lions.

'I was training five times a week. There was no way I was not going to be fit and even Judy my wife used to come out in all sorts of weather and hold a stopwatch. I used to do hill-running, sprinting up and jogging back down. I was so determined I was not going to be found out. I wasn't the biggest of players, of course, and they just used to make a beeline for you – so the first three or four tackles you are literally trying to break someone's ribs just to let them know.

'I played till I was 33 until I got a cartilage injury. I had a good run, because at 26 you think you are almost past it. The '70s was the golden age of British rugby. Every team had great players. Against England I would be up against Alan Old, who played for Yorkshire, and we used to have these interesting conversations on-field. He had to kick all the time, because his centres didn't want the ball, whereas for Yorkshire we ran every ball. He knew that I knew what he was thinking.

'The 1974 British Lions were the best handling side ever, so good we used to apologise if the ball was even slightly off. We scored one try in a Test from a set-piece just by handling under pressure and giving J.J. Williams the overlap – just quickness of hands. We scored ten tries to one in the Test series which just about says it all. The nicest thing in '74 was J.P.R. Williams saying he liked playing behind Dick Milliken and myself. This was a great compliment from a guy who had been to New Zealand and done it in 1971. Sometimes it just happens, you build up a special relationship: you would look at each other and know exactly what was required.

'I learned more in '77 about what not to do. It was the wettest winter and some players did the minimum, which you can't do in New Zealand. Dougie Morgan and Bruce Hay were tremendous tourists and I remembered all these lessons for later when I became a coach.

'I still feel like a player at heart. I don't feel any different at all, except I'm not up to playing any more! I try to work it for the players' benefit. You're trying to make things, or manage things, to improve them. The experience of those tours was priceless.

'In the Lions selection of 1989 Clive Rowlands, who is the best manager I have ever toured with, picked me to coach the Lions when I was assistant coach with Scotland. I coached Scotland for one year, then took the '89 Lions. Coming to selecting the last two or three players for that tour, one of them got a very poor rating from other coaches so we didn't take him. He was a class player, very influential, but you couldn't rely on him and he didn't go.

'We lost the first Test in '89 because the balance of the side wasn't perfect. We wanted to put a lot of pressure on the Australians at source, the scrum and the lineout. I just looked at videos and picked out their strong points and then decided on five main things we had to do. We made some changes. Wade Dooley and Mike Teague came into the pack; Jerry Guscott and Scott Hastings in the centre; and Rob Andrew at stand-off. After that, their coach Bob Dwyer said he had to change the forward play of Australia. And he did, of course, because they won the World Cup two years later. That has always been an unobtrusive tour, but it was massive for the players because none had ever beaten Australia. Fin Calder was brilliant as tour captain. He never put himself above the players. Any problems, Fin would sort it out. At one time after the first Test he said, "Drop me if that would help the Lions succeed." You have to be a big man to do that.

'The Scottish captains I picked – Fin, David Sole and Gavin Hastings – became great players. A bit like Ian McLauchlan. Everyone was telling me Fin was not a captain, just a great team player, but I felt there was something in there.

'When I went back to South Africa with the '97 Lions, that tour broke new gound because of the film crew. We weren't happy about it, neither Jim nor myself. It was a decision by the Lions committee and we only agreed because the film crew agreed there would be some things they could not film. In the end, we forgot the microphones and cameras. It was a commercial arrangement made by somebody else. They couldn't film the coaching. We also had some editorial influence and Jim and I got used to the technique of covering up the microphone.

'They did a good job in the end, but they missed some of the key things. After the first Test win the captain, Martin Johnson, said the Test players would come down to carry the bags for the players who were playing Orange Free State in midweek. So the film crew missed some significant reasons why the Lions succeeded. All the players were there in the morning – the film crew weren't. When everyone else was in their bed, here were the Lions back out again, ready for the next job.

'That would have been pretty powerful on a Sunday morning, when it's raining and the streets are deserted and there isn't one person missing when you're getting on the bus to go training less than 15 hours after winning a Test match against South Africa.'

24. CRAIG CHALMERS

'Who's Craig Chalmers?' asks the uniform on the South gate of Murrayfield. 'Does he work in the office?' Chalmers, you could say, is the forgotten man of Scottish rugby, although he will never see it that way. After a succession of injuries and personal setbacks that would have had less confident personalities in despair, Chalmers in 2000 is not only aiming to get his Scotland place back, but is also hell-bent on a tour spot with the 2001 Lions. 'I'm not that kind of person who relies on one game for the Lions,' he declares. 'I want to have more and I still feel now that I could commit to the level I want. If I didn't have that desire inside me, I'd be as well giving up – I wouldn't be the kind of player I want to be. People might laugh at that, but if I look around, I don't see a player who instills fear in me.'

Chalmers has never lacked that vital self-belief since bursting onto the international scene as a 20-year-old in 1989 – at the time, the youngest-ever Scotland cap. The same year he was selected for the Lions tour of Australia and 12 months after his début he played a leading role in the Grand Slam win over England at Murrayfield.

Too much too soon? Not according to Chalmers. He has always been precocious.

'I was born in Galashiels but brought up in Gattonside, where I live now, and being brought up in the Borders there was nothing else but rugby. No side distractions like computer games. Any spare time you had, you were out kicking a ball about and if it wasn't a rugby ball it would be a football. John Collins comes from the same part of the world and is about the same age as me. But I never really thought about playing anything else than rugby.

'My late father played football when he was younger, but then got involved in the committee at Melrose and coached there for quite a few years, so I ended up getting dragged along. You tend to follow your dad, like my kids, Sam, Ben and Robbie, do now. They want to come training with me and occasionally, if I'm soft and they are moaning at me, I take them to the gym with me. One of them is mad on rugby, another mad on football and the other one is just mad. That's the truth: just mad.

'But Melrose is a very family-oriented club and I was lucky being brought up with a lot of players with the same attitude as I had. Craig Redpath, Bryan Redpath and Graham Shiel – all these guys, there's just a year or two between us. There has always been a good team spirit at the Greenyards and we have had good coaches in Jim Telfer and Rob Moffat. We managed to win six titles in eight years, but we all thought it should have been eight. You're never quite happy.

'When you're coming into the first team there are all these stories about Jim being a disciplinarian and you know you would have to have a pretty good reason to miss training. Sunday morning after my first cap, I still had to be at training because that was the kind of ship he ran. But it did help your discipline to go out and train on Thursday night if it was snowing. Then we started training Monday nights and Sunday morning and other teams started following suit. Most Saturday nights all the young kids go out and have a few beers, so Sunday morning was more a question of Jim making sure we were out running it out of our system.

'I had a swift rise. In '86 I was playing for Melrose Seconds. In 1987–88 I got into the South team and then onto the bench for the Scottish trials, when I went on for the second half. I got games for the A team and B teams that year and then I went to Zimbabwe. It was between myself, Andrew Ker and Richard Cramb, who was sort of the holder of the stand-off position. But I played well in the trials that Christmas with Gary Armstrong and we both got picked for the Welsh game in January 1989. That day, the first five minutes I just wondered what was going on there – "What are we doing here?" I got hit by a big Welsh forward and then I got stood on after that. But I did pretty well. I got a drop-goal and then scored a try in the corner and Fin Calder said, "You'll never play as well as that again." That was Finlay – a pretty straight talker.

'From then on that was the start of it. You get chances and if you take them you are going to do all right. Certain players in the past have been full of talent and good at the game, but they've not taken their chances and they have lost out simply because of that. There's still a lot of luck involved, and I think that some players are lucky and some players aren't lucky, but the ones that put the hard work in do get that extra bit of luck at the end of the day. I look on myself as one of these people who put a lot of work in. I work very, very hard at the game but I think that being in the right place at the right time is important.

'I'm certainly glad that I wasn't professional the whole time. It wasn't nearly as much fun. The first tour to Zimbabwe in 1988 was a great tour, but the Scotland squad could have been wiped out. A concrete mixer came through a red light, clipped the back of the bus and could have killed us all. It was a pretty eventful tour, actually. On the way back, three planes were off the runway with hydraulic failure and the fourth one's hydraulics weren't working, but they were going to get it right. We found out afterwards that Robert Mugabe, the Prime Minister, was supposed to be on the same flight as us to London. He finished up on a private flight and he came through and gave us a little wave.

'The '89 Lions tour was brilliant. At that time I worked for Scottish Power in Galashiels and it came up on the radio that I was in the squad. It was the first I heard about it, which was obviously fantastic. The official letter arrived next day. It's amazing to be given the opportunity to be in the Lions so young with all those great players. I think seven out of the top ten players were Scottish, which was a big lift, as it turned out, for the 1990 Five Nations. I got in the first Test team and didn't have a bad game; but the whole midfield got dropped and to this day they haven't told me why I was dropped. I was pretty gutted, I suppose, but it was a new experience for me and I think I reacted to it pretty well. I was 20 years old and glad to be there, but I wanted more. It was a pretty happy touring party and Donal Lenihan really held the Wednesday boys together.

'In 1990, against England, there was a bizarre start to the day. On the morning of the game we went down to Murrayfield. Gavin, myself and Gary were kicking balls back and forward up and down the park when I turned round and Gavin's ball landed straight in my face. My nose burst and when I went to the changing-rooms there was blood all over the place. And this was the morning before the biggest game of my life. I was sharing with John Jeffrey at the time. JJ was like the father figure for Gary Armstrong and me, the young whippersnappers in the squad. He kept us – well, I wouldn't say kept us on the straight and narrow, but he looked after us. Everyone talks about the slow march before the kick-off. Scott Hastings actually wanted us to walk out with our kilts on! That night we didn't have to drink – we were on a high on adrenaline anyway. It couldn't get any better, really, to be honest.

'I have suffered with injuries. Most of them have come in March/April time, so I've missed tours abroad – Argentina '94, Australia

'98 and the Lions Tour in '92 because of a broken arm. It was a big disappointment missing out on the last World Cup as well. I thought I was really hard done by, not to be involved. I'd been told by certain members of the selection committee that I was number 2 and the next thing you know, you're not involved in the squad.

'There's politics in rugby, definitely. I think players in the past have spoken about certain things and it has gone against them sometimes. But you know, I think I should say what I feel.

'It's strange seeing all these young guys I'm playing with now. Cammie Murray was actually in the bus as a ball boy at my first international at Murrayfield. It's nice to know the young guys will have the same memories as me.'

25. ALAN TOMES

Meeting Alan Tomes and Doddie Weir for the first time together at Kingston Park, home to Newcastle Falcons, one's first thought is that the world was never built for men of this size. Even a rugby clubhouse. The two giants are squeezed around a small coffee table, knees high in the air, barely contained by their seats. The temptation is to laugh. Not something of course you would risk, even in front of two of Scottish rugby's favourite happy chappies. Tomes, who down the years has initiated several tyros into what Derek White calls 'the dark arts of rugby', is still playing at the age of 48 and even claims to have played against Doddie, a mere stripling of 30.

'Tell me, Mr Tomes, were you playing in the days of the three-point try?' asks Weir irreverently. 'Three-point, four-point and five-point, you must have seen them all.'

Indeed he has. After 30 years in the game, Tomes has returned to his roots at Gateshead Fell, his first club. 'To be honest, I'd rather go and watch Gateshead play now than one of these big teams,' he says. 'It's a proper amateur rugby club and I can watch someone I know play, or the son of one of my mates. When one of the professionals makes a great tackle or scores a try you just think, "Well he's being paid £40,000 a year so he should be doing it right."

'I was a big fish in a small pond at Gateshead Fell. We were one of the worst sides around. One year we won one game in January and won the next in September. People used to make jokes about them, but I'm still there. That's in the blood, too. There is actually a guy at Gateshead and I played on his 60th birthday. That is what it's all about for me.'

Tomes played rugby completely without frills and he would like you to think he has little or no sentiment for the game. Many of his contemporaries will say differently and his sentiments about Gateshead seem to tell a contradictory story. But for now he can tell you in no-frills

136

Geordie: 'I remember when we won the Grand Slam in 1984, we got on the bus and there's fans crying. I couldn't believe it. I'd just won it and I'm not that bothered. Fans hate that cynical attitude in players, but I've always been hard that way. If we lost, you'd get stick off them, so don't expect sentiment when it goes the other way. I am not a great one for going back. Once you're finished, you're finished. You're soon forgotten.'

To which many would remark that it would be difficult for the players he played with and against and the fans who watched him turn out for Hawick and Scotland to forget the big, bearded second-row. The Tomes accent may be pure Newcastle, but the heart still belongs in Hawick, home to his father and grandfather and the club he served for 20 seasons, travelling down with his 6ft 6in. frame compressed inside an ancient Morris Minor twice a week for the first seven of those years.

'I was at Gateshead Fell in 1970 and playing for Durham County. My grandfather was living and working in Hawick and he would talk about me to people in the factory where he worked. One day Robin Charters phoned up my old man, whom he remembered from his Hawick days, and said, "Hello, Charlie. I hear you've got a big son, do you want to send him up for a trial?"

'The rest is history, as they say. I went up for a trial and that was it. I couldn't play straight away because I didn't have any money and I didn't have a car. I played one game at the start of 1973, because they played against Northumberland up here, and I guested for them. I even scored a try. Right then I started saving for a car. Until then, Dad lent me his for six weeks so I could get down there. In that Morris it was a bit risky in the middle of winter at times, but it never let us down. The Hawick trial was quite an eye-opener. My old man drove me up and we met Robin Charters and I didn't know anyone. I wasn't a confident person, but Dad just told me to get my kit bag and go into the dressing-room and introduce myself. I went in, turned left in the tunnel and went into the first changing-room. When I walked in the door Jim Renwick – I recognised him because I'd seen him on TV – was halfway through a joke and he looked round and the joke stopped and I read his mind: "Who's this big bastard?" It was a horrible experience at the time and Jim still tells jokes about that. I played with Jim for 20 years. We are the same age. I brought him down to Newcastle when he held the world record of caps for a centre and he just behaved like one of the lads. Just a great unassuming character and, at the end of the day, he could play. Jim packed it in, but he played for Hawick Harlequins against his son one day and let his lad have it: "You shouldn't have stepped inside me," he told the boy.

'Since that first day at Mansfield I have never regretted anything in 20 seasons – not a thing, the travelling, nothing. I go back to Hawick now and there's still people who remember you, people who probably pushed you in your pram, folk who remembered me dad or me gran.

'At Gateshead the background was all drinking, good crack. Then I went to Hawick where it was almost professional. Derrick Grant was coach and I had a lot of time for him. In the five years I was there with him in charge, he missed one training session. He used to bike down and then bike back home, I mean serious commitment. He was as good as Jim Telfer, maybe better as a club coach. I honestly loved that sort of approach. You have to have a dictatorship, you can't have a committee. Derrick's approach was way ahead of anybody at the time. When Gosforth won the John Player Trophy we beat them twice, once down here and then on their own ground. The English club champions beaten by a team with every player born in Hawick – can you imagine that now?

'I loved those games with Gala in those days. They were the best two teams in Scotland and there was always something at stake, usually the championship. It was real blood-and-thunder stuff with some real characters playing. Hard men and known villains. In the lineout there was things you could do then, dirty stuff you couldn't get away with now. A lot of punching and incidents off the ball. You expected it but you didn't whinge about it. It's a man's game. If you don't like it, don't play. And don't let your mother watch it if she doesn't like it. If you went down you knew you were going to get kicked, so you learned to cover up.

'I never had any thoughts of playing for Scotland. One of the Hawick coaches once told me that if I stuck in I would play for Scotland. I replied, "If I do I do, if I don't I don't." He didn't like that attitude. But I really meant it. I wouldn't have lost any sleep over it. I was just being honest.

'I won my first cap in '76 against England. It was a lovely day, the Queen was there and the game was so fast. When the whistle blew I thought, "I'm capped. Whatever happens, I've got that cap." My actual cap arrived in the post a year later – the day I got dropped.

'I'd have paid to go on tour. I loved it. It was like being back at school, a bunch of young lads travelling the world. I did ten major tours and I wish I could do it all again. Some people get homesick on tours, but I could never understand that. Every night you're out drinking if you're not playing. That's entertainment, as they say. Scots are great travellers; the

Welsh used to be really bad for getting homesick. On tour I could put up with anything except the snorers. Norrie Rowan was bad. Gordon Brown was the worst. The first time with him I didn't dare complain until I'd had two nights without sleep. Someone once told me that if you whistle it stops them snoring. So I tried it and Gordon woke up and said, "What are you whistling for?" I just looked stupid.

'I first went out to New Zealand in 1975. Nine months before, I had been playing with Gateshead Fell and there I was, going in against Canterbury, one of the hardest, toughest teams in the world. I knew nothing about rugby, really. Did international players eat the same food and that?

'I wasn't a great trainer, but funnily enough I started training harder when I got older. I had ability at the start; then when I got past 30 I started training, doing road runs at 33. When I got capped my mum started buying us steaks because she thought that was the right thing. I never got any proper training advice until I was 21 and went to Hawick. The secret of all good players is to learn fast. I found I could go up through a level no bother. It's keeping a good average that gets you caps.

'You see a lot of rough stuff in the second row. I was stood next to Bill Cuthbertson when he got decked by Tony Shaw in the match against Australia at Murrayfield in 1981, but Billy took the fall. He wasn't hurt. He probably deserved it. You know when someone has been hit hard: you can tell by the colour of their face. It's quite easy to tell. Billy took a dive there, no doubt about it. The ref probably thought the same as I did.

'Another time, in Paris, Donald Macdonald got knocked out by Gerard Cholley, who was French amateur heavyweight boxing champion or something. Donald was poleaxed – I was on the bench and I thought, "I'm on here" – but he got up and played on, so how badly was he hit? Cholley got a penalty against him. Nowadays he'd get banned for life. Anyone who can punch in rugby can do some damage, but there's not many who can punch. There are more teeth knocked out or stitches by accident. I broke my hand once trying to hit someone.

'You can always get your own back at rugby without the hard stuff. There was one time we were playing Gordonians. This guy went past us and sidestepped me for a try. As he ran back he laughed at us. They won and they were going mental at the finish. A year later they came down to Mansfield. It finished 102–0 and it was all because of what happened up there. I'd had to wait a year, but I'd never forgotten.

'I remember how hard the French game was in 1984. In some ways we were lucky to win, but we hung in and the longer it went on the better we got. It was the collective spirit that won it. I could see the try coming – it was so obvious it was going to happen.

'Man of the match was Iain Milne. He won the Grand Slam that day. It was a dirty game and he took so much hammer. I could hear the thuds coming in, but he kept at it and kept at it. He was not the type to retaliate, but what a brave person to take it. It never got noticed. The crowd wouldn't notice. The unsung hero – he won it. I feel a bit guilty thinking about it now, because I should have done a bit more to help him.

'I actually got sent off for hitting Iain Milne, my worst moment in rugby. It was a club game for Hawick at Goldenacre against Heriot's. It was a really niggly game and I'd already been warned, but I was really pumped up. It was getting touch and go and I thought that if I made the next tackle we would win the match. They had a penalty, they had to run it, and they popped the ball up to Iain. I didn't know it was him – whoever had the ball was going to get it. I thought, "Right, I'm going to take him right out of this game. I'll hit him so hard it will really turn the game." I went in with everything. Elbows, knees, the lot. Iain and I, we're good pals. I'd pushed behind him in the scrum for Scotland, toured with him, roomed with him. I apologised to him afterwards, for what it's worth. I think he forgave me, but I never forgave myself. I still feel bad about it all these years on.

'But there were more great moments than bad ones. We used to play Jed at Jed on Boxing Day and the crowd had all been down the pub. I always used to get stick from the crowd in one of the corners there. Hawick had this short penalty move where I used to be involved, so there I went, up the middle, and there was this tiny guy stood in the way, about 5ft 6in. He tackled us round the bootlaces and just before I hit the ground this voice from the crowd shouted, "Tim-ber!" It made their day. Go in a bar then and the crowd would be there supping pints and pulling your leg. It never happens now.

'Looking back at the Grand Slam of '84 there was no collective thought about it. You couldn't bottle it or plan it. Sometimes in rugby you catch the moment, the right place and the right time. Like all the great things that happen to you in your life, four or five things that happen to you make that a special day. You only get one of those days and that day at Murrayfield was one. I've fished all my life and someone once said to me, "You'll get one good day in ten years." And he's right.

It's that atmosphere in the changing-room. Why is it there one day and not the next? It's the same players, the same coach and he may even say the same words. But there's something unrepeatable.

'Someone should try and bottle it – but they never will.'

26. SEAN LINEEN

When you get down to it, rugby's is a remarkably small world. Sean Lineen's father Terry played for the All Blacks against the 1959 British Lions and the Scottish full-back Ken Scotland – the same Ken Scotland whom Lineen regularly meets these days in the clubhouse at Goldenacre or Meggetland, when Boroughmuir play Heriot's. Says Sean, 'My nickname back home was "SOT", Son of Terry, until I started playing for Scotland and my father became "FOS", Father of Sean. Dad loves his rugby, he loves talking to the guys – JJ, Fin and the Hastings – when he comes over. He's met Ken, too, of course.'

Under different circumstances, Sean Lineen may have followed his father into the centre spot in an All Blacks team, but he insists now he was too fond of socialising to wear the jersey with a silver fern. Instead, he became the original Kilted Kiwi. But one difference between him and some of the others is this: there has never been any dispute over his qualifications. His grandfather came from Stornoway and Lineen first arrived in Scotland with no thought of playing for the country. Nor has he made money out of playing for Scotland.

When we meet it is a subtly different-looking Lineen who faces me for his interview in Edinburgh. The luxuriant black hair has vanished, to be replaced by a fearsome skinhead. This is, he explains, the result of a bet before Boroughmuir's BT Cellnet Cup win over Glasgow Hawks four days earlier. He also claims to be suffering from a severe hangover from the Murrayfield celebrations. Lineen may be a coach at Meggetland, but he is still definitely one of the boys.

Lineen enjoyed the traditional ultra-competitive sporting upbringing in New Zealand although, as he points out, 'Dad never pushed me into rugby. It was only much later that I realised how good he must have been. In 1960 he scored ten tries on the tour of South Africa, but he dislocated his shoulder and retired at 23. I still talk to him every week, always about rugby.

'Growing up in New Zealand, the first thing you find is you have to be competitive. In a streetful of kids my age you get in fights every day. You don't wear shoes until you are 9 or 10, even in winter. Every school had a field and in winter, when the weather was too bad to use it, a red flag would go up. As soon as the red flag went down all the kids sprinted onto the field. In New Zealand you are a poof if you play football; over here you're a poof if you play rugby. I want my kids to play sport. It's important. It even helps your social skills. Scotland has great supporters, but in New Zealand it's participation. I had my first game of rugby at four. I picked the ball up and ran the wrong way and scored, but I loved it. It was tough at times. As a skinny white guy, you would come up against 16- or 17-year-old Maoris or Islanders who were huge. You'd see them arriving and we thought they must be the kids' parents. The game would have to be stopped 20 minutes before the end because they were murdering us. In the changing-room later you would see them with their electric razors.

'After I left school I went into the police force and between the ages of 18 and 21 I was at an officer's training college in Wellington. Remember the film *Once Were Warriors*, based in Otara? That's where I was and it was just like the film. Very challenging. I used to see a couple of dead bodies a week and there were fights every second day. I remember one incident, a domestic dispute. I was with a female officer and I walked down the driveway to this guy's house where there was supposed to be screaming and shouting. Suddenly this 6ft 4in. Polynesian with no shirt and a huge Afro came out with a table leg shouting, "Come on, pig!" I had the baton out and smacked him, with no effect at all. He ran back inside and set fire to the house. Another guy once hit me with an iron bar.

'There was so much poverty, but a lot of humour, too, and it was a lot of fun. I was on duty when the Springboks arrived in New Zealand in 1981. There were running battles in Nelson and Wellington and it was frightening. I was in the cordon at Wellington when the police ringed the field and I got told off by my sergeant because I kept turning round to watch the game. In Auckland the All Black prop Gary Knight got hit by a flour bomb dropped from a plane. There were some well-meaning protestors but also a lot of hardened criminals. New Zealand had a huge gang problem – the Black Power, the Mongrel Mob, the Head Hunters – and they started getting in there. They had razor blades stitched along the edge of their shields. It was a real bad time for New Zealand rugby.

'I did manage to play a few games. Being in the police qualified me for New Zealand Combined Services and one coach had even said I'd be an All Black, which took me by surprise. The police shift work killed me and I wasn't that disciplined as it turned out, so I got out of it. I moved from Paparanga to Papakura and managed to get in the Counties side in 1982 when the All Black centre Bruce Robertson retired – an impossible act to follow. But I won 72 caps for Counties and even played against the 1983 Lions, marking John Rutherford, whose head I almost took off in a tackle. Afterwards I was having a beer with the Lions and thought, "My God, what a bloody ugly pack of forwards."

'In 1984 Counties almost beat France and I scored a try. They had guys like Lescaboura, Sella and Cordonnieu in the centre. Esteve scored two tries. Who'd have thought I would be playing against Sella and Blanco five years later in the Five Nations?

'In 1985 the old Kiwi wanderlust set in and I had a season at Pontypool where we caused havoc. Ray Prosser was coach and they had in the pack Graham Price, Bobby Windsor (his last season), Eddie Butler, John Perkins, Mark Brown, Jeff Squires and David Bishop. But they had no backs. They put us in a nice little house in Uisk and we had a great time. There were parties every Sunday and it was my first experience of a house that wasn't detached. I played against guys like Jonathan Davies then, but Bishop would be in my top three as an athlete. He liked to enjoy himself too much and he could be uncontrollable: a hard, hard man and in his prime, the ultimate rugby player.

'When I came back over to Europe I finished up at Boroughmuir through Norrie Rowan. They were on the look-out for a centre. My first 24 hours in Scotland were interesting to say the least. I arrived in Edinburgh and Norrie was going to pick me up in his car. It was 4 October 1988 and Norrie was an hour late. I had flip-flops and shorts on and I had never experienced such cold. Norrie arrived in a Porsche and asked if I wanted a drive. We went straight to training that night and Bruce Hay, who was coaching, really put me through it. Whether it was to prove a point I don't know, but I remember I threw up. That was the start of the making of me, because Bruce was very influential – not so much in coaching, but in attitude. He certainly got me in the right frame of mind.

'Norrie took me to his house in Balerno and the first thing his wife said was, "Who's this?" He hadn't told her they had a guest. I went back out with some of the boys from the club, who got me drunk. Norrie had a Dobermann pinscher at the time and this dog took an instant dislike to me. When I got up at about three in the morning on the third floor the dog came racing up the stairs, so I bolted into the loo. I could see the dog outside through the glass front of the door. There I was, the first night in a foreign country, I didn't know anyone, I was in the nude freezing my bollocks off, with a bloody huge dog outside. Every time I went to the toilet, after that, I took a book and a T-shirt.

'I remember my third game against Hawick, who were unbeaten in three years down at Mansfield Park and we beat them 22–7, I think. It was an eye-opener to see how annoyed the Hawick folk were and how elated Boroughmuir were. It really hit home. City teams basically expected to go down there for a kicking.

'Things moved on quickly after that. I had been there a month and met my future wife, Lynne, at an aerobics class. Then I was asked if I would play for Edinburgh against the Aussies and it was after that I got the call: would I make myself available for Scotland? I believed my mother's father had been born up in Stornoway, rang her up and she confirmed this.

'I hadn't a clue where Stornoway was, even, but I went up there to meet my grandfather's brother Murdo, who was still alive at 89. It was amazing to see where my grandfather was born, in a little croft house in a place called High Borve. All the relatives were there. Before I went up, Finlay Calder and JJ had told me that they only speak Gaelic on Stornoway. Being a naïve Kiwi, I believed them and they gave me some phrases to use. You can guess the rest. The people are lovely there, but no wonder my grandfather left at 17. Murdo was great. He had his arm round me, then I went to speak to someone else, and when I came back he had his arm round the *Daily Express* photographer and was saying, "So, Sean . . ."

'As far as Scotland goes, I know I was in the right place at the right time because I am not a great footballer. Alan Tait had retired, Keith Robertson was coming to the end and there was a gap. I was very lucky. I got a trial and had a shocker, but then I was selected to play against Wales. We beat them and the two stars were the youngsters, Chick Chalmers and Gary Armstrong. Then down to England, where we drew 12–12 and Scott Hastings, myself and Craig just tackled ourselves to a standstill. It was definitely one of our best defensive displays. We beat Ireland, but then got shafted in Paris. Laurent Rodriguez, the number 8, had punched someone: I went flying in a rage and took a big swing at him, smacked him and he didn't even flinch. Then he smacked the first guy he saw – Derek White!

'The Grand Slam apart, the crowning moment for me was scoring a try against the All Blacks in 1990. It was an enjoyable tour, but my biggest regret was not beating them in the second Test. The first thing you had to do was earn their respect and I had to play twice as hard, because otherwise they would just have turned round and said, "Oh, he wasn't good enough to be an All Black."

'By then I saw my future in Scotland and started *Scottish Rugby* magazine in 1990. Through the years we have had ups and downs. I retired after Australia in 1992. I was almost 30 and I'd had a good four years, but you lose your hunger. It's about timing, and it was time for someone else to come in and I wanted a few seasons with Boroughmuir. I got married to Lynne in '92 and that was me, I was going to make Scotland my home. I became coach at Boroughmuir, but I always only saw myself as backs coach and they brought in Iain Paxton, who has done a great job. I'm a firm believer that players make good coaches and I'm only on the first rung at the moment. We went down to Division 2, but it was a very good side, they matured and we got back in style. Then we won the Cup and I lost all my hair.

'During the 12 years here I've been very lucky. I should think I will need a hip replacement within the next year or so. It's the wear and tear. But I have two healthy boys and a lovely wife. And I still manage to get back to New Zealand every year.'

Doddie Weir has long been portrayed as Scottish rugby's big daft laddie, but be warned: that image displeases him greatly. One journalist who overstepped the mark with too many jokey asides in print found himself totally ostracised. Weir won't even acknowledge his existence any more. Weir explains, 'It was just a funny sort of article in a way and I didn't think there was any need for it because this was in the stages of my starting to be a professional and I was the daft laddie still. That was still there, but he just took it a stage further, so I don't speak to him now. It's my loss probably, at the end of the day, but I feel much better for it.'

So the beaming, wisecracking figure of popular mythology has a mean streak? Well, he does give Marius Bosman a kicking every night, Bosman being the Mpumalanga lock who almost ended Weir's career on the 1997 British Lions tour of South Africa: 'Somebody gave me a wedding present of one of these hedgehogs that you clean your shoes and boots on and they mentioned I had to call it Bosman. So every night when I go home, he's still there and he gets a bit of a kicking, so I'm sure I've got the last laugh.'

Weir, as you can imagine, is entertaining company, even if marriage, forthcoming fatherhood and the captaincy of Newcastle Falcons has given him large measures of responsibility. The humour is strangely old-fashioned and structured: he calls everyone either Mr or Sir or by their full Christian names. It's Mr Tomes, Mr Calder, Mr Leslie and Mr Wainwright; Jim Telfer is James Telfer and Dougie Morgan, Douglas. His vocabulary is a throwback to the manic compere on *The Good Old Days*. Not surprisingly, playing ability in the second row apart, Weir has long been considered one of the most valued tourists ever to represent Scotland and the British Lions. And, as the video of the '97 Lions tour showed after Bosman's dismantling of Weir's cruciate ligament, he has bucketfuls of courage. His stoical reaction to the doctor's news that his tour – and maybe his career – was over is far and away the most moving part of the film.

He begins the interview in typical style: 'Good afternoon. My name's Doddie Weir, short for George. I was christened George, but I just noticed the other day the bank cards, the driving licence and even the passport have Doddie on them. I was born on 4 July 1970. I have one sister who is a year younger than me, one brother who is four years younger than me and one brother who is 14 years younger. They've all got ginger hair, which is a bit unfortunate for them, and luckily I don't have that. The sister is married with two kids – I'm a godfather to the eldest one Alex – and I got married to a local lass, Cathy, three years ago.'

Weir's story is interesting in that his career has spanned both sides of amateur and professional rugby. He was born in Edinburgh and went to Stewart-Melville College, but his background is rural Borders and it appears likely that he will finish on the family farm in Stow when his rugby days are over. He puts his hobbies down as eventing, clay-pigeon shooting and point-to-pointing.

'My old man, John, used to play for Gala when he was young, but because his father (my grandfather) died when he was young, he had to man the farm – very tricky at an early age – so that curtailed his rugby. But he has got the programmes still to show he played for Gala. He's a big lad as well, 6ft 4in. and 18 or 19 stone, and I think that's where I get my height from. When I played with the school I was a wee bit taller than the average person, so I think that's the only reason why I ever got picked. I was very slight, probably no thicker than the pen you're holding, and all you could see was the ears and feet. There was a boy called Sandy Fairbairn, whom I was in the Duke of Buccleuch pony club with, and it was Sandy who got me to go down to Melrose. The old man wanted me to go to Gala and follow in his footsteps, but I went down to the Greenyards at 14 and was there for the next 12 years.

'There's one major difference at Newcastle, of course, because we do it for a living, so what we put in has to be to the maximum potential. Or else we get a P45. Being a professional allows you to work at your strengths and weaknesses and, as Mr Tomes will tell you, my weakness was definitely one of weight. He was a big mentor of mine, a great legend. You learn off him, Wade Dooley and those boys. I was about 19 at the time and I said to him, "How do you get so big, Alan?" He said just to wait till I got to about 24 and it would come on. And I just waited and just progressed and did as much as I could and certainly when I went professional the weight did come on.

'When I did some weights in Scotland beforehand, I would be lifting maybe 8 kg above my head and I'd be lucky if I could do it three times. And there was me thinking I was strong. But now we're up to about 26 or so kilograms. That to me is a big change, because it was a major weakness of mine.

'Training in sunshine hours was nice, too. In the amateur days I was at East of Scotland College of Agriculture in West Mains Road in Edinburgh for three years, doing my HND, and I tried to combine rugby and college. For me now, the rest and relaxation is important to keep the mind fresh.

'We had a very good side at Melrose. We were fortunate because when I broke through, Bryan Redpath was there, and Craig Chalmers and Graham Shiel. My best pal was Carl Hogg. Jim Telfer was coach, of course, and I was playing number 8 then. In my younger days the second-rows were just sort of the power horses; I was very slight and slender, so I was disadvantaged by my weight. I played in the back row maybe 11 games for Scotland and it was great to be involved most of the time. Today's game has progressed so much that a second-row gets involved as much as any number 8 now.

'My first cap was against Argentina. Youngsters getting their first caps always got support from the likes of John Jeffrey, Finlay Calder and Derek White and some of the old heads the Bear, Chris Gray and Damian Cronin. Chris Gray helped me on the pitch and if there was any fracas he would be there to stand in and help. I've got a lot to thank him for.

'Derek White was a notable character for me. We went on tour to New Zealand and I would be 19 at the time. Two years prior to that I was touring with the schoolboys and we were billeted out to families. With the seniors it was premier hotels and business-class flights and everything.

'The training was at Gleneagles and Finlay Calder and Derek White were in the library there, thinking they could get away with a whisky and a cigar. In walked Jim Telfer. They said it was like being back at school. They fed the whisky to the carpet and tried to eat the cigars so Jim wouldn't see. That night, after a few more whiskies, Derek White came into the room we were sharing. Being young and keen, I had been a good lad and gone to bed early because we had a fitness test the next day. Derek came into the room about one or two in the morning and tried to do a superman act, diving over my bed onto his – he missed and landed in the middle of the floor. He was lying splayed out and didn't do very well in the fitness test the next day.

'On tour it was a great experience being thrown in the deep end. Alex Brewster was captain of the Wednesday team and Jeremy Richardson was sort of my partner in crime on and off the field. I would never turn back the clock, but I didn't enjoy training too much. It could be an absolute nightmare at Melrose. We had a friend called Tubby Craig who was the stalwart of the Melrose pack – not very tall, but huge and a great technician. He had to come with his tractor and clear the pitch of snow just to train when Mr Telfer wanted a session.

'If it's snowing on a professional day, we can put it on hold because we've got another day to catch up.

'After a few years' involvement with Jim I still have utter respect for the old man and if he says do it, you do it still, even at his tender age of 60. His verbal onslaught was quite amazing at times and he's a great man for putting players in their place. He could scare the living daylights out of you. I learned a lot from the opposition, too. Dooley and Paul Ackford were a partnership that I didn't like – especially the first year I played them, because Mr Dooley perforated my eardrum the first time with his elbow. But if I had to play against him tomorrow there'd be no problem.

'I'm not so much the "daft laddie" these days. I've got three years left of the Newcastle contract and I would probably like to end rugby there because, touch wood, I've had a great innings and seen some great places. The best would be Lapland, when I was invited with the BBC for *A Question of Sport*. Unfortunately we never got to see Santa Claus because he was too busy answering letters.

'With the Bosman thing in '97, I didn't know the extent of the damage and played on for five minutes; then the knee wobbled a bit out of control and when the medics looked at it they told me I gotta go home. But if it happens it happens: you've just got to get on with things. That is my attitude to things. The annoying part was that it was Mum and Dad's sort of first real overseas trip for 20-odd years. The Lions management would have let me stay out, but I didn't like it when you're not involved. I did get back out for the last Test, though.

'If I do the three years with Newcastle I'll be very pleased looking back on the experiences. I wouldn't ever go back to starting it all over again at 19. I feel sorry for the young boys nowadays with the increased competition.

'We've been lucky and it's good that I'm getting to the tail end of my career. Now the young boys come up to me to ask for advice, just as I did with Mr Calder and Mr Tomes. I would certainly recommend professional rugby. I had my doubts at first – but if you don't try it, in ten years' time you'd be kicking yourself. You should see a goal and go for it.'

28. KENNY MILNE

Amid all the stomach-churning build-up to the 1990 Grand Slam decider with England came a much-needed moment of light relief from the Scotland hooker Kenny Milne. Scott Hastings recalls: 'You know we had the Five Nations, the Triple Crown and the Grand Slam and the Calcutta Cup all up for grabs. Someone in the dressing-room had reminded us that all this was at stake when Kenny piped up, "Well, we should at least win one of them."'

Milne is not as scatter-brained as some would like to portray him – although it must be said he had forgotten the time and the place of our appointment in Leith – and his discourses on what he considers the lost art of hooking are enlightening. He was also director of rugby and coach of Heriot's for a time.

'Hooking is definitely a dying art these days,' he says. 'It's a skilled art but do you often see ones against the head these days? Some of the most exciting balls you get are against the head. I would like to see them get back to the old scrummaging laws of the ball going down the middle and making it a skilled contest. What they're starting to do is just pick three big guys in the front row. I was quite lucky because I was very flexible and I could hook the ball. But I played against guys, supposed hookers, who wouldn't survive on those terms. The New Zealand captain Sean Fitzpatrick was highly rated, but if you put him under pressure he couldn't move his legs. Because he scrummaged with a dominant pack he was never really tested; but I know on occasions I had him under pressure and he couldn't move his legs and the ball just sat in the tunnel on their put-in.

'These days the referee and the rules aren't giving them a fair chance to win the ball. Scotland for years and years have played channel one and that's maybe why they did so well. If you put Fitzpatrick in a pack that's going backwards, I don't believe he would be able to hit channel one. It takes a skilled player to hit the ball down channel one under pressure. I could do it and Whitey [Derek White] would be waiting at number 8 and I could give him an extra half-yard.'

In virtually every way Kenny Milne spent his career in the large shadow of his brother Iain. They played only twice for Scotland in a cap international together although the Three Bears – middle brother David was a loose-head prop for Heriot's and won one cap as a replacement in the 1991 World Cup – did team up in a Barbarians front row in 1989.

'Really,' says Kenny, 'I always sort of followed in my brother's footsteps. With Iain there it certainly made life an awful lot easier, especially at club level, because in international terms Iain was a tremendous prop. At club level he was two or three times that because he was against people who were very inferior, strengthwise. But he was one of these guys who was always a gentleman. Often he would do just enough to make sure we won the game. Teams like Watsonians didn't have a very good pack and opposing props always appreciated that Iain could probably have murdered them. But he didn't. I suppose if everyone's pushed far enough things will happen, but in all my time I can't ever say that I've seen him do anything dirty. A couple of years after school he started to get really big and I suppose something similar happened to me. I was tall and skinny and then two or three years after school I filled out as well.

'David was very keen on the weights and built up his body through weight training but Iain and I trained hard in our own way and I concentrated more on the running side than the fitness side of things. David was shorter than me and probably a wee bit smaller build, but he built himself up with the weights.

'My ambition was to get one game in Heriot's 1st XV with Iain and David and when that happened I just set myself other targets. The coach was Andy Irvine in those days – or rather, he was player-coach along with big brother Iain. It was only later that they started bringing in formal coaching guys like Alan Lawson, Bill Dickinson, John Foster and Ian Barnes.

'Andy Irvine was an absolute inspiration to train alongside and to have as part of the side – a phenomenal athlete. I played against Dougie Morgan in his last game for Stewart's-Melville and thought it was great to be actually playing a game against somebody of that stature at the time. Colin Deans was the number 1 hooker for Scotland, with Gary Callander close behind him, and I was sort of third choice for a number of years. Then Colin retired and Gary had a season playing for Scotland. Then I took over from Gary. To this day I would say Gary was the best hooker I ever played against. He was a big guy and technically very astute. He wasn't as flashy as Colin in the loose, but he worked a lot harder in the scrums than Colin Deans did. Colin in the scrummaging was adequate but he didn't really pressurise you, he didn't really make you think. In many ways he was like the modern-day hooker. Gary Callender made you work every single time for your own ball and he and I had some very close matches.

'I had problems on my throwing-in the two or three years before I retired. I had such a long, slow action: by the time I was getting the ball in, the opposition jumpers were up. I had to change my style completely.

'I was 14 st. 4oz. when I first got capped and picked for my mobility. That's ironic, because later on I went up to 16 stone and got picked for my scrummaging! I pushed myself very hard in training because I had a great belief that if you were down at training, you were only there for a short while, so you may as well give it your best and not muck about or skive.

'In 1989 I got the big call. I was working in a bakery at the time and my wife came into the bakery with the letter from Murrayfield. I remember opening it and getting a big cheer from everyone. That year if we'd won in France we would have won the championship and that is still the hardest game I've ever played. They had a big front row and we were just absolutely knackered at half-time.

'In the early stages of my career for Scotland I felt very much a follower in the shadows of the Finlay Calders and the David Soles and these sort of guys. When they disappeared you then took the responsibility on yourself. In my early days I'd run over the ball and let someone like Finlay pick up and go on because he was better at it. It was a confidence thing. When they retired I actually got the confidence to start taking the ball on and it's amazing the difference it made. You started getting noticed a bit more.

'However, despite all that, I got dropped for the first Test in New Zealand in 1990. I remember being really disappointed. We beat Canterbury and got a pushover try and I got dropped and felt pretty hard done by. It was John Allan who came in and we got stuffed. The only change in the second Test was me back in for John.

'I learned a lot out there. It was camaraderie and great fun: we played hard off the pitch and played hard on the pitch. Things like that seem to be missing now, but I'd love to have been given the opportunity to see how good a player I could become as a full-time professional. When I started rugby I was working in a pie factory six days a week, getting up at five in the morning and working till four or five at night. I would come home, have a coffee, go out training, come back, have my tea and fall asleep and get back up. On a Saturday I worked till an hour before kick-off, or ten minutes before the bus left for the Borders. One Saturday I was delivering pies in Rose Street before an international and two weeks later I sat on the bench for Scotland. You know, a lot of people went on about how poor Gary Armstrong was – the poor lorry-driver from Jed – but he was actually earning a damn sight more money than I was at the time!

'When I was coaching Heriot's I took some lessons off most of the coaches I played under. They've all got different styles and I think Scotland has been very fortunate with the coaches they've produced. You would probably live in fear of Jim Telfer's coaching and I think that in the early days he may not have got the best out of me, because I was so nervous and so worried about doing things wrong. When Richie Dixon took over he certainly got more out of me than Jim did.

'I retired after the 1995 World Cup. My feeling was that I'd had great fun out the game, but I had a young family and I wanted to spend a bit more time with them. The old body was starting to pack up, too. But I'm still playing club rugby.

'Looking back, I would love to have played in a front row with Alan Sharp as a loose-head and big brother as a tight-head. Sharp was immensely strong, but it wouldn't be the most mobile front row. I think I'd nick a few against the head, though.'

Until the arrival of Gregor Townsend on the international scene, there is little doubt that John Rutherford was the most extravagantly gifted stand-off to play for Scotland. Although tall for a number ten – over six feet – Rutherford was a devastating runner, particularly in open play. But even a genius has to have a work ethic and Rutherford's pre-eminence did not arrive by accident. Early on in his career he had targeted his weaknesses and worked ruthlessly to try to eradicate them.

He says, 'I had good pace off the mark and I was quite a good runner, but I was a crap kicker. I was actually a very poor kicker when I got my first cap and I'll never forget, because in that season I played against Gareth Davies of Wales and Tony Ward of Ireland, both superb kickers. I knew that if I didn't work on that part of the game I wouldn't survive. So when I was teaching at Watson's in Edinburgh I used to go out every lunchtime and take a couple of kids with me and I'd spend hours kicking. They would punt the balls back and even when I moved away from teaching I used to go out to Murrayfield: Dougie Morgan or Nairn McEwan and John Roxburgh, who was the technical coach, used to come out and I would kick hundreds and hundreds of balls every lunchtime.

'So I made myself into an international kicker, but really in my first season, although I played all right, I wouldn't have blamed the coaches for saying, "We're gonna have to pick somebody that can kick a wee bit better."'

Like so many players from his era, Rutherford is unreasonably modest about his worth to Scotland and the British Lions. It's gratifying to know that, given his current role as backs coach to the national squad, tomorrow's Scotland internationals should learn more than simply the timing or length of a pass and defensive formation at set-pieces.

Born in Selkirk, Rutherford retains a soft spot for the Philiphaugh side. He was spotted in the crowd at Musselburgh when Selkirk went there for the definitive Division Two relegation battle at the end of the 1999 season.

'I went to Selkirk High School and even when I went through to Jordanhill College to train as a PE teacher I used to come back every Thursday night for training and then drove back on Friday. Just about everything I know about rugby comes from Selkirk. When I started playing you really never thought anything other than playing for your town and going through school. That was my only ambition. I didn't play for anyone else. When I was at Jordanhill Bill Dickinson was one of my lecturers, so there was a lot of pressure on me to play for them; and when I taught at Watson's they were keen for me to play for Watsonians. That was quite hard because they were my employers, so I had to keep putting off. "Maybe next week," I'd say. It's hard to play anywhere else when your dad is on the committee and your mum's one of the tea ladies.

'We always relied on three or four players coming down from Edinburgh – like Iwan Tukalo and Iain Paxton – but that was the only way, because Selkirk would probably have the least number of players to choose from, of the Borders clubs.

'I made the logical progression through the ranks, Scottish schools and Scottish Youth and Scotland Under-21s, and always had good coaching. I was very lucky, even at primary school. There was a guy called John Torrie who coached me. He was fantastic, an ex-Selkirk player, and he really instilled a lot of good values. Then when I played youth rugby there was a guy called Jock King, who was an ex-Scotland hooker, and he coached the Selkirk Under-18 team. At national level there were the likes of Colin Telfer and Nairn McEwan – a lot of good people looking after me.

'It was John Torrie who got me to number ten. My first game of rugby was as a hooker and John saw me running with the ball and he just said, "You're a stand-off." And that was the way it was ever after, although I did play centre for the '83 Lions and once on the wing for the Barbarians.

'Wales was my first cap in 1979. I must have been fourth choice, but all the others were injured. I'll never forget it because at that time the Welsh team were world famous. It was the Pontypool front row and Steve Fenwick, JPR, J.J. Williams, all these guys. You never get to see them until you actually run out the tunnel and when I saw them it was like cardboard cut-outs. Suddenly you're on the same pitch as these guys you've watched so often on TV.

'They had Paul Ringer at 7 and it was his first cap. He later got sent off against England, of course. The ball came out and I passed it to Jim Renwick and Paul Ringer came running past and clobbered me and he went, "I'm gonna get you today." I wasn't used to sledging because it just didn't happen in club rugby, so I turned round to Renwick and Irvine, sort of looking for some help. They just laughed, they were so used to it. After the game Paul couldn't have been a nicer guy.

'We drew 7–7 against England: my second cap and my first international try. What I remember about that game was coming off really disappointed and the senior Scottish players were celebrating. I was sitting in the dressing-room, gutted, not realising that to some it had been a pretty good result.

'A lot of people will tell you the big turning-point in Scottish rugby was the 1982 match in Cardiff. I remember the famous Roger Baird break-out and then Jim Renwick scored, but I also recall Gareth Davies at dinner afterwards. You would expect the Welsh boys to be down because that was the first game they'd lost in the Five Nations for ages at Cardiff, but Gareth stood up at the dinner afterwards and asked all the Welsh boys to stand up and sing "Flower of Scotland", which was a fantastic moment. They'd just been whipped and lost their record, but had the humility to stand up and do that. You know, things like that unfortunately don't happen very often.

'New Zealand in '83 for me was a fantastic tour. I knew I was going out as number 2 to Ollie, because Ollie was such a phenomenal goalkicker, but you always fancy your chances. In London they put us through these fitness tests and they always put you against your opposite number. The tests were a 600-metre run, a 100-metre shuttle run (which is 20 metres back and forward five times), as many press-ups as you could do in a minute and the same for sit-ups. Well, we did the 600-metre run and Ollie blew me away, he must have beaten me by 100 yards, and I was gutted. But come the 100-metre shuttle I blew him away. Then I beat him at sit-ups and he beat me at press-ups. We shared a room together and Ollie's a lovely bloke, but when we were leaving the next day he put his hand out and said, "I'll look forward to doing battle with you over the next three months." Then he just walked out the room. I don't think he meant it to be that way, but he totally psyched me out.

'I actually got very close to the Irish boys on tour. Trevor Ringland and David Irwin – I still keep in touch with these guys. What's really nice is we've all had families at the same time, so they're the same age and I go over Belfast to stay with them and they come over to Selkirk to stay with me. These are friendships that have lasted from that tour.

'The first time I played with David was against Wairapa Bush and all he wanted me to do was put a high ball up and he would just kill the full-back. I thought, "This is the guy I want in my team." David was a doctor, a bright bloke, but put a rugby jersey on him and he was crazy. Funnily enough, John O'Driscoll was a doctor, too, and he was as bad. Roy Laidlaw had to work really hard to make the team, but for Scotland we had a special partnership. We knew each other's play really well. We knew each other's weaknesses as well, which is important in a partnership, so you always play to each other's strengths. But we discussed all that. It didn't just happen on the pitch.

'Roy and I sort of grew up together through the side and there are incredible similarities between us. He's the middle son of a family where it was actually his mother who came down from Glasgow to settle in the Borders. We had two sons each, so I phoned him up and said, "Aye, Laidlaw, I've beaten you now." And he said, "Why's that?"

'"Alison's pregnant, we're expecting a third."

'The next night he phoned me back: "You're never going to believe this. Joy's pregnant!"

'He had this amazing try-scoring record against Ireland. In 1984 Roy went off with concussion and Gordon Hunter, from my club Selkirk, came on. Running off the field at the end, Gordon collided with a fan and had his cheekbone broken. It was only two weeks before the French game, so we couldn't say that Roy had concussion   you're out compulsorily for three weeks with that – and it was announced that he had a migraine!

'By 1984 that team had been together for a few years and there were a lot of strong personalities. Jim Aitken the captain, Colin Deans and the Bear; Calder, Paxton and Leslie and then Roy and me at half-back. I always thought we had a chance against England at home. They'd beaten the All Blacks, so they were very confident, but again we just got our tactics spot on there against them. With all Jim Telfer's teams they wanted you to take them on physically up front – which we did – and we noticed that their wingers, John Carleton and Mike Slemen, were really, really flat. So we put the ball behind them and we had great chasing wingers in Roger Baird and Lucky Jim Pollock. It put a lot of pressure on their full-back Dusty Hare. We played territory and got the points on the board: we scored just after half-time through Euan Kennedy, which was a six-pointer at the time.

'So we went to Ireland for the Triple Crown. I think the Irish made a lot of mistakes. It was a gale-force wind and they chose to play into it. We had 25 points by half-time. Roy scored two tries down that blind-side, so it was really all over by the break.

'The French game was at a different level from the other three, but when Jim Calder got that try I don't think they were ever going to beat us. It was a really physical game. I was pleased for Jim Telfer because after the Lions tour he had proved himself. He didn't need to prove anything to us, but he was ecstatic in his own way. On the Monday we all got together for lunch. All except for Roy – he was away rewiring the public conveniences in Jedburgh while the rest of us were pissing it up in Edinburgh on champagne.

'Of that team I think David Leslie would be the hardest player I ever met. He was ruthless and played with his heart on his sleeve. Some of his tackles, he just killed guys, wiped them out.

'My last season was actually 1986 when we had potentially the best team I ever played in. The coaches were Derrick Grant and Ian McGeechan and we had the Hastings brothers, Iwan Tukalo, Matt Duncan, JJ, Finlay, Packy, Jock Beattie, Derek White, David Sole, Deano and the Bear. But I got injured.

'It was just silly. Trips abroad to play were the only perk you got and there were four of us invited to Bermuda in 1987: Matt Duncan, Tukes, Packy and myself. It was right after the last game in the championship and, of course, the day before we went there was an announcement that you were to play no rugby up until the World Cup. It was a long weekend, Easter weekend, for just one game of rugby and it was a nightmare. I knew when the knee went that it was bad, so I was hoping to get back and see the SRU doctor before I reported it. But what actually happened, we got back to Heathrow and Spain – who were playing Scotland a week later – were at the airport and I knew there would be SRU officials there.

'So I just sat in the aeroplane with the other boys and waited till the dust had settled and later had an operation which they thought would get me back to playing again. But six minutes into the first game of the World Cup, against France, I got tackled and really I knew it was curtains. I never played again.

'I'd have loved a few years playing at Selkirk. That's what I really wanted to do. But I got a good run at it and I suppose it helped me in a coaching sense. Because I couldn't play, I got into coaching right away. Initially you've a hell of a lot to learn as a coach and you really never stop learning; but when I first started I wasn't a particularly good coach. I probably expected players just to be able to do everything, but then you learn to place strategies around your team, rather than your team around strategies, and play to your strengths.

'A lot will depend on the next few years and at the moment I'm happy to be an assistant to Geech. I'm a director of an insurance brokerage company and I've been doing that 11 years, so I would have to think a lot about giving it up.

Putting aside his wife and two children, there is little doubt that the most important person in the life of Finlay Calder is his twin brother, Jim – and vice-versa. If you ask for the life story of one of them, you get the other's too. 'Are you doing us together?' asks Finlay of the Calder chapters in this book.

Differing personalities though they may be, the rugby fortunes of each were forged to a large extent by the other. Says Fin, 'Jim decided from an early age that he would play for Scotland and although he did it in stages, that's all he focused his energies on. He is so determined in anything he does. If he starts on a project, he will take it to an almost fanatical extreme until he has taken it as far as he can, or gets bored with it. I suppose that sums up the difference in our personalities. Once I'm into something I will do it, but he has always been so determined and focused – even to the extent that when, as boys, we were playing in the field in front of our house in Haddington, he was always Jim Telfer scoring in Paris and I was the Frenchman supposed to stop him (and failing). I was never allowed to be Jim Telfer.

'I remember an incident when we were in primary 7 at Melville College. We had played Leith Academy in the morning and had won 18–3. In those days a try was worth three points and between us we had scored them all. The truth was that I had scored four to Jim's two. However, Jim was captain and one of his duties was to record the scorers on the team sheet and pin it up on the notice-board the following Monday. Clearly Jim was wrestling with the fact that I had scored more tries than he, so on the way home on the bus he managed to convince me that he had in fact scored four! What was worse was our father used to reward a try with a shilling. Bad enough conning me out of my tries – Jim even took my extra money to boot!

'This clearly bothered Jim over the years and on my wedding day he finally confessed his guilt. That sums Jim up. He always knew he struggled to have the pace and power to compete, so when all else failed, he'd always find a short-cut. He would go to extraordinary lengths to win.'

I had contacted Finlay early in the spring of 2000 to offer my support for the Struan Kerr-Liddell Appeal of which he had recently become Patron. As well as this, unseen and unsung, along with many others, he has been doing voluntary work driving aid to Eastern Europe. Most of this information, it has to be said, needed to be levered out of him.

'I have been very privileged,' he says. 'I don't want this to sound saintly, but I would be the first to say I've enjoyed a life that few people live. I've had to take a bit of a rain check over the past couple of years due to a combination of reasons – mostly burnout and pure exhaustion. I've had a bit of ill health and, lying in my hospital bed, I decided that when I returned to full health I would try to do a bit of good in the next chapter in my life. Due to various circumstances I have been lucky enough to be in a position to put a bit back and I'm doing it in my own sort of way. I firmly believe that you can't take all the time: you've got to give a bit back. I also believe that what's for you will not go past you and you don't have to be forever chasing.

'Coupled with giving a bit back, due to a change in my working life, I now find that I have much more time to be with my children. Everyone has a philosophy about bringing up kids. However, I think that between 15 and leaving home they are at a very critical and vulnerable age. I'm fortunate in that I now find myself in the position of being able to be there for my kids during this stage in their lives, able to give them a wee bit of guidance. Sadly, very soon they'll be gone and then I will have to think of what else to do with my life.'

It comes as a surprise to find so much introspection in one of Scottish rugby's great extroverts, but Calder freely admits that even in his late 20s he was plagued with self-doubt.

'In '84 Jim was part of the Grand Slam team, but then got injured and I went to Romania instead of him. By then I was 27. I played in the Wednesday match in Constanta alongside Sean McGaughey from Hawick, who turned in an outstanding performance. Sure enough, when the team was announced for the Test match, Sean was picked alongside John Beattie and David Leslie. So I came back after my ten days out there thinking that my time was over and that the selectors would continue to look at younger players. I wrote to the SRU, saying that I had taken on a demanding new job and asking them to count me out of the squad.

'It was the following summer, when Jim and I went on that training run together at Riccarton, that my turning-point, my "moment of truth" changed events. Before I knew it, I was invited to play in the trial of 1986 by Jim Telfer and the rest, as they say, is history.

'I've played alongside some wonderful players in my time. I believe that you can manufacture a quality player, but there is no substitute for class. A John Rutherford or a Jim Renwick is born with a gift – I really don't see that you could train or coach talent like that. Sure, you could always make them fitter or perhaps kick off better, but you could never coach their basic instinctive ability.

'What Jim Telfer could do, though, is take a journeyman at district level and turn him into a presentable forward on the international stage by pure hard work, technique and discipline. We never had the bulk of an English or French side, or for that matter, most international sides; however, the rucking game we developed from the late '70s allowed us to compete as a nation. I genuinely believe that by the 1990 tour of New Zealand we were better at rucking than the host nation.

'We also had a hard edge to the team. Derek White, David Sole, Damian Cronin all possessed that element of hardness, essential to compete. To be honest, I think there is an element of badness in everyone – there has to be. I must say that in everyday life I would rarely intentionally offend anyone. But pulling on a Scotland jersey, lining up against the white jersey at Murrayfield, I'm afraid a different person comes out for the afternoon!

'In 1990, the week before we played England, I had been reading an article about Micky Skinner, the English flanker – "Mick the Munch", as he refers to himself. He had described himself as "the thinking man's hit man". For some bizarre reason, about 20 minutes into the game, I said, "Micky, I was reading about you in the *Telegraph*. I see you describe yourself as the thinking man's hit man. You can't be thinking today, my boy – you haven't hit anybody." This was going on in the middle of an international. The guy was looking at me, convinced I was on drugs!

'International success is very often down to selection. I suppose, in truth, that's the key element in most games. When England picked Brian Moore, Dean Richards and Rob Andrew, we knew that they were going to spend 80 per cent of the game camped on our goal-line. In March 1990 Dean was not in the side and we knew we had a chance: they picked Mike Teague at number 8 and, great player that he was, he certainly wasn't a number 8 – we knew that from the Lions tour the previous summer. More importantly, Mike knew he wasn't a number 8.

He liked coming onto the ball, with it up in his arms, not round his feet. That was England's first and crucial mistake.

'The day belonged to Scotland. It was a privilege to have been part of it. Whilst most of the English drifted back south, Brian Moore went to a lunch at Watsonians the following day. He wanted to take all the ribbing, goading and teasing – basically, to hurt, so that he could go away and nurse his wrath for the next occasion. It took Scotland another ten years to win another game against the Auld Enemy. Did they hurt, or what!

'The 1989 Lions tour set the Scots apart as far as attitude towards training. We simply knew that to compete we had to be fitter than the opposition. We brought that edge to the tour and when you then combined our attitude with the talent from the other nations, we had the platform for success. Captaining the side was a dream when you had players like Dean Richards, Mike Teague and Brian Moore to play alongside. Brian is probably the most single-minded man I have ever known (including my twin brother!) – he had a limited physique, but what he lacked in physical stature he more than made up for in attitude and he was absolutely fearless. When you have been in difficult situations you remember the people who stand by you. Brian is one of those people.

'Brian and I have remained friends over the years. I was recently an usher at his wedding in Knightsbridge. He asked that I would do him the honour of wearing the kilt, which I was delighted to do. The fact that the marriage was held in a Scottish church in London added a lovely irony to the day, considering his long-term relationship with our nation! There I was, dressed in the full highland gear. I think some of the guests thought I was some sort of flunkey: they kept piling coats onto my arm and asking me to "see to this, would you, darling". I never let on.

'To have played for Scotland makes anyone feel pretty humble. Most seek no greater reward than just having done it and retiring in the knowledge that you did your best. Jim Telfer used to say, "Anyone can play for Scotland, but that's not enough – you have to win for Scotland."

'He's very probably half right. Not *anyone* can play. It must be a combination of talent and manufactured ability. If you stuck the Calder family somewhere in there, it would be about right. Jim worked very, very hard, whereas I perhaps had more natural ability; and what I lacked in attitude he more than made up for. You know, if there had only been one of us, we would have been the complete article. But I would still prefer to have my twin than his 27 caps.'

31. SCOTT HASTINGS

The best-documented ramble in history – Mao's Long Walk out of China aside – will forever be the Scotland team's spine-tingling march down the Murrayfield tunnel on 17 March 1990. But it could have been so different. The captain, David Sole, had wanted to make a statement to Will Carling and England about the intent of the underdogs in blue and there had been a number of suggestions – some more realistic than others. Sole himself hadn't been so keen on the walk idea, because 'the British Lions had tried it in Sydney in the first Test against Australia in 1989 and it had failed miserably'. Another suggestion was to have a piper lead the way onto the pitch and a third idea had been for the 15 Scotland players to march out in kilts and whip them off, Buck's Fizz style, before the anthems.

The latter suggestion came from the fertile, patriotic mind of Scott Hastings who, with his puffed-out chest and proud defiance at the singing of 'Flower of Scotland' for over a decade, and a Scotland record of 65 caps, came to be considered something close to the reincarnation of Wallace himself. Fortunately for the sake of history and the destination of the Grand Slam, Sole settled on The Walk in 1990.

Hastings, however, still holds the copyright to his idea: 'It was useful just talking about it in the build-up because it kept our minds off the match and its consequences. In the tunnel the expectation was not only that of the Scottish rugby folk in Murrayfield, but also that of the Scottish team's following throughout the world. You suddenly realised that Scotland's sport can bring people together and hopefully on that day we brought the Scots throughout the world together.'

Scott Hastings's enthusiasm for anything he is involved in comes tumbling out of any conversation with him. While his elder brother Gavin is more deliberate and measured in his approach, Scott retains a boyish *joie de vivre*. And although both played for Watsonians, Scotland

and the British Lions and work together at Hastings International in Edinburgh's West End, they are really not a bit alike. What they did possess in their playing careers, above everything else, was a daunting self-belief. Says Finlay Calder: 'We would be sitting there in the dressing-room going through enormous self-doubt and there's Scott and Gavin flicking the ball to each other, with the muscles on their biceps. There was no doubt in their minds that they were the best thing since sliced bread.'

There are, in fact, four Hastings brothers. The youngest, Ewan, played with Scott and Gavin at Myreside, while the eldest, Graeme, emigrated to Australia and played for Melbourne and Victoria State. If Gavin and Scott believed in themselves, so did Graeme. Colin Deans remembers, back in the '80s, meeting an exiled Scot in a Melbourne bar who told him, 'My brothers are going to play for Scotland.'

'We were certainly a sports-mad family,' says Scott. 'If Wimbledon was on we'd be out with the tennis rackets and if the Test matches were on the cricket wicket would be cut in the back garden. The amount of costs the old man paid in terms of window breakages was quite extraordinary. In winter, out came the rugby kits and we would go down and watch Watsonians on a Saturday. Family walks were very much part and parcel of the scene as well. Once we had a clearout in the garden and we found 27 footballs. It was never two-a-side, it was always three against one (usually my younger brother, who regrets it a bit).

'We were all very close, though. In 1990 we were at the second Test when Scotland played New Zealand. Graeme flew over from Australia and Ewan from Scotland and it was great sharing a beer and being in each other's company – all four of us on the other side of the world. I suddenly realised what a strong bond as a family we'd always had. Gavin and I were always fighting with each other as kids. We fought on the rugby field and now we're fighting in business. That's the rivalry between each other. As time went on we recognised each other's strengths. One game across in Dublin, he had misfielded a ball and I had purposely gone back to cover him. I collected the ball and thumped a 50-metre touch upfield, a real bit of a fluke. We were standing in the middle of Lansdowne Road and he said, "I probably owe you a pint of Guinness for that one" – and the next morning in Dublin Airport he tapped me on the shoulder and handed me a pint of Guinness.

'We've also had great support from our mother and father, who toured with us over the years. Up to even the 1995 World Cup they were right there, supporting us at each and every game. I'm sure they were proud of us, but we were equally proud of them and grateful for their support.

'When I was young I looked up to people like David Johnston, who was my hero and he played for Watsonians, of course. Andy Irvine, too: we all went along to Murrayfield to watch him either turn a game or lose a game for Scotland. It wasn't just Scotland players. There were people like Phil Bennett, Gerald Davies and Gareth Edwards.

'I think, to be honest, I've come through the best period of rugby, especially from a Scottish perspective. I've had two British Lions Tours and played during a period when the game was amateur and you could get away with things. I think the professional game has put a lot of pressure on guys, ensuring for example that if they are going to drink, they drink moderately. You know, when we celebrated, we celebrated well into the middle of the night; and even in the build-up to internationals guys would still have a beer or a glass of wine. I know the guys don't touch alcohol in the build-up to a game these days. The nutritionists are involved, saying it can affect performance and it is detrimental to your body condition. But I feel that in many respects a drink in moderation has done nobody any harm at all. It's part and parcel of the fabric of the sport.

'I look back and think of my first cap. It was a great day, a great family day, because Gavin and I both got capped on the same day. So when the letters came through we had a big party and the champagne was flowing. Nowadays a squad doesn't get announced until three or four days before the game, so the players can't go out with their mates and celebrate with a beer. For me, the tradition of getting recognition for playing for your country wasn't complete without waking up with a sore head.

'Our first cap was against France in January 1986. All of a sudden I was playing alongside some of my heroes like John Rutherford, Roy Laidlaw, Colin Deans and Alan Tomes. It was certainly a baptism of fire, but the big man knocked over six penalties to ensure that all the points were kept in the Hastings household. So, rather than Scotland winning 18–17, it was Gavin Hastings 18, France 17!

'I've obviously had a long relationship with Jim Telfer since then. He can be a dour man at times, but again his passion for the game is unrivalled. There are times when he has frothed – literally – from the mouth. I was sharing a room with Kenny Milne prior to the 1988 Scotland–England game down at Twickenham and Jim had kept the forwards back for five minutes for rucking practice. Kenny was always one of these guys who used to wear match shorts on the morning of a game – obviously getting his nether regions used to these tightly crimped shorts. Well, he came in with his shorts absolutely ripped to shreds. He was bleeding from a cut on his leg and Telfer had the forwards rucking over each other. Three or four hours away from the game and each of the Scottish forwards had been kicking shit out of each other.

'I was perhaps one of Telfer's strongest critics in the 1996 New Zealand tour which he managed on behalf of Scotland. Richie Dixon and David Johnston were supposed to be the coaches, but Telfer wanted to coach and he didn't manage the tour properly. For me, it spoiled the tour. We had a couple of confrontations on that particular tour. But if you look at Telfer's coaching record you know it is second to none; I hold him in high regard as a coach, rather than a manager. I don't believe he is a good manager of people, because he is so dedicated to the cause of rugby and not many others are. I think he rubbed some people up the wrong way and didn't quite strike the balance with some others. But he was a helluva good guy and I think that, latterly, more humour came into his demeanour and that's not a bad thing.

'The Murrayfield crowd was very much part and parcel of the psyche of Scotland's success in the 1980s and '90s. In many respects that was the sort of contributing and catalytic factor in the performance that we produced that day in 1990. I think there was a great belief in our overall game plan. It was certainly part of our strategy to try to outthink the English. For example it was a great shock when Finlay walked down the front of the lineout and said, "Hi Ackford" and Paul Ackford turned round to look at Finlay, thinking, "What the hell's he doing here?" – by which time the ball had already been thrown in and was in Gary Armstrong's hands.

'I once had to interview Will Carling for a Radio 5 series. Now that our playing days are over, we can ask questions about what happened in the English dressing-room. You rib each other about some of the tales that went on and it's interesting to see how each team would have prepared for the Scots in a different way.

'Rugby is a great sport for friendships, no matter who you played for. It's nice to say to guys like Phil Bennett or Gareth Edwards that I was a kid when I watched them at Murrayfield; and I hope in some ways somebody will come up to me and say likewise and tell me they have derived a bit of inspiration from me. I've been part of Five Nations rugby for so long, it was a very special period in my life. I used to go to Cardiff Arms Park as a kid and think how lovely it would be if it happened to me. And it did. The dream came true. There's no harm in dreaming, because it gives you motivation and objectives to hang on to.

'In many respects I am at a crossroads at the moment with rugby coming to an end. You actually dream, now, of success in business and success in the family and that's what I'm looking for for the future. I've always said that if I want to, I can pick up the phone next year and have a game. Well, I can, but not at 1st XV level. It's time to move on. Now I can wake up on a Saturday morning and decide what I want to do with my Saturday and not what rugby dictates. But at the end of the day I recognise it's still all about fun.'

32. STEWART HAMILTON

The nearest Stewart Hamilton got to becoming a Scotland international was a couple of Scotland B caps in the mid-'80s. Of the 40 players in this book, Hamilton is the only one who never appeared in a full international. But to many, Hamilton is the archetypal rugby player, certainly the definitive club man, and it was at the insistence of Finlay Calder – and on the advice of a number of others – that he qualifies as a Giant of Scottish Rugby.

Physically he certainly fits the bill, although he is down from a playing weight of over 19 stone to around 16. A clue to his popularity in the rugby fraternity can be found in his description of the aftermath of his second B team appearance, against France in 1987, where he 'finished up getting drunk and dancing on a table'. It is the same reason, he believes, for that being his last representative appearance.

Hamilton still plays at the age of 44. Though coming from Larkhall, near Glasgow, he is closely linked with the emergence of Stirling County as a force in Scottish club rugby during the early 1990s – which culminated in the Scottish Club Championship in season 1994–95.

'I got invited to a stag party in Stirling one night, for the late Hamish Logan. There were quite a few farmers playing for Stirling at that time and I think they noticed my size. I was 22 and hadn't touched a rugby ball. Where I came from you were a bloody poof if you played rugby. In certain areas it is still viewed like that. At this stag party it soon became clear this was my kind of place: they were stood there at the bar with their trousers round their ankles singing bloody songs, you know. After ten pints they were still managing to put them down in one. I thought, "This is for me." A fortnight later I went down for the training and never looked back. For 15 years I probably never missed a training night.

'In 1984 I went to Heriot's for three seasons after Andy Irvine phoned us up, about the same time as Jocky Bryce went there. I was in the second row behind the Bear, not that he would have noticed, right enough. That season or two, if he wanted the scrum to go forward or the scrum to go back, there was nothing either I – or whoever he was propping against – could do about it. And that was towards the end of his career. He was a bloody great lad off the field, too.

'It was obviously a different culture and a different background for me, but I mix with everyone. With a wife and kids, though, it was a hell of a commitment, because you would go over on Saturday morning and usually get back on the Sunday afternoon. So that was when I went back to Stirling. I became captain and we got to the First Division. I was 40 at the time and slowing down a bit, but I still trained hard. No matter what I'd been up to the night before, I'd still be up at six or something for a run. We had a great side then, particularly the pack. The front row was Brian Robertson, Kevin McKenzie and George Graham. Brian unfortunately had a bad neck injury, but of course the other two got to play for Scotland.

'Stirling was a tremendously social club. The two years before we won the league, we went to France. Maybe I shouldn't mention some of the stories from that – although we were all dedicated to the game on the field. Club training was Tuesday and Thursday and we ran through all the moves on a Friday. On the Sunday we went down to run off the beer. So we were together four times a week. It was such a great team and I don't just mean McKenzie, Graham, Ian Jardine and Kenny Logan. We all know about Kenny. He's a fine player, but he has also made some bloody howlers. At Stirling you wouldn't get away with it, because there was always someone to keep you in line. The majority of folk, it must be said, were delighted when he started doing well and went down to Wasps.

'Kevin McKenzie has had a lot of tragedy. His boy didn't make it and he also had a bad injury. Everyone has a chip on their shoulder, but I think Kevin sometimes had a whole bag of tatties on his – I think that's helped him achieve a lot. For the size of him he was tremendous. I remember him as a wee toerag 20 years ago and from seeing his career start to seeing it end you wonder where the time goes.

'George Graham: I always think his missus should have taken up rugby, although the bark is often worse than the bite. She's from the bottom end of the town – a notorious place and rightly so. George was a breath of fresh air after he came back from the Army. You could see he was an absolute star, just the way he got about the park, and he was as strong as an ox in the scrum. He was also a guy who could handle himself. He would have six on your chin before you could blink, or as you were blinking. It was part of life where he came from.

'We were lucky as well because Richie Dixon would come through and help with the coaching. He played a big part. Ian Jardine was always a bit of a quiet man, but for the two or three years Stirling were doing well I can't remember anyone getting past him in the centre. He was one of the best tacklers I ever saw. But if there was one player you could single out for the success of Stirling County it would be Brian Ireland – the amount of work he did and the tries he scored that year in 1995. He was always a great pest to us when we were not playing, but for the 90 minutes on the park he was a pest to the opposition.

'I joined Stirling County when they were in the Sixth Division and have been right through to the championship. We had some great laughs. We were playing Bridgend one Friday before a Wales–Scotland game and it must have been the Thursday night. I was playing pool in the bar and I think we were short of players. This big Welsh guy was there; I asked if he played rugby and the next thing, he'd agreed to come down and turn out for us. What I didn't know was that he was the bloody village idiot. He had seemed all right, and sure enough he turned up, but just before the kick-off Brian Ireland turned to me and said, "Have you spoken to that guy?"

'"Aye, he plays a bit of rugby."

'"He's a bloody nutter. He told me he's just out of the jail for murdering somebody." It takes all sorts.

'Before all the new rules came in, the lineout was a battleground. The rule changes were maybe for the better because it could hardly have been a spectator sport – a bunch of forwards punching the shit out of each other. But when lifting came in I think that ended my hopes of getting any further, because while they might not want beanpoles, no one is wanting to lift someone who weighs 19 stone.

'The B caps I got were both against France. Looking at the photograph afterwards, everyone on it got a cap on it except me: Gavin Hastings, Kenny Milne, Tukalo, they all got capped. You'd swap everything for a full cap. I'd have died for Scotland, definitely, and I suppose I was there or thereabouts. I suppose what didn't help was where I came from.

'After that game in France I'd got pretty drunk and I was giving them a few songs on top of this table and the table broke, which definitely didn't help my Scotland career. But if you were away from home you did that. If I'd done it when I was a bit more established I'd have got away with it. It's the Larkhall mentality they didn't like. Larkhall is an old mining community and my old man told me this story about walking down the street when some old guy stopped him and said, "I saw your Stewart on telly the other day. God, he's getting a size. How big is he now?"

'"He's 19 stone."

'"Nineteen stone," said the old guy. "F★★★ me, that's only a stone off a ton."

'I also had a season with Glasgow Caledonian Reds – and played in Europe – until Hugh Campbell took me to one side one day and told me my services were no longer required. But I'm still playing down at Hamilton. I went there as player-coach, but then my life was in a wee bit of disarray, so I resigned and just decided to carry on playing.

'Next year I'm going back to Stirling. There are nine or ten of the old school going back: they've been spread around the place, but we are all heading back. I always said I wanted to play a senior game with my oldest boy, Gregor, and that's him 17 now, so it shouldn't be too long. What senior game that is going to be, I don't know. But then the youngest, Scott, he's a big lad and he said he wanted to play in a game with me if I kept on playing. So you never know. You just get involved and it becomes a way of life.

'There's bloody more to life than rugby, no question. But I'm buggered if I know what it is.'

33. IWAN TUKALO

Iwan Tukalo is a bit like the Brad Dexter character in the film *The Magnificent Seven* – the face you can always recall from the 1990 Grand Slam team, but the name you can never remember in the pub quiz. The Selkirk and Scotland wing, it appears, will always have to lurk in the shadow of the likes of Calder, the Hastings, Stanger and Armstrong. Gavin Hastings rates him 'possibly the most underrated wing ever to play for Scotland'.

Tukalo, however, remains one of the most popular members of that Scotland side, an uncompromising opponent on the field and an entertaining character off it. For Tukalo, like so many others, rugby has been a lot of fun. It still is. He enjoys touch rugby and can be spotted at Inverleith on Sundays regularly helping coaching with Stewart's–Melville juniors.

'I started playing my rugby at Royal High in Edinburgh,' he recalls, 'and when I was playing for them I was actually going to university at Edinburgh to do civil engineering. At the same time Selkirk had asked me to go down and play there because a couple of the committee had seen me play for the Co-optimists down at Walkerburn. In that particular game I played at scrum-half. I turned Selkirk down because I wanted to concentrate on my studies and Selkirk is a bit of a hike. But Royal High had got relegated and I wanted to keep up my standard.

'Selkirk had a lot to offer with John Rutherford and Iain Paxton playing there and Gordon Hunter at scrum-half, so that was it for ten years. My first tour was with Scotland to Romania in 1984. I thought, "Fantastic." But then you got there and it was awful. We took hampers with us with our own meat and Mars bars. At lunch you would get your ration of a Mars bar and just whoof this down. I thought, "If this is touring with Scotland you can stick it." I shared with Jim Renwick. It was his last tour and I said to him, "Jim, you've been around for a long time. How does this compare with other Scotland tours?" And he said, in his broad Hawick accent, "It's the pits."

'My first cap at B international level was in France and after two minutes I scored a try and I thought this was it. My international career was launched. Forty-one unanswered points later, I began to think that maybe there was a little more to this game than I'd realised. A lot of us suffered from that; a few careers got put on temporary hold.

'But I got capped against Ireland in 1985. I put this cover tackle in on Hugo MacNeill as he was going over and he spilled the ball. "Are you looking, selectors?" A couple of minutes later my opposite number Trevor Ringland just shot past me, so I was back to zero. In the changing-rooms afterwards Hugo came in and said, "Congratulations on your first cap. I know you won't want to swap your jersey, but here's mine." And he handed over his jersey. Then he added, "And by the way, if I had seen you coming you wouldn't have stopped me scoring."

'I went to Bermuda for the Easter Classic with Hugo a couple of times – once in 1987 when John Rutherford did his knee in and finished his career. Four of us, Matt Duncan, Iain Paxton and John and I, got carpeted for that. It was funny, because we were on opposite sides. I thought I couldn't be doing with playing against Matt, this huge guy in your face all the time; so I said to this local guy, Tommy, "Look, I'm not going to learn anything playing opposite Matt, you go in and have a go." So he did. And next minute, there was Matt coming down the wing – the first time he got the ball. I could see him getting ready with the elbow. Then Tommy just got right at Matt's ankles and got both legs and the look of surprise on his face as he went over!

'When John got his injury no one had touched him. He just planted his leg and his knee went. When the SRU found out, all hell broke loose and they were threatening to expel us from the World Cup squad. They got John ready for the game against France, but he didn't last long and that was that. His knee was well shot. I remember – and this shows the courage of John – he was limping before the match but still went in there.

'On a lighter note, Scott Hastings had these T-shirts made up, really well done, with a map of New Zealand on the front and all the players' names on the back. The back was all autographs. Duncan Paterson was the tour manager and his name was in the bottom right-hand corner. Scott, as a little joke, put this fictitious name on, "A. S. Hole", and it just so happened to be right under Dunc's name. Now Scott doesn't have the brain cells to have done this on purpose, it was just totally by chance, but we had 1,000 of these T shirts with "DUNCAN PATERSON, A. S. HOLE" on them. So Duncy saw it and said, "Right, you're not selling a single one of those until they've all been changed" and we had to sit there changing them all to "A. S. Haley" or something. The thing was, the alterations were all done in marker pens, so after a couple of washes they were all back to "A. S. Hole".

'On another light note, I remember when Colin Deans got his 50th cap on that tour. It was a game against Zimbabwe and there was going to be a presentation beforehand with Roy Laidlaw making the speech. So Roy got all pumped up and made this magnificent, moving speech and of course Deano wasn't there – he was away doing a TV interview.

'We've had some great trips abroad and not just with Scotland. I was in Japan in 1986 to play for the President's XV against the All Blacks. That's where John Jeffrey formed his friendship with Dean Richards – the pair who ended up kicking the Calcutta Cup round Edinburgh in 1988. There was myself, JJ, Dean Richards, Paul Rendall of England, Micky Harrison and Phil Orr from Ireland: these were the invited guests. The rest were all local Japanese players from their national team.

'The flight going out went via Anchorage. We got off to a bad start, because we were all sitting around at Heathrow having a few beers and we missed the call. They actually came looking for us. On board, the stewardesses were being very hospitable and Rendall, the Judge, wangled us a few seats at the back of the plane and a tray of gin and tonics. Pretty soon there was a bit of a session going on. Then the stewardess started getting a bit twitchy and asked us to sit down. The Judge told her to go away in so many words, so she went for the pilot. Of course, Rendall told him to go away as well. We were now over American airspace, where it's a federal offence to threaten the captain, so at Anchorage they were going to arrest him.

'We managed to talk them out of that and promised to keep Rendall quiet and fortunately when he got back on board he fell asleep. Great. But then all of a sudden there was this commotion: he had woken up and gone into the galley up in business class, where there were all these drinks, and he'd grabbed a couple of bottles of wine. Of course he was swaying about, with wine going all over the place. So that was the Judge.

'When we actually got to Japan we dumped the stuff in the hotel, freshened up and then went to watch Japan play the All Blacks. We were in the president's box and I always remember seeing the TV next night – Japan got hammered 103–0 – and there was this shot of us sat there, thinking, "What the hell are we doing here?"

'In rugby I've been lucky and I had the best of both worlds. People ask me if I missed out on the professional era. I did have a couple of offers, when I was playing, to go to rugby league. But the way I tended to look at it was this: if I had a lousy day at work I could go down to the rugby field at night, knock hell out of a tackle bag and then go back and start work the next day. But if you're a professional and you have a lousy day on the training pitch, what do you do to unwind? There isn't anything.

'I always had a career to fall back on with British Gas at the time. I started to get quite a bit of press coverage when I played for Edinburgh and got interviewed by our own in-house magazine. They asked me, "What do you put first, your job with British Gas or your rugby?" Being totally focused on where I was going, I said rugby, of course, and I just saw this jaw drop to the ground. So I quickly had to dig myself out of a hole!

'I know that if I'd made a conscious effort to concentrate totally on a career, I would have been a few more steps up the ladder with British Gas. But I also always maintain that if I had chosen to go down that route I would be sitting here wondering, "What if . . ?" I could be sitting here looking at videos of the 1990 Grand Slam win and some other punter's in the number 11 shirt.'

Is there life after professional rugby? Meeting Alan Tait a few months after his retirement at the end of the 1999 World Cup, there doesn't appear to be. He's still in a tracksuit, but the only exercise he has had that morning is to take his two lurchers for a walk around the fields by his home in Stichill, a few miles from Kelso. He's suffering from a heavy cold and, it must be said, looks severely at a loose end – which is perhaps understandable after over two decades of playing both codes of the oval-ball game and with nothing discernible on the horizon.*

His original trade of roofing doesn't seem an option with a wear-and-tear back injury which plagued him throughout his last couple of years in the sport. He has also to come to terms with the daily business of hanging around the house. His wife is away doing the shopping and he says, 'I wish she'd hurry up, I'm bloody starving.' Despite the Cumbrian twang – he went to primary school in Workington when his father signed for the local rugby league side in the late 1960s – Tait is Kelso-born and he built his bungalow in Stichill when he was still playing league himself in England. He called his autobiography *Rugby Rebel*, but anything anarchic about Tait has always been in the minds of others.

After a club career in union with Kelso and eight Scotland caps before heading for Widnes and, later, Leeds, Tait was simply doing what every top player in Britain did in the mid-'90s – playing the sport for money. In 1997 that career came full circle when he became the first professional league player to return to Scottish international rugby and he was chosen for the 1997 British Lions tour of South Africa. Rebellious or not, Tait's life has simply been about finding the right options for himself and his family. And while 'professional' was once a dirty word in Scotland, it has now become almost like a badge of merit: these days no

---

* Tait was appointed technical consultant to the Scotland team in September 2000.

one gets anywhere without a professional attitude to virtually every facet of the game.

After the Lions tour of 1997 Tait signed for Newcastle, won the league with them and then joined Scotland's first 'professional' side, Edinburgh Reivers, then known as a superdistrict. It was not a happy marriage, however: 'It was another new venture for us, but the fixtures were few and far between and when the European Cup came round I was dropped by the coaches. It was a bit of a downer because I'd had a bit of conflict with them and I think they were trying to show authority, that they could drop anyone they wanted. It might have been a bit of a statement. They never asked me for any advice and it was always the same thing, the same training, the same tactics, the same mistakes, even the same comments to the press before and after a match. You'd look at Ceefax and you couldn't tell one after-match comment from another. They just weren't prepared to move off the spot and everyone up here seems too proud to ask for advice.

'You can learn from anyone. The man who had a massive influence on me was Ellery Hanley and I was 28 years old. What can you learn at 28? The four years I played alongside him at Leeds were an eye-opener. He was the first professional before professionals. He never drank, didn't smoke, ate the right things and trained hard. He set examples on and off the field. Especially on. Every week, he went out there with guys wanting to knock his head off and he just took all the punishment and came back for more.

'At the Reivers I never got downcast about it because I was still involved in the Scottish set-up and Jim Telfer had a lot of faith in us. At the start of the 1998–99 season I was put on the bench for Scotland with Gary Armstrong. Bryan Redpath came in for Gary and Jamie Mayer for me. I thought it was the beginning of the end. Jim called me an "impact player", but I think it was after the Maoris game that I had a word with Gary in his room and told him I was seriously thinking of retiring. I got a couple of minutes against the Maoris and scored a try near the end, but I thought, "What's the good of a 34-year-old fella coming on for two minutes at the end of an international when they could have younger players coming on?"

'To be honest, I was a knock-on-the-door from retiring and if I'd had the courage to knock on Jim's that would have been it. Gary was as sick as me, but he reminded us we'd been in this situation before. Gary had set his sights on the World Cup a year later. A year sounds a long time, but it's nothing in rugby because the build-up starts so early. I just bit the bullet in the end and was glad I did, as it turned out, because things turned round. Gary got back in when the home nations came round and I was on the bench for the match when Duncan Hodge broke his leg in a district match and I got 25 minutes of the second half against Wales. They put Gregor Townsend in at 10, Johnny Leslie at inside-centre and me outside him and everything just clicked – you'd have thought we'd played together for 20 years. It was tough on young Hodgey, but it was almost like fate.

'I knew it would be probably my last game at Twickenham when we went down to England and I was asking myself all week for a big performance. I wanted the youngsters in the team to think the same way. I think Scotland had a bunch of guys there who were ready to take on anybody and we should have won.

'The Ireland game, that was where Gregor got his try in every match and I missed out. Gregor's a world-class player, there's no getting away from that. You get the stand-off experts like John Rutherford who will tell you how a stand-off should play; and you have the classical number 10s that can put a ball where they want to put it and read the game. With Gregor maybe you haven't got the perfect 10, but you've got an extra attacking flair which you otherwise wouldn't have. Another guy I can think of like that is Steve Larkham of Australia. He started at 15 and he doesn't kick a ball great, but he's a phenomenal player. You'll always have your arguments with Gregor because he's not your rock-solid 10, but I would always take a gamble with him.

'John and I hit it off straight away, his attitude and everything. I knew 100 per cent where he was coming from. If he has a bad game he's desperate to play again, like me. The only way to put it right is the next game. Some put their tails between the legs, but the good thing about rugby is that you can go and put it right.

'The French game was my last in the championship. I knew that. The French weren't performing and Scotland were on fire. I was expecting a backlash and they were coming out in front of their home crowd and in a new stadium; but again our confidence was sky high that day and everything just clicked. It was unbelievable. I remember we called a move in our own 22, and nine times out of ten I wouldn't have been giving the pass, but the ball just left my hand; Glenn Metcalfe came onto the ball, he just hit it at pace and he was gone. Everything we did just turned to gold. We seemed to outrun and out-think them. Jim Telfer couldn't believe it either at half-time. Then we just kept them out for 40 minutes, which to me was more pleasing than all the points we'd scored in the first half. I don't think anyone was thinking of winning the championship, but you could say we were chuffed to bits.

'The Sunday morning we were all rough at the edges with the wine and the beer and that's when we started thinking about Wales playing England for the championship. I came back home and we went down the Black Swan for a pint. All the lads were shouting for Wales and I can just remember turning round talking, because there was no way Wales were going to win. Then Neil Jenkins put a long ball out to Howarth and they were back in it. In the end it was almost a carbon-copy move that I'd scored against England – when the centre hits the line on a straight ball – and Gibbsy did it perfectly. The pub went mental. I was actually dancing on the bar. It never, ever entered my head that Jenks wouldn't kick that goal. The whistle went and I bought the lads four bottles of champagne. They were even more shocked than I was when I got the bill. Then the phone started. Doddie rang up. He was at Bryan Redpath's in Melrose. There was a big party at Gregor's bar, the Sports Café in Edinburgh, and they were wanting us to come up there. But by then the only place I was going was home, because I'd had enough. I knew that was my last Five Nations: I knew I wasn't going to play after the World Cup. This was the big one for me. It was the last time in the jersey.

'I was actually left out of the World Cup game against Western Samoa and the lads played really well. I thought Jim might not change a winning side. My back was killing me and I was on these anti-inflammatory pills and, really, I had to call on all the experience of my 35 years to get through to my grand finale. Everything I'd learnt and knew was geared up for that match.

'It was Gary's last game, Jim's last game and mine and Paul Burnell's. The other players sent us back out. It was unbelievable. My nine-year-old lad Michael came on the field just when I was hugging Jim and that's when I broke down. It was all getting too much. My dad was there as well. He'd been there at Old Trafford for my first cup final in rugby league, the Premiership final for Widnes, and he was there for me at the end. Michael got a bit of a shock when he saw us in tears and he ran back to his mum and said, "Mum, Dad's crying!"

'But I wasn't the only one. Back in the changing-room, Gary got us in a circle. He was going to say a few words, being captain, but he couldn't speak. The emotion that was in that room was incredible. It was a fitting way to go out – the World Cup, against New Zealand – but to be honest that finished me mentally and physically. The Reivers gave us a couple of weeks off, but when I went back to training there was nothing there. Just a shell of my former self.

'The injury would have finished us anyway, but the motivation had gone: the will to play rugby had gone. Everything just fell to bits after that game. I can tell you, when the time comes to stop, you know about it all right.'

Peter Wright, the Bonnyrigg blacksmith, is rugby's classic poacher-turned-gamekeeper. Notorious in his playing days for problems with referees, he now gives talks to Scotland's leading officials on how to contain recalcitrant front-row forwards in his role as Development Officer for Dumfries and Galloway. Those who can remember Wright giving away ten yards time after time for back-chat in internationals can only gasp at this outrageous piece of role reversal. It's also a great irony that the SRU should take on board a man they once fined for foul play in an international match – and that the same reformed bad boy, in his days coaching Murrayfield Wanderers, should lecture players on indiscipline.

He says, 'Part of my job now is to lecture to referees. Down at Largs one weekend for a coaching course, I was in there lecturing them about front-row play. It's quite funny, but the majority of them do listen. There's a guy called Bill Calder who refereed in the First Division when I played. He's now Referee Development Officer down in the Borders. He told me the problem with me was that when I used to argue with referees, nine times out of ten I was right. So it's good to talk to them now and not get penalised ten yards.

'I also think I am quite good at being a coach because I knew all the dodges. I was always at the back of the pack in training, unless there was a punishment for being last, in which case I'd be second last. I know when people are not putting it in. It's sometimes difficult to give guys a row, because you've been like that, but at the end of the day you can't get over that kind of thing. The funny thing for me is to talk about discipline, to tell the guys to keep their discipline and not to argue with referees, and they look at me really funny. But of course, just because I did it doesn't make it right.'

Wright started his career at the age of 15 with Lasswade rugby club, to the south of Edinburgh, where his precocious bulk earned him an automatic place in the club's front row: 'We lived very close to the club and although Dad was a soccer fan and on the committee at Bonnyrigg Rose, a couple of teachers dragged me into rugby. I played hooker and back-row and people kept pushing me towards prop. I was so big, I was just running through people. I would score eight tries in a game, 80 tries a season, because I was that size and no one fancied getting in my way. Once I got into prop I thoroughly enjoyed it and made the first team at 15. The guy who was hooker, Davie Pringle, was actually older than the two props put together.

'I had the size to compete, but I certainly wasn't mature and I was terrible for giving away penalties for arguing. I was dead quiet off the field, but on it my personality took over. I just felt I was never wrong. I was seeing things the referee wouldn't see, but I'm very passionate about rugby. I find referees very difficult to talk to. I have watched them on TV and at times felt hatred for these people.

'When I left school blacksmithing certainly helped with my strength and I never really did weights. I was fitter when I wasn't a professional because I was doing physical work and was on my feet all the time. Bryan Redpath said the same thing. When he was a joiner he was fitter than when he was full time. The other thing was that doing manual labour brought you back to reality. In the game against England in 1994 I got yellow-carded for rucking Will Carling; I was on a building site on the Wednesday before that match and this brickie from Glasgow had said, "Mind and give that Will Carling a good shoeing for us."

'What actually happened in the game was that Will Carling was on the wrong side. I rucked him really well and the next thing was the referee giving us the yellow card. I couldn't believe it. Jim Telfer came up to us after the game and said, "You should never have been yellow-carded, it was a great piece of rucking." That made me feel better. Then when I got back to the building site on the Monday morning, this big fella patted me on the back and said, "Well done, that was brilliant!" He honestly believed I had done it for him.

'One minute you're away down at Twickenham, the next, you're back at work amongst ordinary people. You're not Peter Wright, international rugby player – you're Peter Wright, bloody useless blacksmith. A lot of guys like Kenny Logan could learn some humility coming onto a building site and working alongside guys making £120 a week. When I was 15 or 16 there were a couple of guys there who basically taught me to drink and I was going out with them on a Saturday night and spending all my wages. I'm still great pals with them and they taught me that they're far more important that all these middle-class folk.

'My dad was the same. He didn't watch the game; he would just watch me and point out all my mistakes. He'd be the first to point out that talking back to refs never worked for me and I think it probably cost me my international career, so I know what I'm talking about. We played England in '96 at Murrayfield for the Grand Slam and I gave away the penalties for ten yards each time. I also got fined for something that happened in that game. I was pulled for supposedly stamping on Dean Richards when someone from Aberdeen wrote to the SRU after seeing it on TV. It was the same game Jason Leonard allegedly punched Rob Wainwright, but because nobody saw the fist connecting with the face, he got off with it.

'Then this guy from Aberdeen wrote in and said, "Instead of complaining about other teams, why don't you keep your team in order?" Basically it was the 43rd minute and I was walking back from a ruck; Dean Richards was lying on the ground and I didn't stamp on him, I stood on his ankle. I got fined two thirds of a match fee, which was a bit harsh.

'Funnily enough, I didn't get a bollocking for that match. I would have certainly given one. Coaches are scared to do that, to be honest, because they are afraid players are going to go off in a huff or come out with a torrent of abuse. There are a couple of guys I coached at Murrayfield Wanderers I wouldn't go out for a drink with, wouldn't socialise with – but they are quite good rugby players and I don't have a problem coaching them to be a better rugby player.

'I retired in 1996 with a wear-and-tear injury. But the enjoyment was going out of it anyway. I went back to blacksmithing for a time and coached Murrayfield Wanderers. Then, when one of the DO jobs came up, I applied for that. Since then it has been great, a whole new life. It's different from coaching and playing, because you are talent-spotting, coaching kids, coaching adults, getting structures in place. Dumfries and Galloway isn't a rugby stronghold and there's a problem with employment. A lot of guys drift away at 18 or 19 because there's no work. But there are six or seven clubs and there are incentives. Duncan Hodge is from Lockerbie and when someone like that comes through it gives everyone a lift.

'I want to be Scotland coach one day. Jim Telfer asked me at my interview how I saw my long-term future and I said, "Sat in that chair asking some poor bugger the same question." You have to have long-term goals. At five I said I was going to play rugby for Scotland one day and now I say I'm going to coach Scotland one day. Why not set yourself targets?

'I've been very lucky because I have been with some wonderful coaches – Jim, Ian McGeechan, Dick Best, Richie Dixon, Bruce Hay, Sean Lineen – and I think I can take a bit from each. A lot of people are bothered about borrrowing from other people. But there's only so much you can do because, when you get down to it, there aren't many new ideas floating around.'

Big Gavin certainly fills office space. Following rugby, you become immune to being dwarfed by flankers and locks, and even the odd prop, but aren't full-backs supposed to be lean, nippy and close to the ground? Even younger brother Scott, who is six-foot something and 14½ stone, calls him the Big Man. The Gavin you see and hear on the TV screens is also a tad different in the flesh. The public earnestness often turns into intolerance if you ask a daft question or get a fact slightly wrong. Perhaps it comes with being in the public eye for so long, or maybe he's had a bad day on the golf course.

The Hastings siblings, as described elsewhere, have maintained some sort of rivalry – usually in sport – since they were old enough to walk. In rugby terms Scott holds a slight edge, with his 65 caps to Gavin's 59, but Gavin is the senior business partner at Hastings International. And as he is happy to point out, 'I always kid Scott on how many caps he has got, but I always say that if you actually equate it to how many minutes he actually spent on the field then I've got far more than him, because he's won a couple of caps and he's been on for about ten seconds. Anyway, I think in this day and age we should go back to having in brackets how many minutes and hours you played international rugby. There are guys coming on as subs for five minutes here and five minutes there and all of them sporting their 40-odd caps.

'Yes, there has been sibling rivalry. Jim and Finlay Calder may get on like a house on fire, but we always had our odd confrontation. It always used to be me who tidied everything up. You would have your collection of beer mats, or whatever you did in the early days, and Scott would just come in to annoy me and just bloody well flatten the lot. So he got a clip round the ear for that.

'We got selected at the same time, of course, in 1986, and we went out to the pub that night. In the good old way of celebrating, we got

absolutely plastered and it was great   a few friends and the pub and
that's the way you do things most days. Actually winning was great, too.
We were piling into the champagne and we had two big long tables and
the French were utterly disconsolate. We were up to all sorts of nonsense.
Bacon and tomatoes came along but they were sort of stuffed tomatoes
and everyone kept piling these bloody things onto my plate; so I put one
on a dessert spoon and flung it over my shoulder. About 30 yards at the
other side of the room it landed on someone important at the top table.
Later in the week the the SRU President arrived at training saying he
had a very grave matter to report and went on to tell this story about the
stuffed tomato. Gary Callender was sitting next to me. He punched me
on the ribs and said I shouldn't have done that. The story that went
around was that it was me, but I'm not so sure. I think it was Scott, but
I have a sort of forgetful nature after a few glasses of champagne, so it
maybe was me.

'I had a similar embarrassing incident after a Scotland B match against
Ireland over in Galway in 1984. I didn't play very well that day and we
got beaten by a few points. I dropped a high ball and they scored under
the posts. The next one, I dropped it again and didn't release it, so they
got a penalty. There was a party at night, but we were leaving at some
ridiculous hour like 6.15 the next morning and I got back to the hotel
five minutes after the bus had left. They were flying to Shannon and I
missed the plane. I eventually got hold of them and I told them I'd fallen
asleep, which was actually true. I had to get a train from Galway to
Dublin and had about six hours in Dublin on my own. Then I flew back
to Glasgow, eventually getting home about midnight when I should have
been home about midday.

'Dad made me sit down and write a whole bunch of letters to a lot
of people, but after that it was two years before I got capped. Someone
must have forgiven me – maybe it was my letter-writing – but that was
a bit embarrassing, I have to say. The story goes that there was a guy,
Paddy Flynn, driving around all the housing estates in Galway knocking
up all the people that he thought I might be with. But he never did find
me.

'That first Scotland cap didn't begin in the best way. I put the kick-
off straight into touch and I thought the boys wouldn't be very pleased
about that. The forwards were jogging back to halfway for the scrum and
I was jogging back towards the posts; then I heard a noise and the crowd
were going nuts. France had taken a quick throw, unbeknown to me and
everyone else, so I turned round and found about seven French guys

running towards me. You kind of take the guy with the ball, or try to intercept it, but sure enough they scored at the right-hand touchline. Thirty seconds into my international début.

'Fortunately things got a wee bit better after that and I kicked a few goals. I always say I missed a few goals as well and I think I could have set a new world record for penalties. I've never watched a video of that game, but I reckon I must have missed six penalty goals. I could have had twelve in my début, then. That would have been a good day!

'In 1989 I got injured and Craig Chalmers came in and took over the kicking. At Murrayfield in 1990 I was lying down, holding the ball steady in the wind for him to kick, and some cynics suggested that was the only way I would get on camera. I did score one penalty against France in that 1990 season, but that was all; three points was my contribution. In fact, there were quite a few internationals where I wasn't first-choice kicker and Craig wasn't going to pass up a chance. He was a fairly difficult guy to get the ball off, sometimes.

'There are many people who are shit-scared of Jim Telfer, but I certainly wasn't one of them. To my mind, it's not a healthy situation to be in. Anyway, I found Jim a very honest man and you can't say any better than that. You knew he would listen to you. My abiding memory of Jim Telfer is the loss to England in the '91 World Cup. He was absolutely devastated. We had to go down to Cardiff the next day. We were staying in the Angel Hotel and we didn't train that day. The guys were having a game on the Tuesday or the Wednesday against the All Blacks in the play-off for third place, so we decided that we'd all go out on the Sunday night in Cardiff and have a few drinks. So we were all buying Hawaiian shirts, or whatever, and getting dressed up and we had a team meeting just before dinner. Some of the guys came in with these shirts on and that's when Jim arrived.

'He said, "You've just played the biggest game of your lives and you've got the biggest game of your lives in two days' time and no Scottish side has ever beaten the All Blacks. You've got a chance to make history and if any of you think you are going out in Cardiff tonight then you've got another think coming." Basically, we all looked at one another and thought, "Well, that's us not going out." That was just the power of the man.

'The Lions tours were brilliant, real adventures. They come around only once every four years and you spend the intervening period trying to beat the hell out of one another. Then you go on the Lions tour for eight weeks and suddenly you've just got to gel. I found that fascinating, the huge contrast.

'Finlay was a brilliant captain. You'd walk to the ends of the earth for him. I've got this photo of Finlay. It's after we won the last Test and the series against Australia: we're up at a vineyard in Hunter Valley, all getting completely smashed, and there's Finlay standing there with the owners of the vineyard and he's got a look of quiet satisfaction on his face. To my mind it sort of sums him up.

'David Sole was a great captain and also led by example from the front. Finlay was more engaging as a person. I always remember, before we left we were training down at London Irish and I'm raced against Chris Oti about 250 yards round the rugby field. Well, there was never any danger that he was going to beat Chris, but he bet the shirt off his back and I tell you what, he bloody well ran it out. He wasn't going to win, but sure as hell he was going to have a go.

'I thought I was the right man for the captaincy job in 1993. At the first training session the guys were pretty nervous and I was quite nervous and I said, "Right, come on boys we're going training." I was really quite chuffed when they followed me!

'We weren't far away from winning that series – but for the whim of an Australian referee we probably would have won the first Test. We won the second Test and everything would have changed round, but that's life. There were some close shaves off the pitch, too. The Welsh flanker Richard Webster was on that tour and we went off shooting clay pigeons one day. Peter Winterbottom was there and Webster must have been wandering around at the back of him; suddenly a bloody shot went off and missed Winters' foot by about two inches. Winters was just shitting himself and Webster and all his Welsh cronies were all having the biggest laugh. There were a few characters and that's what you want. You room with the Irish guys and they all get the parties well organised; the Welsh guys are forever on the phone; and the English guys are doing their hair. It's a good contrast of style and background.

'All my career I played before professionalism and people say, "I bet you wish you were playing now." That's a joke. No way. I think the one thing that amateur rugby players will have over professionals is longevity and in other ways the fire has gone out. I suspect that if someone is appointed captain, or becomes a new cap, these days, he goes out and has a celebratory cup of tea.'

Frame. What a totally apposite name for a 6ft 1in., 14½ stone centre who always picked the shortest way to the try line. A man who proved a massive physical presence in the centre for Gala and Scotland. It made up for a lack of pace, he insists: 'I'm coming now, ready or not!'

As with so many strong and aggressive rugby players – many of whom, curiously, were schooled at posh Glenalmond – John Frame turns out to be a cerebral character with a great gift for mimicry, a stockbroker with a large house in sight of Murrayfield and a large walled garden where he serves me tea. Frame comes originally from Inverness ('not a hotbed of rugby') and after Glenalmond he studied law at Edinburgh University. It was the late Jock Turner – 'a fortnight before Davie Chisholm tried to persuade me to go to Melrose' – who persuaded Frame to go to Netherdale, where he finished up as captain.

The Borders, he said, were a totally different culture for a Highlander living in Edinburgh and he was the 'first city slicker' to play for Gala: 'I think there was a slight air of apprehension when Peter Brown and I arrived. It was a bit like a foreign international playing for Rangers, but I was made enormously welcome.' Perhaps Gala had simply never seen anything like Brown and Frame, before or since.

Brown insists Frame would read poetry before a match and there are rumours that he has embraced Buddhism. 'Did he say that?' asks Frame. 'I think he must be getting very old and senile.

'I remember Norman Pender of Hawick on the New Zealand tour of 1975 – this was two years after I had last been capped and I think even my wife believed I didn't play any more. He and Ian McLauchlan, the captain, didn't see eye to eye and I think Ian regarded it as very amusing to put me in with Norman Pender as often as he could. I recollect it was my final season with Gala and heaven knows how I got picked, it was clearly a mistake. But I got to share with Norman Pender, the Hawick prop, more often than anybody else: I had to listen to his poetry on biking, which he always used to make a point of reciting just at those moments I was trying to get to sleep. It maybe beats snoring, I'm not sure. It was on that tour that I realised prop-forwards weren't stupid because I taught him how to play cribbage; by the end of the tour he was beating me soundly.

'Props carry a great macho burden with them and I often thought their ability to perform on the pitch was based on their opposite number's expectation of them. Tom Kiernan, the former Ireland and British Lions captain, told a story – which may be apocryphal and may on the other hand be true – about the relationship between Syd Millar of Ballymena and Davie Rollo, the Howe of Fife prop who was one of my heroes as a young man:

'Davie Rollo came in for his first cap against Ireland, propping against Syd Millar. Syd was saying, "Jeez, who's this so-and-so from Howe of Fife? I've never heard of him and I've never heard of his f*****g club. I'll chew him to bits." They went down in the first scrum and Davie Rollo was there with his socks round his ankles, as always. So Syd gave him a little poke with his boot in the shin: "Jeez, I tell you, I hit him right in the middle of his shin and I could feel the pain go halfway up my backside. I knew it hurt the bugger, but he never moved an inch."

'At the lineout Davie Rollo pulled Syd towards him with one finger and said, "Er, I wouldnae do that again if I were you." So at the next scrum Syd hit him as hard as he could on the other shin and this time the pain went right up to Syd's head.

'So they got to the next lineout and yer man looked at Syd with these funny f*****g eyes and leaned forward and pulled Syd towards him with one finger, put his face up close and said, "Er, I really wouldnae do that again if I were you."

'And Syd said later, "I tell you what, I have never been so f*****g terrified in all my life."

'Now in my day people like Syd Millar and Davie Rollo never had to threaten. That game against Canterbury when Sandy Carmichael got his cheekbone smashed? Things like that didn't seem to happen with these sort of guys. At Twickenham in 1971 Fran Cotton came in against Ian McLauchlan in the first of two games in eight days; I remember Cotton complained at the dinner about McLauchlan's lack of sportsmanship and McLauchlan's response was, "Well, you've got seven f*****g days to sort it out."

'A lot of the humour I recollect was built around the seven-a-side game. There was a young man called Duncan Paterson who played in the same great Gala seven-a-side side as myself and Peter Brown. We had won at Selkirk in the sevens there, where the home support was very vociferous in favour of the opposition. We had beaten an Irish team and we came into the dressing-room after the final and we were accustomed to winning, to be honest. Dunc had a very sharp sense of humour and invariably after a match there is a silence for a time and he spoke up: "Well, you've got to hand it to they Selkirk. There's twae thousand of them between a semi-final and a final learned to boo in an Irish accent." You go to Langholm or Melrose, with Gala they were very hostile, no matter who you were playing against.

'There was no quarter given in the Border leagues, but there was an awful lot of humour, too. I have a philosophy which I attribute to a team-mate called Johnny Gray, who later went on to coach Gala in the year I became captain – the centenary year. We were training at the back pitches at Gala and I was a very bad trainer, doing running followed by press-ups. Eventually I gave up and collapsed in the mud. The next thing there were these size-12 boots next to me and Gray said, "Aye Frame, get up, life gangs on, life gangs on." And since then I have often thought in times of tribulation you can either lie there and die, or get up and carry on. I think that's what rugby teaches you.

'The first time I got picked for Gala in 1968, we won the Gala Sevens and we beat Loughborough in the final. It was all the more joyous because they wore maroon like Gala and had to borrow Hawick's jerseys.

'Before that, we had been training on the Thursday and the guys were a bit nervous about the match because Loughborough had Gerald Davies playing for them and I was supposed to be marking him. Someone said to Dunc, "That Gerald Davies, he's awfa fast, how's Framey going to hold him in?" And Dunc said straight off, "Gerald Davies is nae so f*****g fast with 14½ stone on his back."

'At Gala we lost occasionally, and in a Scottish jersey perhaps more regularly, because there was a great Welsh side around at that time. I was never on a winning side against them, but the games were remarkably close. We hadn't a coach until Bill Dickinson came along and he was introduced as adviser to the coach. It was Jim Telfer who did most of the shouting – a very inspiring captain to play with, but of course I had the arrogance of a centre three-quarter and just assumed he knew nothing about centre play.

'He was certainly a different sort of captain to Peter Brown. Peter saw himself as a great psychologist. In fact, he spent a lot of time inside his own mind, but he was a very, very fine player – a magnificent lineout jumper, spring-heeled and, like his brother Gordon, not a man to give ground. Ian McLauchlan was a different sort of character altogether, a very aggressive character in his manner, a very difficult chap. Obviously people would take to him because of his track record, but he would push people away. I could never understand it.

'Rugby, I think, has taught me to behave with integrity and honour. I've always thought that I'd never want to be in a situation where I was walking down a street and have to go down a side street if I saw someone else coming. Those people who behaved irresponsibly on a rugby field were, I found, not trustworthy off it either.

'I'm a great believer in cause and effect. I believe in doing things in a straightforward way and have tried to follow that philosophy. I've been very lucky in my marriage. I have four lovely children, one of whom is special needs – that in fact makes him special, because you learn a great deal of tolerance, having to support someone in an unequivocal way. I have had a life of enormous richness.'

Until John Leslie's effort against Wales in 1999, Frame held the record for the fastest international try ever – scored against England at Murrayfield in 1971, in a game to celebrate the centenary of the first Scotland international (at Raeburn Place). 'You never want to beat England on superior play,' he says. 'You want to beat them with a disputed penalty in the last minute of the game and win by two points. So in a way the try fitted that criterion.

'John Reason, after the game at Twickenham seven days before, had made great play about England losing because they'd failed to use their superior three-quarter line. This hadn't gone down too well with the so-called inferior three-quarter line. When Jock Turner kicked off way deep, a big bugger called Jeremy Janion caught it; and instead of passing it to Bob Hiller to boot back downfield, he started rampaging off across the pitch. The whole of the Scottish pack were coming up towards him and he obviously thought, "Bugger this for a game of soldiers" and started passing infield. All I had to do was keep running and when John Spencer dropped it, it happened to drop at my feet and I happened to pick it up and run ten yards over their line. It all took about 11 seconds.

'Funnily enough, when John Leslie scored his try against Wales, I was seated there with my son. and he turned round and said to the guy next to him, "My father's record has just been broken." So I had to sign some programmes and confirm who I was. Then someone said, "You must be really sad at your record going."

'"Wait a minute," I replied. "Who cares about the fastest try scored against Wales? Tell me who holds the record against England!"'

Andy Irvine freely admits that when he finally retired from international rugby in 1984, after one of the most luminous careers in any sport, there was a large measure of relief in his decision to hang up the boots that had made him the highest points scorer in Scottish rugby history: 'In some ways, although I missed the game, it was nice not to have all the hassle with it, because I didn't get much free time. God only knows what it must be like for the top footballers. I just have so much sympathy for the George Bests and the David Beckhams. They just have no life at all. They may have millions of pounds, but they can't spend it, or they can't spend it in any privacy at all. It must be dreadful. And I remember the Welsh boys, even in the amateur era when there was no money: Gareth Edwards, J.P.R. Williams, Phil Bennett couldn't go out about Wales without people pestering them. After a while it does wear a wee bit thin.

'To a certain extent I haven't had the same attention, because rugby's not a big game in Scotland. I actually had less freedom in New Zealand than I ever did in Scotland. I was stopped much more often going down Queen Street in Auckland than I was in Princes Street in Edinburgh, which is nice because I like to enjoy my sort of privacy with my family and so forth and it must be bloody awful to be "somebody" like the real superstars. People would say it would be great, but some of the superstars crack. Look at the likes of George Best.'

It's not totally invidious to compare Irvine with Best, although the similarities ended the minute both left the playing arena. On it, Irvine was just as capable as the soccer player of turning a game single-handedly with an instinct for joyful running that was mind-boggling at times. Unlike Best, Irvine was also the sort most girls would have been happy to take home to meet Mum. He still is.

In his pristine offices on George Street, Edinburgh, where he is managing director of a commercial property company, Irvine looks every inch the city businessman. There is a boardroom table with room for 20, a smart suit, an air of gravitas and a tan (possibly from skiing). Only a slightly squint nose gives the game away. Although he is still involved in rugby with the mini set-up at Heriot's, Irvine is famously publicity-shy – normally he demands sight of an interview before publication - but in fact he seems totally ambivalent about how he is viewed in the annals of the game. It was, he insists, just a lot of fun.

Most of his contemporaries are happy to acknowledge him as the greatest Scotland back ever, although there are the odd codicils. Peter Brown would say, of playing for Gala against Irvine and Heriot's, 'If you put up a high ball and Andy managed to catch it, you were in severe trouble. Fortunately, he would drop as many as he caught.'

Andrew Robertson Irvine was born on 16 September 1951 in the port of Leith. With two brothers some 15 years older, he was effectively an only child and he says, 'I didn't really see them when I was a kid. They had gone off to work by the time I was of an age where I could communicate. My mother used to tell me that she was quite a good sprinter in her day at primary school, or something, and that's about it: there's no sporting background in our family at all, really. Soccer was my sport at Gillespie's Boys' School, where they didn't play rugby, and the only reason I played rugby was because I went to Heriot's and it was compulsory. So I never really touched a rugby ball until I was 13 years old.

'At senior school I was much more interested in how Hearts were doing, but once I went to Heriot's I took a bit more interest in rugby. I'd been to Murrayfield once, to see the All Blacks in 1967. The next time I was there I was actually playing against them. Once I had left school and got into the FP side I started to make pretty rapid progress. I got into the Edinburgh side within about three months of playing. I started in the September and in the December or November I was picked for the Edinburgh team, so it was only after that I thought, "I might be able to do something here." But it was purely an enjoyment thing. I just loved playing the game, it was as simple as that. Basically we were only playing for our own enjoyment and our own pride – and there is pride in representing your country, or British Lions, or Edinburgh.

'I always wanted to play full-back. I played it a couple of times at school and you had an awful lot more space and an awful lot more room and you could see everything in front of you. I was a good trainer. It's really quite natural that the more you practise, the better you get. John Rutherford wasn't a particularly good kicker when he started. He was a brilliant runner, but he'll probably be remembered more for his fantastic kicking now, because he worked so hard on it.

'Neither Jim Renwick nor I won a Grand Slam or even a Triple Crown, but that's life. We both went down to Twickenham in 1973 and '75 to win the Triple Crown, but we lost on both occasions. In fairness we were quite well beaten in '73, but two years later I felt we were robbed. England were awarded a very dubious try and the guy that got it, Alan Morley, admitted later that he didn't touch it down. In the '70s Wales were very, very strong and when Wales weren't strong there was a great French team with Jean-Pierre Rives and all these sort of boys.

'The competition was quite fierce. Jim and I both just missed out on the '84 Grand Slam, but really we had just finished our careers. I was actually brought in as a sub for the last couple of games, but I had been injured all season – so had Jim – so we were a wee bit unfortunate. We were 33 years old and quite a number of that Grand Slam team – chaps like Iain Milne, Alan Tomes, David Leslie, John Rutherford and Roy Laidlaw – were a wee bit younger than us. We'd just lasted a bit longer, that's all. Anyway, it was still great to see a Grand Slam.

'When I came in, in 1972, P.C. Brown was captain. But then he lost the captaincy to Ian McLauchlan a year later. Physically, Ian wasn't very big at all, but he was so dedicated that he used to do a huge amount on his own. He was a gym teacher, so he had the facility to do weights but he was an incredibly dedicated individual and hard as nails. He had real serious aggression for a wee chap.

'In the second row we had Alastair McHarg and Gordon Brown. McHarg could only do what he did because he was the other half of a duo where the other boy was a great big solid so-and-so. You couldn't get away with two Alastair McHargs. He was a sort of Scott Murray type, very mobile, very athletic and he could run all day. But you also needed the workhorse.

'I was very fortunate to get three Lions tours – in '74, '77 and '80. The first one was the most enjoyable because it was the first rugby tour I'd ever been on. I had no idea what it was like. I had no family responsibilities; I was single; I had no real sort of business responsibilities, either, because I was just a junior graduate – in that sense it was almost like one big holiday. I was in a fantastic country with fantastic weather, great hotels and great food, playing the game I love, in the sunshine. And although you didn't get paid you certainly weren't out of pocket. Everything was laid on a plate. Ironically, in those days I think that we got an allowance of 50p a day that was our expenses – £3.50 a week – and yet you couldn't spend it, such was the hospitality. All you spent money on were postcards and stamps.

'I learned an awful lot on that first tour because we had a fantastic back division with Gareth Edwards, Phil Bennett and JPR. A lot of the backs moves I later introduced to Heriot's and to Edinburgh and to Scotland as well, and a lot of them worked fantastically well for ten years. There were a lot of dummy scissors and double-dummy scissors and dummy runs and loops and so forth that we certainly used at Goldenacre and it was fantastic, just brilliant. We were a good side, but probably not as good as we were cracked up to be because you have to weigh it up against the calibre of the opposition. In those days South Africa had been starved of international competition. The history books will show that we were undefeated, but I think there are reasons for that.

'Business restricted my involvement in rugby after I retired. On Sunday afternoons I coach the mini-rugby down at Goldenacre, but that's about the extent of it. There were also other things that I was quite keen to do in life. For instance, when you played rugby you could never ski because you just couldn't take the risk of damaging your knee; and because of rugby I never went on a family holiday until 1983, because every year I would be on tour.

'The way I played, I was always going to make some mistakes, just like the way I play golf. But you know you hope that you can make up for it. You have your ups and downs and hopefully your ups will be more frequent than your downs – but I had a fairly cavalier attitude towards rugby. I still believe to this day that the best place to attack from is deep in defence and I get disappointed at the lack of flair today.

'I was always pretty keen on goalkicking in those days and whenever the referee blew for a penalty you had to get there early. If you didn't, P.C. Brown or Douglas Morgan would do. But that's a good sign, because all too often these days you see people shying away because they don't like the pressure. I think probably I kicked better on Lions tours, because there was more chance to practise. I very rarely practised in Scotland, because when we trained on a Tuesday and Thursday night it was always dark and the balls you got were like footballs. Nowadays all the stands are completely enclosed, so you've not got wind whistling round each end. And all the balls have a plastic coating.

'The condition of the pitch is an awful lot better, too. When we played at Murrayfield the grass was really long. It's like a bowling green now. I never played at Murrayfield, not even at the end of my career, when you could go out and practise. We were never even allowed to go out and walk on the pitch. Now they have curtain-raisers before the game and I just find that mind-blowing. Once, you'd have been shot if you'd walked on the Murrayfield pitch on a Friday afternoon.'

Coffee Republic, a popular café in Edinburgh's West End, throws a narrow glass frontage onto the city's Queensferry Street. At 12.30 p.m. on 23 May 2000, customers there – including the author, and he expected it – are alarmed by a sudden darkening of the room, as if a cloud had passed by. It's not, however, an eclipse of the sun, but simply the arrival of Iain Milne in the doorway.

The mighty Bear of legend is even mightier these days, possibly four stones above his playing weight of 16½ stone in the days when he was the best tight-head prop on the planet. Coffee Republic's chairs are not wide enough to contain him and he suffers manfully and without complaint for an hour perched atop a ridiculously small stool. The definitive gentle giant.

Many have said that Milne's fondness for the social side of rugby would have made him an anachronism amid the strictures of modern-day professionalism. Finlay Calder insists the Bear could be 'uncontrollable' on trips abroad, but he also adds, 'They would have found it impossible to drop him.'

The eldest of the Three Bears was born on 17 June 1958, the son of a GP (who hailed originally from Aberdeen and 'moved down to Edinburgh forty-odd years ago'): 'Heriot's was the catalyst for rugby. I always played prop, although I had one season at hooker at school. I never progressed beyond these two positions. Believe it or not, the PE teacher at Heriot's thought I was too light and it was my mobility that got me noticed. I always enjoyed the ball to hand and I tell a few jokes against myself regarding that. I spent 90 per cent of my time at tight-head and you tend to take more of the pressure there because you're up against their hooker and loose-head; but they are both technically difficult in many ways and both are pretty demanding.

'I got thrown in at prop at 19 for the FPs and I took a few pastings in the early days – Ian McLauchlan and people like that. He was obviously very mature. But although I got badly beaten in several head-to-head competitions, I never got down about it and going in at that age I learned quicker. I think McLauchlan thought I was an easy ride to start off with. He didn't want to bother with scrummaging that much, he just enjoyed running round the pitch with the ball in his hand. But latterly I probably gave as good as I got against him. The others I had good battles with were Jim Aitken at Gala, Hector Barnfather at Langholm and, internationally, some of the French props – Gerard Cholley, guys like that. My second cap was against Cholley, a pretty fearsome character, but I didn't have many problems with him that day: I just basically kept out of his way. Everyone in the Scottish team had told me about him, but it went very well, really. Ian McGeechan played too, so I am probably one of the few players who has played with Ian and been coached by him.

'I left school in '74 and played for the FPs that first season. It was a golden era for Scottish club rugby if you like. I have a lot of fond memories of that period. Hawick were the dominant force early on and then there was a time in the late '70s and early '80s when ourselves, Gala and Hawick were supplying much of the international squad. These games were as high a standard as there has been in the amateur era. The South v. Edinburgh game was almost like another Scotland trial. There were crowds of five or six thousand and a hell of a lot of interest.

'My first cap came in 1979 a bit out of the blue. Bob Cunningham was the incumbent; Sandy Carmichael had just retired; Norman Pender was still floating around; there was Norrie Rowan . . . I was way down the pecking order. I was probably lucky in that Heriot's won the championship around that time, which probably helped get me noticed. I don't think I even played a trial, certainly not a B game. I was as nervous on my last cap as I was at the first – physically sick at times. In the early '80s quite a few players came together at the same time, but there's no doubt the major influence was Jim Telfer. Jim used to have a go at me and Jim Calder more than most. The quiet ones. But I can't say I took the game as seriously as Jim and I think he learned a lot on the tours he was on – how to handle people and get the best out of them.

'There had been no thought about winning a Grand Slam in 1984. Ireland were going through a poor patch and in the early '80s England had a very poor team, although they still fancied themselves. They had some good players, but some of their selection was very haphazard and I think that showed in the results. I played a couple of seasons down at Harlequins and the talent was there, but there was no one around to harness it. It was only when Geoff Cooke and people like that came in that they got their act together.

'In that Scotland side we had balance and experience. Jim Aitken wasn't that great a player, to be honest, but as a captain he was a good organiser and liaised well with Jim Telfer. I had a lot of time for Jim Calder. Iain Paxton was an 80-minute player, David Leslie was not, and I don't think a team could have sustained two Leslies – but he was totally committed.

'It has always been in my nature that I'm not overly aggressive and I always thought if someone did react with punching or kicking it was a sign that I was getting on top. To be truthful, I never got really hurt. Against France in 1984 I finished up with a black eye, but it was just a sign they were getting frustrated. I don't think anyone tried to take advantage if they were on top of me, which didn't happen very often anyway.

'Heriot's had a very strong front row, but a tremendous back division, probably as strong as any club side have ever had: Andy Irvine, of course, but also Fraser Dall, Jimmy Craig and Harry Burnett, all B-level internationalists. They could have held their own with anyone at that time. The front row was Jim Burnett, myself and Callum Munro and we had a good rapport for many years. We gave the backs a good platform, but with Andy there we scored innumerable tries from our own half. It was a great time to be playing.

'Andy was probably the most influential person for me. He made me vice-captain at the age of 20 or 21, one of the youngest in the team at the time. Andy was influential everywhere. Speak to the treasurer at the time and he will tell you you could guarantee an extra 700 or so on the gate if people knew Irvine was playing. He was a tremendous enthusiast, too, and I think latterly he got more enjoyment out of playing for the club and seeing the boys develop than he did playing for Scotland where people expected so much from him.

'It was strange how Edinburgh public schools managed to produce these families playing rugby. Quite a unique situation. I got to play twice with Kenny, my brother, for Scotland. The first was in 1989, my last Five Nations game, when we were together against Wales (and got a pushover try, incidentally). The second was in New Zealand in 1990. I never got to play internationally with David, my other brother. I half-thought of retiring in 1987, but made a comeback and then it was in the back of my mind that if I went on to the 1991 World Cup there was a chance of us all three playing together. If it had ever happened, it would have been against Zimbabwe.

'There's no doubt in my mind that the way the game is progressing, the influence which the scrum can exert is getting less and less. I think this is to Scotland's detriment. There were certain individuals involved in selection and coaching who got it into in their minds that the front row was all about being mobile; but they forgot about the basics. We suffered for that for a number of years. New Zealand have always had mobile forwards, but go back through the history of All Black rugby and the back five have usually been crucial. There's always been that platform from the front row.

'There's no doubt that New Zealand brought out the best in me. I went there twice and I think I played some of my best rugby against the All Blacks. That final game against them in 1990 was one of the highlights of my career and I thought we were unlucky to lose. When I got back I sat on the bench against Argentina and I think there was a feeling among the selectors that I wasn't fit and they gave Paul Burnell a game. I never really got to the bottom of what happened there. I wasn't all that pissed off at the time, to be honest, because old age was telling and I had picked up a few niggling injuries. But I made a big effort to try to get back for the World Cup in 1991. However, a week before that I damaged my neck in a scrummaging session and my biggest disappointment was that we did some very heavy scrummaging when I knew we weren't quite ready for it. You need to build up to it.

'So that was it. Yet I can still look back with pride on what I achieved. And I've made a lot of friends. I should really make a bigger effort to stay in touch with them.

'I think if I had been a professional I would have been a far better player, but whether I'd have been stimulated sufficiently is another matter. I certainly wouldn't be teetotal: there is no need for it and I still think I would have enjoyed the odd night out. Believe it or not, I did train very hard – Andy Irvine would bring out the best in you in that respect – but I also thought that it wasn't unreasonable to let your hair down on a Saturday night. I don't think that would be acceptable nowadays, more so because the media would get hold of it and you wouldn't be allowed to do it anyway. But over the years there have been some good parties. I just hope I didn't cause too much damage over the piece.'

40. GREGOR TOWNSEND

Gregor Townsend thought he had seen everything in his career until he arrived at Castres in the summer of 2000. His first French club, Brive, had been an eye-opener – for example his rival for the stand-off shirt, Christophe Lamaison, had a clause in his contract saying he could not play in any other position – but when the club owner at Castres arrived to watch a pre-season friendly 300 feet up from his own helicopter, the lad from Galashiels probably realised how far rugby had progressed from his days in the mini ranks at Netherdale.

'He is a multi-millionaire and owns the third biggest pharmaceutical company in France,' says Townsend of his boss. 'I couldn't believe it at first. I thought of putting up a high ball for him, but then thought better of it.'

Townsend and his wife, Claire, live in a second-floor apartment in the town, a few yards from the River Tarn and an hour's drive from the Pyrenees. There are are sixteenth-century weavers' houses and the traditional French market square. Claire is currently doing a degree in sports management from Leicester University by video and correspondence and spends two or three hours a day on that. Gregor, after a not totally happy time at Brive (rugby-wise at least) is focused on yet another stage of his multi-faceted career. Long thought of as the laid-back, wayward genius of Scottish rugby – a man, like Andy Irvine, just as likely to lose a game as win it – Townsend in fact is deeply critical and analytical of his own game. He is still, he says, looking for a perfect 80 minutes and hasn't come close so far.

Many of the critics who label him an 'enigma' may be surprised to hear him say, 'Everybody is affected by confidence and I am very critical about my own. If there is a missed tackle or a pass that doesn't go to hand, you're fuming with yourself all night and all next day.'

The move to France, in fact, he regards as the latest chapter in an extended rugby education that began at the age of five at Gala where his father, Peter, played alongside John Frame in the Maroons' centre – and is continuing to this day: 'My first serious game was at the age of five when my brother's Under-10 side were short of a player and I was stuck on the wing. I was the only player who didn't score a try. There's a photo at home with this tiny little boy stuck among all these tall kids and I remember going to other people's houses that night with the cup.

'I actually played more soccer as a kid and joined Hutcheson Vale Boys' Club. Mum and Dad used to take me up there every weekend to play. When I went to Galashiels Academy at 15 I played for the school team in the morning, youth team in the afternoon and Under-16s on Sunday. I used to be in agony by Sunday night.

'All my ambitions then were in a Gala context and I never dreamed of moving away. That's how rugby has changed, but my wish is eventually to go back and be involved in the coaching there. I first toured Australia when I was 19. It was my first experience of playing abroad and it really opened my eyes. With Graham Shiel I arranged to stay on, but I had to come back and play in the Students' World Cup. Next year I went back to play for Warringah and it improved my handling, passing, everything. It also made me determined to see as much of the world in rugby terms as I could.

'My first cap was against England, when I came on as replacement for Craig Chalmers. It was a bit weird, because I had never played inside-centre in my life and that's the position I came on at. It was a game of two halves, as they say. I missed two or three tackles early on and wasn't even doing the right technique for tackling. But then I started getting used to it and I started wanting to have a go at the English defence. I found my feet in the second half and wanted more of this.

'I remember, after Craig went off with a broken arm, running up the touchline at Twickenham with the stands going up and up. Before a game I used to be really pumped up. Then I went to Australia and it was like a breath of fresh air. They were all chatting away before the match and pretty laid-back, then during the match really physical. Over here it's very different. You have ten minutes before the kick-off, with the anthems and everything, so it's a bit of a waste of energy getting worked up. I get nervous quite early in the morning, but after that I am quite looking forward to it. Some people get physically sick, Neil Jenkins being a good example. The guys you would think are very calm are often the worst. You would think Derrick Lee is the most laid-back guy in the world but he gets very, very nervous.

'I finished my business studies in 1995 and that gave me the scope to travel. The idea was to go to Northampton, become a better player and then come back to Gala. But then when I was down there the game went professional. I would hate people to think I was moving around because I was not loyal: really, all my moves have been to different countries, except for the last, and that was because we wanted to stay in France. My ambition was to play in every country. I remember speaking to Cardiff after my second season at Northampton – I wanted to play stand-off, which wasn't always possible at Northampton – and pick up something from every country that plays rugby.

'I never used to play flat until I went to Australia and in France it's more about angles and it's more physical. In Australia they are into wrist passing. In France they like long passing with players coming from behind each other on long, looping runs. My experience of France is that the coaching hasn't moved on much, but the players have. Here they view a coach as someone who is a bully and it used to be either a scrum-half or a prop. At Brive they were both props.

'A French training week is nothing like a Scottish or English training week. Every Wednesday we used to have a full-contact game, which is unheard of over here. It's easy to coach a game; taking a rucking or lineout session is much harder. But that is changing. There are three Australian coaches in France this season and they realise that coaching will have to be more successful. They didn't want to be Anglo-Saxon, deliberately – they wanted to be more spontaneous. But that hasn't brought much success. Hookers in France used to be basically big props who couldn't throw in the lineout, but now they realise they can't get away with that. They also have to be professional, for example in turning up to things on time and looking after their bodies. At one time they could get away with drinking and smoking. Not now.

'Over the last couple of years French teams haven't done well in Europe, or the Five Nations, so they have to catch up. They realise you have to be more technical. When I spoke to Jeremy Davidson, the Irish captain of Castres, that was one of the reasons I went there. I was on the verge of coming back to England: I wanted to stay in France, but I was disillusioned with the coaching there. However, the coach at Castres had had two years at Harlequins so I am more in tune with him. I loved my time at Brive, although I was unhappy with some of the selections and they had a bit of a foreigner thing. Lamaison played in the World Cup semi-final win against New Zealand and had to come back, but we were winning more games with me than him. It affected my confidence when he came back and for the first time in my career there was nothing I could do. Not having the chance to play was very frustrating.

'That affected my confidence with Scotland, too, and it's hard to find confidence in internationals. I had a month's spell where I was doubting myself until I sorted things out in my head. But then I wasn't at stand-off for Scotland any more!

'I have analysed it from a personal point of view and a public point of view. My first senior year, I played very poorly. In a Scotland B match I threw an interception and that's where the enigmatic stuff came in. The press in Scotland are very different from the press in France or New Zealand. Christian Cullen will drop a high ball then score two tries and the press never come out and say, "This is a guy who will do something good one minute and something bad the next." They'll say that he made one mistake but that he's still a good player. I do enjoy getting away from it. No one likes being slagged in the papers. I am viewed differently in Scotland from how I'm seen in France, Australia and even England when I was down there. It's interesting.

'I have never got close to a perfect game. There are times when you get every kick to touch and make every tackle, but then you start analysing the passing – passing is always the one. At stand-off there are probably 20 options for you when the scrum goes down, then you narrow it down to five or six. You call a move – a move has maybe three options in it – then you can cancel the move, the ball can come out badly and you have to kick. When you have the ball in your hand and you are under pressure, you are down to two, maybe three options. Last Saturday there, early on, I did a mispass and just as I passed I realised the centre had just left the guy outside me and he would have got a space. I was thinking, "Oh, if I had just hung on a bit longer." These are the things that frustrate you after a game.

'I still love the game, the 80 minutes when you are up against your opposite number or the opposing back-row, but it's really the learning thing. You learn from training sessions a lot. You learn more about your skill, getting every pass long, things like that. But in the game you learn about decision-making. In training you learn the tools of the decison-making; in a game you have to realise when that long pass is on, or vice-versa.

'I like to think I'm very structured and very analytical. I watch a lot of videos of teams like ACT in Australia, I always want to know. An instinctive thing is just a decision made very fast. You just see it coming from experience. If you can make that decison early, you get more time on the ball and when you are playing well, you do seem to get more time on the ball.

'I am very lucky to play rugby and can give everything to the game now. Training twice a day, you feel as if you are turning your body into something needed to play rugby. Last year I started thinking about coaching more and I do want to do something with Gala eventually. I was always against having a further career in rugby and wanted to do something new, something challenging. But maybe I'll get that from coaching.'